The Decorative Tile

The Decorative Tile

in Architecture and Interiors

Tony Herbert and Kathryn Huggins

The Decorative Tile

in Architecture and Interiors

Contents

This book is dedicated to nineteenth-century
ceramic tile-makers around the world, and
especially the communities at Jackfield,
Shropshire, England and at Auneuil near
Beauvais in northern France.

Phaidon Press Limited
Regent's Wharf
All Saints Street
London N1 9PA

First Published 1995
Reprinted in paperback 2000
© 1995 Phaidon Press Limited

ISBN 0 7148 3979 5

Printed in Hong Kong

Captions
Page 2. William Butterfield used tiles
bearing Gothic motifs in strong geometric
arrangements for the altar step and reredos
at All Saints' Church, Margaret Street,
London (1849–59).

Page 4. The east end of All Saints' Church,
Margaret Street, London has a rich
polychromatic display of tiles, creating a
finale to a crescendo of decoration which
perfectly fits the liturgical use of the
building.

Initial letters to chapters throughout this
book are nineteenth-century letter tiles
made by Maws and Craven Dunnills of
Jackfield, Shropshire, England.

Introduction

The term 'tile' is bewilderingly vague in the English language. In its widest sense it can refer to any sort of material, whether it is stone, vinyl or even carpet, which is used in a (usually square or rectangular) modular form. The tiles featured in this book have one thing in common – they are all made from clay dug out of the ground and fired to a temperature at which the clay undergoes chemical changes and becomes permanently hard. The term 'ceramic tile' is open to a wide interpretation and its uses range from wall and floor tiles to roofing tiles and even include non-architectural applications such as the tiles on the nose cones of space rockets.

Opportunities for pedantic semantic arguments abound, such as 'How thick does a tile need to be before it is called a brick?' Cultural and geographical interpretations also make their mark; American readers will know the chunky glazed blocks used in building as terra cotta, whereas in Britain they are most likely to be described as architectural faience.

Absorbing though these differences in terminology and language are, they should not obscure the main focus of the book which is the role of decorative architectural tiles. The use of tiles in architecture is an ancient tradition whose roots can be traced back to several different parts of the Middle East and whose branches stretch across Europe. The history is told in outline in the first chapter and, with the passing of the centuries, the contribution of tiles to architecture emerges as the kaleidoscopic vocabulary of colour, shape and pattern develops. The advent of industrialization in the nineteenth century introduced new techniques for producing building materials and new opportunities for using them. For decorative tiles this was a golden age which lasted until the economic and social upheavals of World War I. The second to the seventh chapters explore the fundamental themes arising from this period, seeking to integrate tiles, their design and manufacture with the architectural and social environment in which they were used. This book, in contrast with many existing tile books, aims to avoid the insect collector's approach of mounting individual specimens in cabinet drawers labelled with a particular company or technique. Instead it acts as an ecological guide, encouraging the study of tiles in their architectural habitat. The final chapter serves as a reminder, not only of the need for conservation, but of the ability of the decorative tile to evolve and adapt to the changing architectural needs of the twentieth century and beyond.

Tradition and Sources

's old as knowledge, as universal as learning' is the way in which the largest tile manufacturer in Britain, H&R Johnson, described tiles in its advertising copy of the 1970s. A more detailed examination of the origins of tiles in architecture only serves to support a statement which initially sounds like advertising hyperbole.

The long and geographically diverse pedigree of tiles had a strong fascination for people in the nineteenth century. W J Furnival, writing in his monumental *Leadless Decorative Tiles*, captures the romantic travelogue quality of the tile traditions, showing how 'the ornamental-tile maker's craft has flitted fitfully hither and thither in the wake of early civilisations, leaving indelible traces where once the Babylonian, Egyptian, Persian, Arab Mongul, Moor or monk held sway'. He describes in detail and with enthusiasm how each civilization has been able to 'add their own touch of genius', with the result that the art of tiling 'gathers utility, variety, attractiveness; wins the favour of princes; becomes installed in palaces and temples; and ebbing and flowing with the chameleon tides of national prosperity, advances as genius, enterprise, patronage and fashion supervene, or languishes by dearth of them'. The tile tradition was ideally suited to the eclectic outlook of many nineteenth-century architects and designers. Its archaeological discovery held a strong appeal and its colours, patterns and forms were a Pandora's box of ideas awaiting mass reproduction and creative interpretation.

A large Italian maiolica floor tile (c. 1480) from a pavement in the nunnery of San Paolo, Parma. The youth carries a romantic message in the rim of his hat, inscribed 'To be given into the hand of Zovano'.

Right. The Ishtar Gate of the City of
Babylon (c. 580 BC) displays an early
and impressive use of glazed architectural
ceramics.
Below. The Processional Way leading up
to the Gate was lined on each side with a
frieze of 60 lions in relief.

The Near East, with its tradition of baked or sun-dried brick, was the geographical cradle of architectural ceramics and the use of coloured and glazed materials was a logical development. At least as early as the fourth millennium BC the Egyptians were producing tiles of a siliceous, sandy composition whose surface glaze was stained turquoise-blue with copper. These tiles were used to decorate the jambs of inner doorways in the Step Pyramid at Saqqara, south of Cairo.

Egypt was also a pioneering centre for the manufacture of glass and there may be connections between the development of knowledge about glass-making and the development of glazes for architectural ceramics and pottery. A deep blue glaze was most commonly used in ancient Egypt, the choice of colours no doubt being limited for technical reasons. The widespread use of blue was also probably related to contemporary conceptions of divine power and eternal life. Later, Egyptian tiles were decorated with lines scratched in the clay before the tile was glazed, making the design stand out in a deeper blue against the turquoise colour of the background. Perhaps the most impressive examples are the wall tiles found in the Nile Delta at the temple of Medinet Habu near Tell al Yehudia. Dating from around 1180 BC, they portray captured slaves of different races as well as fabulous beasts, real animals and symbolic signs and ornaments. These tiles are thought to have been used to decorate a small chamber or passageway and, despite their fragmentary nature, they are impressive early examples of architectural ceramics. The dispersal of the excavated material to museums in Cairo, Berlin and London may seem unfortunate today but it undoubtedly contributed to a wider appreciation and emulation of the material in the nineteenth century.

Even more impressive are the coloured and glazed relief tiles and bricks used by the Assyrians and Babylonians in Mesopotamia between the thirteenth and the fifth centuries BC. Due to the work of German archaeologists between 1899 and 1917, the Processional Way and the Ishtar Gate of Babylon later became well-known in Europe through their reconstruction in the Museum of Western Asiatic Antiquity in Berlin and through similar examples in other major museums around the world. The Processional Way, which ran north/south up to the forecourt and the northern main gate of the city of Babylon, was constructed in around 580 BC. It consisted of two parallel walls 20-24 metres (65-79 feet) apart, with a 180-metre (590-foot) stretch decorated with a magnificent frieze of lions in relief. These were produced as moulded bricks, fired and their outer faces glazed in bright colours, although the lions' manes, which were originally fiery red, have now faded to a greenish yellow. Each lion is about 2 metres (6 feet) long and consists of 46 different bricks in 11 courses and archaeologists estimate that there were originally 60 lions on each side.

The lion was the symbol of the goddess Ishtar, ruler of the sky, goddess of love and patroness of the army and, when used in a repetitive frieze, it makes a very strong

Examples of Roman mosaic arrangements,
such as this one from Cordoba, Spain
(top), provided a source of inspiration for
such manufacturers as Maw & Co, who
produced them in a tile form in the 1860s.
The designs shown here are taken from a
printed catalogue page.

image. Culminating the great frieze of lions was the Ishtar Gate, its archway flanked by two towers. The exterior was clad with blue glazed bricks which displayed an estimated 575 relief depictions of animals of two types. An inscription by King Nebuchadnezzar II reads 'I set up wild bulls and furious dragons in front of the gates and thus magnificently adorned them with luxurious splendour for all mankind to look at in surprise.'

Even in its reconstructed form, the frieze is a vivid display of architectural ceramics conceived to demonstrate the power and greatness of Babylon. Thus at a very early date coloured glazed ceramics contributed in an important way to architectural image-building. Although separated by over 2,000 years, some of the late nineteenth-century tiling schemes demonstrate the use of tiles for very similar architectural purposes. The very antiquity of the ceramic tradition they evoke is part of the appeal, adding respectability to what might otherwise have been dismissed as vulgar, gaudy commercial architecture.

Relief-decorated glazed brick friezes reminiscent of Babylon occur again in the fifth century BC in the palaces of the Achemenid Kings of Persia. Best known of these are the friezes of archers from the Royal Bodyguard which decorated the palace at Susa (now in the Louvre). The technique of creating brick friezes died out after the eastern conquests of Alexander the Great in the fourth century BC and the Greeks and Romans generally restricted their use of glazed decorative tiles to semicircular roof ornaments decorated with reliefs.

The most important legacy left by the Roman Empire was the mosaic floors laid in both domestic and public buildings. In Italy the small pieces of mosaic (*tesserae*) were, for the most part, made from marble or coloured stone and these floors are therefore beyond the scope of this book. In Roman Britain, however, ceramic mosaic was commoner and the discovery of its bold patterns and layouts by archaeologists in the nineteenth century was a stimulus for a revival of mosaic floors. Furnival rejoiced that 'under the very feet of our ancestors, unheeded for centuries, lay the patterns from which our most modern ceramic floors are really derived. An art lost to us for 1,500 years is being relearned and restored to practical utility.' In some cases the process of discovery and remaking was remarkably direct. Thus in 1857 George Maw, a young British tile manufacturer, was involved with excavating the mosaic pavements in the Roman city of Viroconium in Shropshire and shortly afterwards he was manufacturing ceramic mosaics at the family tile works only a few miles away at Benthall, Broseley.

After Greece and Rome, the search for tradition and sources focuses on Islam, the great unifying force in cultural terms. The Islamic faith, born in the year 622 AD when the prophet Mohammed migrated from Mecca to Medina, spread rapidly to Syria, Palestine, Mesopotamia, Persia, Egypt and North Africa, reaching Spain in 711.

In Islamic architecture ceramic tiling was to develop as a highly important and extensively used decorative element with a popularity and variety of design greater than was apparent anywhere else in the world. Persia was the cradle of almost all the techniques employed for the production of tiles which were later used in Europe. Islamic tiling is of interest not solely for its own sake but because of the important and almost continuous stimulus which it has provided to architects and designers up to the present day. Islamic tile art developed over several centuries in countries spread across three continents – Asia, Africa and Europe. It varied according to local tastes and architecture, making classification difficult.

By 750 AD the centre of the Islamic world had moved eastwards from Damascus to Mesopotamia. The earliest Islamic wall tiles have been found at the ninth-century palace of the Abbasids at Samarra on the banks of the Tigris near Baghdad. Craftsmen were attracted from all over the Islamic world and, drawing some of their inspiration from the ceramic wares imported from China, potters laid the foundation of a great ceramic tradition. The tiles excavated from Samarra include plain green or brown lead-glazed squares and hexagons but much more important are the pioneering examples of lustre decoration. These tiles have a ground of opaque white glaze with hand-painted decoration in yellow, brown and sometimes red. This decoration is supplemented by a gold lustre which was produced by applying a compound of silver and gold in a medium of liquid ochre. The metallic lustrous sheen was deposited on the glazed surface of the tile by a second low-temperature firing in a reducing atmosphere in which oxygen was restricted. The tiles glittered like gold in sunlight and must have greatly enriched the architecture of the palace in which they were incorporated. The craftsmen responsible for the lustre technique migrated to Egypt in the Fatimid period (969–1171) during which lustre was used on pottery rather than on tiles. Following the overthrow of the Fatimid dynasty by Saladin, the austere foe of the Crusaders, the makers of lustreware left Egypt, many finding their way to Persia, which was then ruled by the Seljuk Turks. As Arthur Lane pointed out in his guide to the collection of tiles in the Victoria and Albert Museum, 'artists went wherever a strong and prosperous ruler offered employment' and 'if cities and their populations were annihilated, the craftsmen were spared as part of the booty and carried off to serve their conquerors elsewhere'.

In the thirteenth century Kashan, which lies about 120 miles south of Teheran, became an extremely important tile-making centre, known especially for its lustre-painted tiles which were exported to many other Persian cities. Lustre- and relief-decorated tiles were used together in architecture in several important ways. The inner walls of both religious and secular buildings were faced with dados of striking interlocking star- and cross-shaped tiles, each painted with a complete design. Along the top of the dado there was usually a cornice of rectangular tiles decorated in blue

The great Topkapi Palace at Istanbul, built by the Ottoman Turks, developed the Islamic tiling tradition of stylized foliage patterns and calligraphic friezes. In the Hall of Sultan Murat III (opposite) the domed room, dating from the sixteenth century, is entirely decorated with blue and coral-red Iznik tiles. Tiles with a repeating arabesque pattern (below) cover the walls adjacent to the main gate of the Harem.

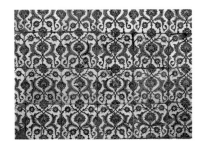

Tiles and tile mosaic played an important role in the decoration of Islamic mosques. They were grouped around the mihrab or prayer niche, as in the Karaouyine Mosque, Fez, Morocco (left), or sometimes covered the inner surface of a dome or portal completely, as in the Shah Mosque at Isfahan (right).

with large calligraphic inscriptions. In religious buildings the finest tiles were grouped in elaborate compositions to form the mihrab, or niche indicating the direction of Mecca, towards which the faithful turned in prayer.

As a non-ceramic form of interior decoration, panels of stucco moulded and carved with figures and stylized plant ornament had been a feature of the Near East since the time of the Sassanian kings in Persia (221–641 AD). Their production in fired clay was a logical development, providing a weatherproof material which simulated the effect of light and shade provided by relief stucco work. These clay tiles are found on buildings in Bokhara and in Samarkand from 1369 onwards (when the latter city was rebuilt as their capital by Timur and his successors). Green or turquoise glaze was applied over most of the surface of the panels, while inscriptions and other decorative devices were highlighted in opaque white, purple or blue. Complete inner and outer walls of buildings were clad in this material, including the columns and capitals flanking the portal, creating a rich effect. Some of the finest glazed relief tiles of the fourteenth and fifteenth centuries are to be found in the mausoleums of Shah Zindah cemetery at Samarkand. The relief decoration stands out very sharply, being chiselled or cut before the tile was fired and glazed, and not cast in a mould as earlier relief decoration often was.

Ceramic decoration of a completely different nature, but one which is equally characteristic of the architecture of the Near East, is tile mosaic. The brickwork of twelfth-century Persian buildings was often bonded to form patterns or Kufic inscriptions on the outer walls by using glazed bricks of different colours. This ornamental brickwork was the forerunner of facing whole walls and cupolas with glazed slabs of earthenware cut into shapes that interlocked and formed a continuous surface of patterns in contrasting colours – tile mosaic. Straight-edged geometric designs (which offered practical advantages in their production) gave way to long and elaborate curvilinear designs and stylized plant forms, the technique reaching its maturity in the Seljuk city of Konya in the thirteenth century. The individual pieces were cut from glazed slabs which had already been fired and were then fitted together face downwards on a drawing of the design. Plaster was poured over the back and in between the bevels and was strengthened by inset canes running crossways. When dry, the panel could be lifted and placed in position against the wall. In addition to adorning mihrabs, tile mosaic became widely used to decorate inner surfaces of domes, transitions to domes, arches, niches and walls. The use of tile mosaic spread throughout Persia in the fourteenth century, with good examples appearing in Isfahan and in the Great Mosque at Yezd (finished in 1375). A later and even more monumental use of the technique can be seen in the portal of the Blue Mosque in Tabriz (completed in 1465).

The other extremely important technique developed by Islamic potters was the

The nineteenth-century pictorial tile panel has its origins in early examples such as this animated garden scene of c. 1600 which decorated the royal buildings of Shah Abbas I at Isfahan.

use of painted lines of manganese-purple pigment mixed with a greasy substance which disappeared during firing. This pigment was used in between areas covered by different-coloured glazes and had the effect of keeping the glazes banked up on each side of the dividing line. This technique, which was later known in Spain as '*cuerda seca*' (dry cord), could be more rapidly executed than tile mosaic and allowed much greater pictorial sophistication. For instance, on the walls of the royal palaces and garden pavilions constructed at Isfahan by Shah Abbas I, around 1,600 '*cuerda seca*' tiles were used to form large pictures which spread over a number of rectangular slabs. A fine example in the Victoria and Albert Museum dates from 1600 and is taken from one of the royal palaces, probably Isfahan. It depicts a scene in a garden in which a lady and two young men are being brought fruit and wine. Here is the partial source of the pictorial tile panel often found in the nineteenth century decorating butchers' shops, banks, public houses and hospital wards, although these panels did not usually employ the '*cuerda seca*' technique. Like tile mosaic, '*cuerda seca*' was originally transmitted to Turkey by emigrant potters and examples of the technique from around 1420 can be found in both the Green Mosque and the Green Tomb in Bursa.

Bursa and Edirne were the early capitals of the Ottoman Empire. Edirne in particular was associated with the development of underglaze painting as an important technique for decorating tiles, a technique which was to blossom into full

Underglaze painting was an important technique which was extensively used for decorating tiles in the sixteenth-century buildings of the Ottoman Empire. These tiles are at the Topkapi Palace in Istanbul.

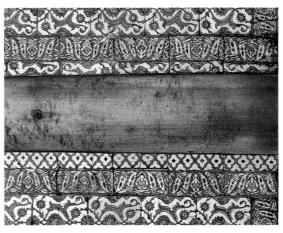

magnificence in the sixteenth-century tiled buildings of Istanbul. Underglaze painting was slow to develop at first because the colours available were too limited and lacking in strength. The original inspiration came from the Chinese white porcelain painted in underglaze blue which was being imported to the Near East in increasing quantity in the fourteenth century and which stimulated Islamic potters to emulation. Syrian potters made blue and white hexagonal tiles which were set point-to-point, with plain turquoise triangles filling the gaps (an arrangement which was frequently copied in the nineteenth century). But the production of underglaze painted tiles of world significance is invariably associated with the town of Iznik. The first Iznik tile period is characterized by the production of blue and white hexagonal tiles in the early years of the sixteenth century. By 1550 there was a marked trend towards rectangular tiles, with an increasing use of olive green as well as turquoise and purple. The third Iznik tile period, which lasted from about 1555 to 1620, employed colours of a startling intensity, particularly a distinctive red which has now become known as 'sealing wax red'. The range of subjects used to decorate the large Iznik tiles is remarkable and includes fantastic flowers and saw-edged leaves, tree blossoms, cypresses, vines, tulips, carnations, Chinese cloud-scrolls and large arabesques. The colour and pattern of Iznik tiles simply cannot be ignored and Arthur Lane

In the Harem of the Topkapi Palace, Istanbul, Turkey, tiles were used in the living areas of both the eunuchs and the princes. The walls of the Courtyard of the Black Eunuchs (above) were decorated with panels of tiles bearing stylized cypress trees and tree blossoms. In the wing (opposite) where the crown princes lived in grandeur and seclusion, this seventeenth-century room with completely tiled walls has a gold-plated fireplace flanked with shutters decorated with mother-of-pearl.

Left. Tiles lining the walls of a colonnade at the Alhambra, Granada, Spain.
Below. Geometrically patterned tiles were often used as a dado to shoulder-height, with more elaborate calligraphic friezes in the plasterwork above.

concluded that their 'improbable and barbarically splendid colour have a cruel fascination like that of hothouse plants'.

In the nineteenth century a preoccupation with Islamic buildings and their decoration coincided with the expansive confidence of the age. The distinctive Islamic use of architectural polychromy, geometric patterns and stylized plant forms exerted a strong influence on architects and designers in several countries, all of whom were eager to seek and exploit new ideas in the eclectic climate of the period. This mood also coincided with rapid advances in the technology and manufacture of tiles, including the rediscovery of lustre glazes, and it resulted in the powerful, unfamiliar decorative tiling schemes which are discussed in the sixth chapter.

Although the eighteenth-century Grand Tour was frequently extended to areas east of Greece, it was not until the early nineteenth century that a systematic study and recording of Islamic styles in architecture began. Interest in bright polychromatic decoration can be found amongst writers and artists too and the pictures of J F Lewis (executed whilst visiting the Alhambra in Granada in 1832–3) caused J S Cotman to lament that his own colours were 'faded by comparison'. One of the buildings that attracted particular attention amongst nineteenth-century architects was the Dome of the Rock in Jerusalem, where the polychromatic tile decoration added as part of the sixteenth-century Ottoman restoration was especially interesting. F Catherwood took considerable risks and was threatened by hostile locals when he made a detailed investigation of the building and its decoration in 1833. Rather more significant, and of considerable later impact, was the meticulous recording work of Owen Jones and his French companion, Jules Goury, who spent months at the Alhambra in Spain making detailed drawings and taking impressions of ornament by means of plaster or unsized paper. Goury died of cholera in 1834 whilst completing the work. On his return, Jones decided to be his own printer and publisher and the result was his *Plans, Elevations, Sections and Details of the Alhambra* in two volumes, published in 1842 and 1845.

The distinguished role which ceramic tiles played in architectural decoration in the Near East from very early times is not paralleled in Europe. Here, decorated tiles did not come into general use (outside Moorish Spain) until the second half of the twelfth century and then they were almost entirely confined to floors. Yet, there had been no significant precedent for this type of tile in the Near and Middle East since floors were more often covered with rugs. In addition, the technique of decorating tiles with coloured clay inlays was unfamiliar, despite the great variety of tiles which had been used in architecture for hundreds of years.

The first earthenware tile pavements were essentially substitutes for the mosaic floors in marble and other stone which were originally created around Istanbul and later used in Italy. Yet northern Europe lacked the variety of coloured stones and marbles and for this reason the inlaid ceramic tile is thought to have been developed

Examples of Moorish tiling patterns at the
*Alhambra in Spain. Geometric patterns
were a strong feature of Islamic decoration
and the many different permutations found
and recorded at the Alhambra provided the
most significant source of ideas for
nineteenth-century tile-makers.*

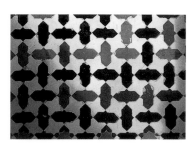

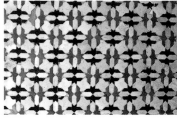

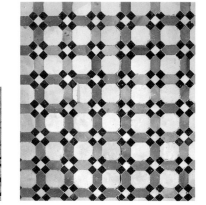

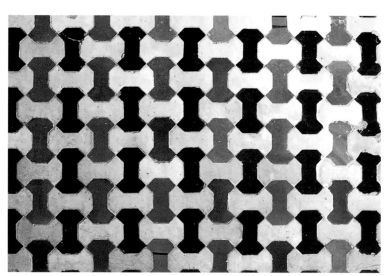

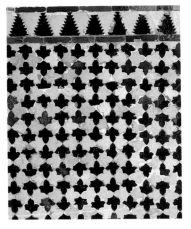

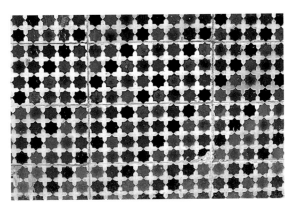

in France in the second quarter of the thirteenth century. Production soon spread to the Low Countries and Britain. It was essentially a technique inspired by inlaid stone tiles known as marquise tiles which originated in and around St Omer in northern France. Their raw material was a special kind of white limestone derived from Marquise in the Pas-de-Calais region. From this stone, tiles were made which were decorated with inlaid patterns and figurative motifs using a technique known as *champlevé*. First the stone was polished, then the design was drawn and the background cut away in shallow counter-relief. The depressions thus created were filled with a resinous mastic composition stained a darker colour than the stone, such as brown, red, blue, grey or black. Details were engraved in fine lines and likewise filled with the coloured mastic, the white stone appearing in sharp contrast to the dark colours. The mastic infill wore quickly, however, and this probably explains why such floors are usually only found in the choirs and chapels of churches. The technique remained popular for tomb slabs which frequently showed the figure of the deceased in outline. The fullest development of the technique can be seen at St Omer Cathedral where galloping knights are depicted against a dark grey background with the details picked out in red.

The technique of making marquise tiles was easily adapted to tiles made from clay. After the clay tile was cut out, a wooden stamp with decoration in flat relief was pressed into the soft clay, leaving impressions which were filled with clay of a contrasting colour, usually white. In the early tiles made in England the white clay was used in a fairly solid plastic state and surplus clay was trimmed off with a knife. Later, in the fifteenth and sixteenth centuries, the clay was introduced into the stamped cavities in the more convenient form of a liquid clay or 'slip'. After a period of drying, the tiles were covered with a thin, transparent lead glaze which on firing brought out the contrasting colours and facilitated cleaning. The firing or 'burning in' of the coloured clay inlays explains the later use of the term 'encaustic' for such tiles. Provided the depth of the inlay was sufficient, inlaid tiles were well-suited to use on the floor and provided a vivid patterned pavement for royal palaces, churches, abbeys and prosperous merchants' houses.

Medieval tiles derive much of their attraction from the variety and quality of the designs used and these included foliage, geometrical forms, heraldry and heraldic animals. In Britain the range was enormous and it has been comprehensively documented in the British Museum catalogue compiled by Elizabeth Eames.

In addition to square tiles, shaped pieces such as rectangles, polygons, quatrefoils, circles or segments of circles were also used to build up floors of tile mosaic. Their beauty lay in the combination of different tile shapes with alternating glaze colours which brought the geometry of the design vividly to life.

One of the earliest tile mosaic floors is in the chapel of Ste-Geneviève at the

The earliest inlaid floor tiles used limestone with patterns filled with a coloured mastic, such as those surviving at St Omer Cathedral, France (top right). This technique was occasionally revived in the nineteenth century, as seen in GG Scott's restoration of the chancel of Lichfield Cathedral in 1857-62 (below right). Medieval English ceramic inlaid tiles developed a range of patterns which were based on foliage and heraldic designs. Top left. Late thirteenth-century floor tiles in the cloister of Tichfield Abbey, Hampshire. Below left and centre. A thirteenth-century tiled pavement in the original frater (refectory) of Cleeve Abbey, Somerset.

Above. The encaustic tiles made by Craven Dunnills for the church of St John the Baptist, Kemberton, Shropshire (1882) were derived from fourteenth-century designs, original examples of which survive at Neath Abbey, West Glamorgan (below).

Abbey of St Denis near Paris, dating from the second half of the twelfth century. The earliest-known use in England was at Fountains Abbey in Yorkshire where the tiled floor was made between 1211 and 1247. Similar tile mosaics occur at other thirteenth-century Cistercian Yorkshire abbeys such as Byland and Meaux, suggesting that the monks of this order had some influence in their distribution. At Byland Abbey the tiles facing the risers of the steps have survived complete with their coloured glazes, making it possible to visualize their handsome effect in the rest of the building. In the south transept chapel a large area remains in situ, with contrasting circular and linear arrangements juxtaposed with dramatic effect. The surviving area is made up of 906 individually cut tiles of 40 different shapes, all but two of them curvilinear.

In France and England both tiles of a single colour and tile mosaic pieces were decorated with linear decoration. Occasionally the lines were individually cut on the surface of the tile with a stylus – and these were known as incised tiles. More common are line-impressed tiles on which the linear decoration has been stamped. A

late, but interesting, group of line-impressed tiles are those made in the sixteenth century at Chateauneuf-en-Bray in Normandy, France, which were exported to the southern counties of England. Two of the designs feature male heads in Renaissance helmets – a rare example of medieval imagery on floor tiles adapting to a new era, particularly in northern France where medieval methods survived in the hands of peasant potters until the nineteenth century.

Other evidence of this survival comes from the borders of west Flanders (now Belgium) and France where inlaid tiles continued to be made and used in a very characteristic way around the fireplace. The production of Flemish inlaid fireplace tiles reached its peak in the eighteenth century during a time of economic resurgence for the southern Netherlands. Most were used in large farmhouses in rural areas and about two-thirds of the production featured lions, of which a hundred different variations are known!

With the spread of new architectural ideas from Italy to Britain in the sixteenth century, decorated tile pavements went out of fashion. They did manage to survive in a high proportion of medieval parish churches and cathedrals but by the nineteenth century many had become very worn, often with the coloured clay inlays completely ground away through constant foot traffic. The great manufacturing revival of floor tiles from the 1830s onwards (which replaced most floor tiles and whose story is told in the third chapter) was preceded by a phase of antiquarian and archaeological interest which provided a vital link with medieval sources and tradition.

As early as 1788 John Henniker was collecting inlaid tiles from the abbey of St Stephen, Caen, Normandy (just before its destruction during the French Revolution), some of which he gave to the Society of Antiquaries in London. Later the excavation of ruined abbeys, abandoned after the Dissolution of the Monasteries in England during Henry VIII's reign, provided not only specimens of individual designs but also valuable evidence of the layout of patterned tiles and floors.

The collection of medieval tiles at the British Museum was initially largely the result of rescue work carried out by dedicated antiquarians and private collectors. Its influence as a source was not restricted to Britain, however, and in fact it was later felt in the United States when, at the end of the nineteenth century, Henry Chapman Mercer sketched the tiles, made notes and took away wax impressions before embarking on his own remarkable Arts and Crafts version of medieval tiles.

The great medieval tradition of floor tiles was largely over by 1550 and was in any case primarily a feature of northern Europe. In its place came a complex and interesting sequence of wall and floor tile traditions which spanned a period of 200 years and in which Spain, Portugal, Italy, Holland, France, Germany and Britain were all to play a part. Developments in one part of Europe can be seen to have had influences elsewhere and the uses of tiles in buildings, showing individual national

characteristics, are the result of a cross-fertilization of techniques, decorative fashions and design influences with history and politics.

The 500-year Moorish occupation of Spain, which ended in 1492, had provided a meeting-point of two cultures. Artistic and technical influences from the Middle East and North Africa, which had been absorbed during the period of Christian reconquest, were to have a lasting influence on the manufacture and use of tiles, not only in Spain and Portugal but in many other parts of Europe too. The fourteenth century raised tile mosaic to its full potential in southern Spain, notably on the dados lining the inner wall of the Alhambra at Granada and the Alcazar at Seville. The patterns were built up from small, glazed pieces of tile cut into various polygonal shapes. By the sixteenth century, however, this laborious process was being imitated by Spanish tilemakers much more cheaply by painting colours onto square tiles using the 'cuerda seca' technique which had long been familiar to Moorish potters. The

Early sixteenth-century Italian maiolica floor tiles of octagonal and polygonal shapes made for the chapel of Bartolomeo Lombardini in the church of San Francesco in Forli.

alternative method of decorating tiles, used particularly in Seville, was known as 'cuenca' whereby moulds were used to sink the pattern as hollows in the surface of the tile, leaving a raised outline to keep the different colours apart.

Later, in the nineteenth century, this technique was easily adapted to metal dies used in a mechanical press, thereby allowing mass production of what had previously been a distinctive regional material.

In addition to *cuerda seca* and *cuenca*, the third decorating technique from the Hispano-Moresque ceramic tradition was lustre painting, with the area around Valencia emerging as the most important centre. Valencian tiles were exported to Italy in the late fifteenth century, one particular destination being the apartments of Pope Alexander Vl in the Vatican. These lustre-painted Spanish wares were known in Italy by the term 'maiolica' and the technique soon became an Italian speciality, with painted decoration being applied over an opaque white glaze containing tin oxide. Painted maiolica plaques, sometimes in relief, were produced as house signs, especially in Faenza, and from the fifteenth century the Italians made colourful maiolica floor and wall tiles with Renaissance decoration executed in the characteristic bright colours of orange, yellow, purple, green and blue.

The sixteenth century brought a greater elaboration of design. A good example of the fully developed Renaissance style can be seen at Siena in the Piccolomini Library at the Cathedral, originally of 1507. In southern Italy, and particularly in Naples, later maiolica tile pavements had adopted a full baroque style by the eighteenth century with carpet-like designs spreading across many tiles. A particularly impressive scheme from this period is the cloister gardens of the Convent of Santa Chiara in Naples. The fourteenth-century cloister was transformed between 1741 and 1742 by Donato and Giuseppe Massa. Maiolica tiles were used to face the hexagonal columns which were

Italian maiolica tiles made in Faenza c. 1530 and used in the Chapelle de la Vierge, Eglise de Brou at Bourg in France.

decorated with plant designs and landscape scenes with figures on the tile-clad benches between.

The architectural importance of maiolica tiles in Italy itself is at least equalled by the influence they and their makers exerted elsewhere in Europe. Tile-makers were among the wide range of migrant Italian artists who helped to transmit Renaissance styles all over Europe. About the year 1500 an Italian maiolica maker from Pisa, Francesco Niculosa, settled in Seville. He soon found that in Spain tile-makers were allowed a greater share in architectural decoration than in Italy and set to work on a monumental scale. In 1504 he produced tile pictures for the altar in the chapel of the Alcazar at Seville, depicting the Visitation, the Annunciation and the Tree of Jesse. The tile picture, spread over many flat, tin-glazed, square tiles, remained popular in Spain and particularly Portugal and still represents an important use of tiles today.

In France, the activity of an Italian-directed tile workshop at Lyons is documented from 1512 onwards and, slightly later, Rouen became a centre for the production of maiolica tile pavements for the great new Renaissance palaces of the nobility. Italian in technique, these tiles were still thoroughly French in style. In sixteenth-century Germany relief-decorated tiles retained their popularity for tiled stoves, although a

Seventeenth-century Dutch tin-glazed tiles decorated with typical flower subjects. The influence of imported Chinese porcelain is apparent in the oriental character of the corner motifs.

new Renaissance influence was added to the previously Gothic designs. Austria and Switzerland, however, now adopted flat maiolica tiles with painted scenes for their stoves. The most famous producers were the Pfau family who maintained a factory at Winterthur during the sixteenth and seventeenth centuries.

The fashion for colourful maiolica tiles spread to northern Europe too at the beginning of the sixteenth century and Italian potters established themselves in places such as Antwerp in Flanders. Most famous of these potters was Guido di Savino from Castel Durante, who, after marrying a woman from Antwerp, changed his name to Guido Andries. His tiles found their way to England in around 1520 and were used on the floor of the chapel at The Vyne near Basingstoke in Hampshire. One of his fellow craftsmen, another Italian immigrant named Pierre-Frans van Venedigen, made the famous pavement for the Abbey of Herkenrode in Belgium (now in the Musée du Cinquantenaire, Brussels) in 1532.

The heyday of the Antwerp ceramic industry may have been of short duration (1520-70), but it had great significance for later developments in both Spain and the Netherlands. It is traditionally said that Flemish potters from Antwerp were responsible for the foundation of the tile industry at Talavera de la Reina in central Spain in the 1560s and also for the painted tile workshops of Seville. A Flemish influence is certainly discernible in the pierced strapwork borders on many of the Talavera tiles. Today Talavera still produces painted tiles and retains many old examples. In the church of Nuestra Senora del Prado it is possible to follow the development of local production from the sixteenth to the eighteenth century.

Links between Antwerp and Spain were quite logical in the sixteenth century since Spain at that time ruled the Low Countries. But the campaign for Dutch independence, with its attendant unrest, caused many artists and craftsmen to flee north to the relative safety of Holland. They took their ceramic skills with them and passed them on to Dutch potters. This 'melting pot' situation resulted in the new Dutch tile-making centres of Rotterdam, Delft, Haarlem and Utrecht, as well as centres situated as far north as Makkum and Harlingen in Friesland. The Treaty of Breda in 1609 brought peace and general commercial prosperity, which also had a beneficial influence on the new Dutch tile-makers.

In *Decorative Tiles Throughout the Ages* Hans van Lemmen observes that, at this time, 'the prosperity of the Dutch middle class led to expanding towns where many new houses were built. There was money which could be spent on such luxuries as tiles, which made homes more hygienic and added colour and decoration to the interior'. There is a striking similarity here with conditions in many European countries in the mid-nineteenth century. It is interesting to see how the uses of tiles, particularly in the home, evolved in Holland in the sixteenth and seventeenth centuries and then underwent a widespread revival in the nineteenth century, aided again by favourable

Flemish influences from the sixteenth century are evident in this elaborately tiled park in the centre of Talavera de la Reina, Spain.

Opposite. Dutch tile panels were used as house signs in the seventeenth century. This example was made for the House of the Three Flowerpots and bears the arms of the Van Arkel family and the city of Gorinchem, where the house was situated. Left. A late seventeenth-century Dutch tile panel decorated with an elaborate vase of flowers sitting on a plinth and surrounded by fantastic and slightly oriental birds.

conditions, chief amongst which was middle-class prosperity, and reinforced by the onset of mass production.

The new Dutch tile industry in the seventeenth century demonstrated a marked swing from floor tiles to the production of wall tiles, which were used to line kitchens, dairies and cellars where they conveniently kept out the damp. In living rooms these tiles were frequently used to decorate the big fireplaces and overmantels, to fill the spaces between windows and doors or to form a narrow skirting, as may be seen from Vermeer's picture of a lady standing at the virginals painted around 1670. Tiles were also used to flank door frames or to line the wall behind a bed. On the walls of staircases they provided a light-reflecting surface which was cleaner and more durable than whitewash. A tiled recess for a candle was sometimes incorporated.

The tiles themselves were hand-painted with designs which have since come to be regarded as characteristically Dutch – flower pots, tulips, animals, depictions of trades and occupations and, later in the seventeenth century, ships, children's games, biblical scenes and landscapes. Anne Berendsen, the Dutch writer on tiles, suggests that Dutch tiles are 'an expression of a middle class people, its folklore, its sentiments and, often, its sense of humour'. A decisive change occurred around 1620-40 when, influenced by the blue and white Chinese porcelain brought back by Dutch sea traders, tile decoration became predominantly blue and white and consequently polychrome decoration, reminiscent of Italian maiolica, became less common. Blue and white 'Delft' tiles have, over the years, become an epitome of Dutchness and were an important source of inspiration in the nineteenth century.

The evolution of the Dutch fireplace and its use of tiles is of particular interest and is the essential precursor of the nineteenth-century tiled fireplace in all its variety and abundance. Dutch fireplaces before 1700 had high smoke hoods and tiles were generally restricted to panels used directly behind the fire. The subject of the tiles was frequently a vase of flowers – a motif which may have had its origin in the custom of standing a real vase of flowers in the fireplace during the summer. Traditionally the smoke hood of Dutch fireplaces was supported by sandstone pillars which were sometimes carved as standing figures or caryatids. As tiles became more common in the seventeenth century, both pillars and caryatids were transformed into flat, painted tile forms, surrendering their true architectural significance and coming much closer to nineteenth-century fireplaces with their tiled side panels. After 1700 it became fashionable to lower the smoke hood to about a metre above floor level. Although this reduced the scope for the tile decoration around the fireplace itself, it did make it possible to tile the whole of the great smoke hood right up to the ceiling. These 'smuigers' were built until the mid-nineteenth century and carried spectacular displays of tiles which might include a whole series of narrative biblical scenes or Dutch landscapes. The hand-painted tiles were the forerunners of the almost

A hand-painted Dutch tile panel made in Rotterdam at the end of the eighteenth century. The panel, which was probably made for a Spanish church, depicts the Crucifixion and is the twelfth in a set showing Stations of the Cross.

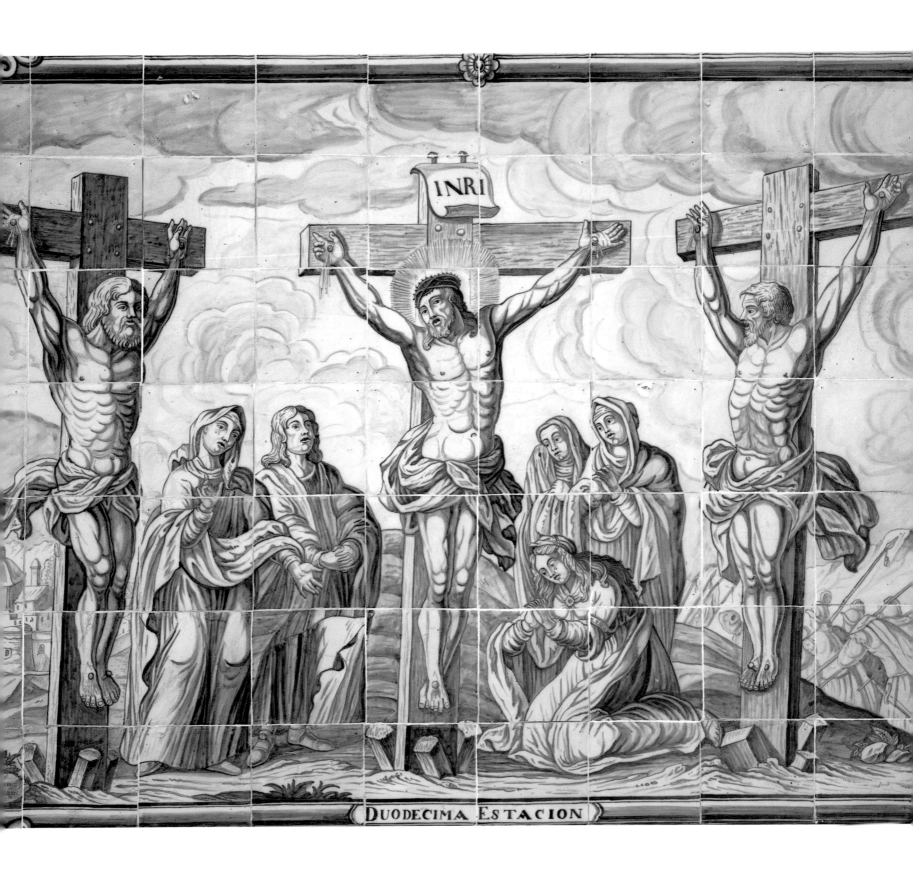

DUODECIMA ESTACION

The octagonal tiled dairy at Endsleigh, Devon (c. 1815). Built for the Duke of Bedford and using plain tiles surrounded by decorative borders, this was one of the forerunners of the fashionable nineteenth-century tiled dairy which reached its zenith with the Royal Dairy at Windsor.

universal picture tiles which were mass-produced as sets for later nineteenth-century fireplaces (and which are featured in the fifth chapter).

Dutch tiles were produced and used in huge numbers in the seventeenth and eighteenth centuries, not only in fireplaces or indeed in Holland. They were exported for use in prestigious architectural schemes in England, Germany, France and even Portugal where they were to influence local production by suggesting the use of designs borne on a single tile rather than spread across several tiles. The Chateau of Beauregard in the Loire Valley, France, still preserves a striking reminder of the quality of exported Dutch tiles. The floor of the portrait gallery, laid in 1646 with 6,000 tiles made in Delft, depicts soldiers copied from Prince Maurice's book *The Handling of Firelocks, Muskets and Pikes*, which was first published in The Hague in 1608. The tiles are remarkably unworn and the overall effect of serried ranks of soldiers (including pikemen, halberdiers, musketeers and armoured cavalrymen) is extremely powerful.

In Germany, several fine tiled interiors survive which consist entirely of imported Dutch tiles. Near Cologne the Augustusburg at Bruhl has ground-floor rooms panelled with blue and white tiles, while there is a whole series of tile pictures in the summer dining room. In the park the main hall of the Falkenlust (falconry lodge) displays Rotterdam-made tiles decorated with a pattern taken from the arms of Bavaria and interspersed with bird tiles. The park at Nymphenburg near Munich has various pavilions elaborately decorated with Dutch tiles, including the Amalienburg Hunting Lodge which was built in 1734–9 and has notable polychrome tile-pictures of vases of flowers.

For Britain the most significant Dutch influence was felt when Dutch potters moved to England in the seventeenth century and English delftware tile-making began to grow in London, Bristol and Liverpool. For the first half of the eighteenth century English designs closely followed Dutch examples in an effort to compete, but after about 1750 English designs show increasing originality. In Bristol the *bianco-sopra-bianco* (white on white) technique was developed which enabled details to be painted in pure white on the slightly bluish-white ground of the tile, thus creating subtle but original effects. Most English delftware tiles were used for fireplaces, although few have survived in their original form. One of the best is the large fireplace at Aston Hall, Birmingham, which has a whole set of chinoiserie tiles.

The most important innovation in English eighteenth-century tiles was developed in Liverpool in 1756 and provided a complete contrast to the Dutch delftware tradition. It was pioneered by John Sadler and Guy Green who successfully transferred an image from a printing plate (at first wood block but later engraved copper) to a tile by means of a transfer tissue. Most images were printed in a single ceramic colour, usually black, red or brown, which was fired on to the white glazed surface of the tile at a relatively low temperature. This printing technique allowed the

Border tiles from the dairy at Endsleigh, Devon. The design of trailing ivy was produced by Wedgwood using the newly available technique of transfer-printing to produce an outline which was then hand-coloured. Wedgwood also supplied the ceramic settling pans and cream coolers for the dairy.

consistent reproduction of very fine detail – impossible to achieve by hand painting – and paved the way for industrial exploitation in the nineteenth century. The subjects, which included landscapes with romantic ruins and figures of fashionable society, evoke a feeling of eighteenth-century England. Even more distinctive and documentary are the images of English actors portrayed in a particular role on stage and often bearing their name and the title of the play.

The greater availability of tiles in Britain in the eighteenth century because of home production led to some important architectural innovations, such as the tiled dairy. The ability of tiles to carry a painted or printed decoration but also to provide a cool and clean wall surface was exploited in a series of elaborate dairy buildings on the country estates of wealthy aristocrats. Wedgwood tiles played an important role in establishing this tradition which continued through to the nineteenth century and culminated in the magnificence of Prince Albert's Dairy at Windsor (see the fourth chapter). The charming idea of the lady's play-dairy (in which, dressed in silks and satins, she pretended to be a milk-maid) originated with Marie Antoinette and her cottage Le Hameau, at Versailles. However, there is evidence that decorative dairies were built in England long before Marie Antoinette thought of the idea. One of the best survivors of the English eighteenth-century dairy genre is the dairy at Althorp in Northamptonshire which was built for Lavinia Lady Spencer in 1786. The brown ironstone building with pyramid roof is complete with its lining of tiles made by Wedgwood. Cream-settling pans and other ceramic dairy equipment were also supplied by Wedgwood and remain in the building. Plain tiles predominate but all the windows, doors, angles of the room, the cornice, and a frieze immediately above the workbench, are decorated with trails of ivy.

The final strand in the history of tile traditions and sources comes with the export of European tiles to the New World. Tin-glazed earthenware tiles from Holland and England were the first to reach America for use on an architectural scale. They were not uncommon used as fireplace surrounds in the homes of the well-to-do in the eighteenth century. A recent survey has recorded 102 such fireplaces, dating from before 1800, scattered across 11 eastern states but with nearly half in Massachusetts. They doubtless provided their owners with a reminder of their European origins and predate the production of decorative fireplace tiles by North American potteries. In eighteenth-century America mass production of tiles and all the changes this would bring to architectural decoration were still not even visible on the horizon.

One of the two fireplaces in the Peirce-Nichols House, Salem, Massachusetts, faced with Liverpool printed tiles. These tiles were taken from the captured British ship 'Revolution' by the brother-in-law of Gerathamel Peirce, who built the house in 1782.

The Marriage of Art and Industry

The central Refreshment Room at the
Victoria and Albert Museum, London
(1868-70). Designed by James Gamble,
the decoration was produced by the leading
manufacturers of the day. The walls are
clad with ceramics by Minton and the tile
pavement is by Maws.

Until the nineteenth century tile-making was essentially a craft-based business and, even though in some places tile manufacture was an important part of the local economy, it was essentially a workshop operation. The Industrial Revolution introduced new techniques for preparing and forming clay into tiles, using such improvements as steam power and iron presses, and these techniques in turn necessitated special factory buildings; even more importantly the changes in industry created an unprecedented demand for decorative building materials. Supplying the dual needs of mass production on the one hand and elaborate decoration on the other required a radically different combination of skills and philosophies from those of previous generations. Thus in nineteenth-century decorative tile-making art and industry were brought together in a new and fascinating relationship.

The effect of industrialization in terms of developing manufacturing technology was less dramatic in the case of ceramic tiles than in many other spheres. Whereas the making of textiles or the smelting of iron were revolutionized in the eighteenth century at least in Britain, tile-making was relatively slow to respond to new technology and the advent of steam power. Although the first steps towards mass production had been taken with the printed decoration of tiles in Liverpool from the 1750s onwards and Josiah Wedgwood's limited production of dairy tiles at his Etruria works, it was not until well into the nineteenth century that tile manufacture started on a large scale, first in Britain and later at varied dates in other European countries. The United States did not really begin to develop its own tile-making industry until the final quarter of the nineteenth century.

Industrialization brought changes to towns and cities which, for the manufacture of ceramic tiles, had a far greater importance than developments in the technology used to produce them. The demand for robust and decorative building materials increased enormously as European cities expanded. The nineteenth-century building boom meant not simply more buildings but buildings of entirely new types and uses and often of an unprecedented size and scale. Railway stations, office buildings, large hotels and municipal buildings such as town halls, libraries and museums provided a novel opportunity for architects to extend the use of ceramic tiles while capitalizing on both their colourful, decorative qualities and their hard-wearing, easily cleaned surfaces.

The other equally important, but very different, reason for the revival and expansion of tile-making came from the needs of both the new churches and of the large numbers of medieval churches then being restored. Here industrial production was stimulated and led by the demands of architectural style, enlightened by archaeology and fuelled by the contemporary zeal for the Gothic Revival. (The resulting story of the encaustic tile is told in the third chapter.) This movement produced some remarkable examples of the fruitful collaboration between art and industry. Herbert Minton, as manufacturer and industrialist, and A W N Pugin, as designer and architect, formed an influential working relationship in the 1840s, to undoubted mutual benefit. Meanwhile in France, the other European country particularly influenced by the Gothic Revival, a similar symbiosis existed between the restorer and architect Viollet le Duc and the Boulenger family, who were encaustic tile manufacturers situated near Beauvais.

The union of art and industry was strengthened on the production side by a number of technical developments. In 1840 Richard Prosser took out a British patent in which he described the making of ceramic buttons from clay dust. Herbert Minton was quick to realize that he could apply this method to the manufacture of wall tiles and purchased a share in the patent. Fundamental to the process was an iron press incorporating a screw thread and flywheel which compacted the clay between two metal dies in a box. By 1842 Minton had over 60 tile presses in operation. This process of mass production soon spread to the Continent and in 1846 the German firm of Villeroy and Boch installed presses at their factory at Septfontaines in Luxembourg.

The pressing of tiles from clay dust offered considerable advantages for economic mass production. With a water content of only a few per cent the pressed tiles were easily dried, taking less time and fuel than tiles made from much moister plastic clay.

An iron encaustic tile press, dating from the mid-nineteenth century and made by W Boulton Ltd of Burslem, Stoke-on-Trent. Presses like this formed the basis for the mass-production of tiles.

A large quantity of nineteenth-century wall tiles were decorated with moulding or some form of relief decoration; this was cheap and particularly easy to achieve by using metal dies in the presses, which formed the clay dust into tile and relief decoration in one process.

After a first, or biscuit, firing the tiles could be made colourful and attractive by applying glazes to their faces using cheap, unskilled and often female labour. The glazes melted in the second firing and gravity caused them to run from the areas of high relief to form thick pools in the hollows, thus highlighting the effect of the relief decoration without any need for costly skilled hand-painting. Tiles such as those decorated with egg and dart mouldings relied for their visual effect on this simple process and were very popular in architectural tile schemes.

Ingenious use of this industrial method of clay dust pressing even led to the production of a tile form of mosaic, patented by Maws in 1862 but later used by a variety of manufacturers. The face of the 'patent mosaic' tile was indented, with lines representing the joints between the *tesserae*. When the tiles were laid on the floor, the indented lines filled with cement and the overall effect looked convincingly like real mosaic. Such an industrialized and essentially sham form of decoration naturally attracted its critics but the *Journal of Decorative Art* in September 1887 was won over by its cheapness, declaring that 'whether the purists who some years ago contended with such fiery zeal that everything in Architecture should be what it appeared to be, would describe these tiles as imitations we do not know, neither do we care; suffice it that they are decorative in the extreme, are durable, and are available at much less cost than the real mosaics'.

The adoption of industrial production methods and the demand for output created tile factories in the second half of the nineteenth century that were increasingly sophisticated in their layout and operation. The making, decorating,

These patent mosaic floor tiles by Maws were used in the hallway of Croesawdy, Newtown, in Powys, Wales. The house was built for the owner of the adjacent woollen mill in 1881.

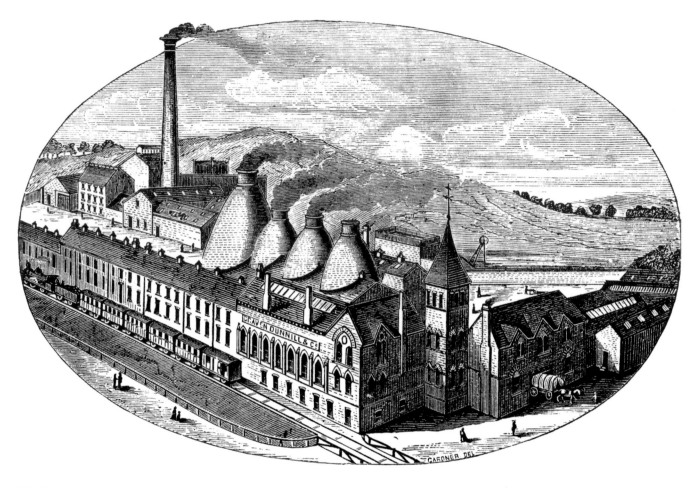

drying, firing and despatching stages of tile production were separated out and were often housed in different buildings, although they were still close enough together to allow an efficient flow of raw materials and finished products. But the buildings were more than mere housing for machinery and workers – in fact they frequently became an expression for the mixture of art and industry which was contained within them. Tiles were used to decorate the factory façades, thereby promoting both the company and its products, as well as the actual cause of tiles in architecture.

In Britain the most impressive Victorian tile factories are all the work of one architect – Charles Lynam of Stoke-on-Trent. The first was built for Minton Hollins in Stoke in 1869 and was intended from the start to be a showpiece in every sense. It not only incorporated the latest principle of linear production but it also allowed its owner, Michael Daintry Hollins, to have unhindered access to all parts of the works in his gig, an important factor when seeking to impress potential clients. The company's geometric tiles were used externally in a striking way, appearing as decorative panels in the semi-circular window heads on the ground floor, with the company name in mosaic above the main entrance arch. The interior, with its offices and showroom, reinforced the visitor's impression of a company whose output demonstrated taste and quality. *Great Industries of Great Britain*, in its third volume which was edited by James McCarthy and published in 1877, enthused about the building, as 'turning sharply to the left and ascending the stairs that lead to corridor on corridor of offices, you see the walls covered with tiles of many designs, but all bearing as the central ornament the monogram of the firm. In every passage, at every turning, in every angle, and in every corner, they are still before you, and the floor on which you tread is inlaid with some of these famous encaustic tiles which, while recalling the classical tessellated pavement, remind you of the world-wide renown which their manufacture has achieved for Messrs Minton, Hollins & Co.'

The architectural presentation of the company as an art manufacturer must have been considered successful since, in 1874, a rival tile company in the Ironbridge Gorge, Craven Dunnills of Jackfield, chose Lynam to design their new works. Geometric tiles were again used to fill in the pointed arches above the windows and the completed building, with its tower and spire, made a striking engraved image which was used on company letterheads as well as on the front cover of the catalogue.

Lynam's third and final opportunity to design a tile factory came with Maws' new works in Jackfield, which were opened with great celebration on 10 May 1883. This factory was larger than either of his two previous works, with buildings covering two hectares. Externally, decorative tiles were restricted to a large panel above the main entrance recording key dates in the history of the firm. Inside, the fine wooden staircase, with a tiled dado punctuated by panels of classical figures representing such

Above. Trade tile for Maws' agents in Chicago. Their name (which should have been Dibble) was misspelt and so the tiles were used on a warehouse floor at the Jackfield tile factory.
Opposite top. Engraving of Craven Dunnill's factory at Jackfield, Shropshire, c. 1875.
Opposite below left. Postcard of Maws' new Benthall Works at Jackfield, opened in 1883.
Opposite below right. Maker and designer recorded on a ceramic block on the 1905 façade of Kardomah Café, Liverpool (now demolished).

The town of Auneuil in northern France has several richly decorated buildings surviving from its nineteenth-century encaustic tile industry, which was operated by the Boulenger family. These include a company house of 1885 clad on three sides with encaustic tiles (left) and the despatch warehouse of the factory (opposite below).

Part of the façade of the Ménier chocolate factory at Noisiel-sur-Marne, east of Paris. Designed in 1872 by Jules Saulnier, the cast-iron structure was decorated with polychromatic infills of coloured bricks and glazed tiles.

virtues as 'Knowledge' and 'Durability', led up to offices with grand faience fireplaces and a top-lit showroom

Flamboyant tile factory architecture was by no means restricted to Britain. The Beauvais region of France also has some fine examples. The best are undoubtedly the former buildings of the Boulenger factory in the small town of Auneuil. Here there are buildings decorated with encaustic tiles which wilfully defy all but the blind to pass them by unnoticed. The despatch warehouse of the factory strides alongside the railway line, each of its 16 arches separated by 'pillars' of tiles of different designs, whilst above each arch are recorded in tiled form the medals and honours gained by the company in the years between 1855 and 1875. Nearby the manager's house has tiled façades which include a *trompe l'oeil* window. But the ultimate tile-decorated building must be the house or 'museum' built by the Boulenger family in 1885 which, on three sides of its rectangular shape, is entirely clad with the company's products like a giant architectural version of a printed catalogue.

The striking buildings of the nineteenth-century tile factories are really only an outward manifestation of the successful union of art and industry. The real driving force behind this unfamiliar combination were the 'art manufacturers' – an innovative breed of entrepreneurs who emerged in a variety of fields to meet the challenge of mass-producing decorative architectural products. In the field of tiles their problems and achievements are epitomized by the Maw family whose tile-making efforts in England progressed from a hand-pressed prototype in the 1840s to the largest decorative tile works in the world little more than 30 years later. From a family journal which has survived, it is possible to piece together not only the sometimes haphazard way in which the Maws became involved with tile-making but also their diverse interests, which contributed considerably to the success of the business. The detail of their story is unique but in broad terms it is a story typical of many family-owned art manufacturers in both Europe and America.

The key characters are the two brothers, George and Arthur Maw, and their father, John Hornby Maw. The family had originally come from a Lincolnshire farming background but the essential financial backing for developing the tile works must have been made possible by J H Maw's involvement in the family's successful manufacturing chemists business in London. Despite the scientific nature of the business, his daughter, Anne Mary, recorded that there was 'always an atmosphere of art in the dingy house at 55 Aldermanbury'. By the 1840s J H Maw had withdrawn from the business and was clearly shaping his artistic taste and talents. An unsuccessful attempt at farming in Essex was combined with lessons from Peter De Wint in sketching from nature. His circle of artistic friends was growing and his daughter mentions 'Mr & Mrs David Cox, who with their young son, were beloved and intimate friends in those days'. Anne Mary's birthday in 1835 was celebrated by a

grand dinner party of artists. Amongst the guests were J S Cotman and J M W Turner who, she recalls, 'took me on his knee and cut a pencil for me out of my new paints-box, that I might draw him a house – remarking "dash it the child draws crows better than I do!"'. A ten-year stay in Hastings gave J H Maw the chance to collect Elizabethan carved oak furniture and contribute to Royal Academy exhibitions for several successive years. He loved 'to paint in the company of Artists visiting Hastings, or to entertain and talk to artistic callers'. Growing up in such a strongly artistic and cultural home setting, it is easy to see how the young George and Arthur acquired skills and attitudes which were later to re-emerge in the tile business.

The tile-making venture appears to have been started almost by chance. A move to Tavistock in Devon was made in 1849, J H Maw 'having heard of certain beds of porcelain clay for sale on Dartmoor, which … he thought might prove a good investment for his sons'. Nothing came of this, however, and, after four months, the family moved to Bideford in North Devon. Here they paid visits to 'the works of a very primitive potter, who used the clay on the river's bank near Appledore to turn therewith jars and jugs of simple but picturesque shape'. What followed is the real embryo of the great Maws tile industry and is graphically described by George and Arthur's sister, who was 20 at the time:

Above left. Photograph of Arthur Maw with his family in the grounds of their home, Severn House, Ironbridge in Shropshire, c. 1870.
Above right. Early watercolour designs for Maws' encaustic tiles.

My father and I had been interested in the roughly made inlaid tiles of a mediaeval church in the neighbourhood, and I had traced some of their designs when after experimenting in decorating the potter's pitchers, incoloured with the contents of our paint boxes, it struck my father that it would not be difficult to imitate the ancient encaustic tiles - which work we all proceeded to employ ourselves in with breathless interest. I think my father first carved a 'die'...this was impressed on a paving tile of the plain clay, while moist, and the imprint filled in with a cream-like fluid of white pipe clay, which being carefully dried and scraped, behold the perfect reproduction of the ancient encaustic tile. The first tiles took a long time to dry, and then the old potter, who also was sympathetic, carefully 'fired' them for us in his small kiln.

Of course our tiles 'left much to desire' - the white pipe clay had shrunk away from the solid background, some of the design had fallen out and our tiles were far from the perfect works of art which we had committed so hopefully to the kiln. But our dear father was not to be daunted and thought he saw even in this failure the germ of the business for his boys, for which he had been searching and praying. I know my mother and I made pilgrimages to old village churches in the neighbourhood where I, prone upon my knees, industriously traced the designs of all the ancient encaustic pavements we could find.

The Maws' proposal of a marriage between art and industry did not have to wait long before its consummation. In the autumn of 1849 J H Maw's attention was drawn

Above left. Five hand-drawn and -coloured designs from Modern Encaustic Tile Designs Vol 3, which was produced by Maw & Co in c. 1860.

Above right. Tracing heightened with watercolour of the pavement in St Mark's, Venice. This is one of a series executed by George Maw whilst travelling around the Mediterranean in 1861.

to an advertisement for the sale of an Encaustic Tile Works in Worcester. 'He at once wrote proposing to visit Worcester with his son and look into the affair, and accordingly to Worcester he and George went, and returned quite fascinated with the possibilities of the Encaustic Tile Business.' The Maws moved to Worcester and took over the remnants of the works which had been established by the Worcester Porcelain Company. Soon after George went off to the Agricultural College at Cirencester and 'the tile business was left to the unaided enterprise of my father and Arthur, who was only 15 years old'. Not surprisingly, they encountered many technical difficulties and George gave up his successful studies at Cirencester to return to Worcester and come to their aid.

In the spring of 1852, attracted by the prospect of good, cheap local clay and coal, the family and its workforce migrated to Broseley in the Ironbridge Gorge. It must have been an extraordinary sight as the young Maws, the tribe of workmen, their equipment, wives, children and belongings all travelled in the same train. Anne Mary later wrote 'I remember thinking there was something patriarchial [sic] about it.'

The first years at Ironbridge must have been difficult, with all the members of the family contributing. Even Anne Mary was involved in copying antique designs and drawing patterns on woodblocks for the catalogues. The Maw family were great travellers and assiduously recorded tile designs and other decorative details on their journeys through many parts of Europe and around the Mediterranean. It is clear that Italian marble pavements provided the inspiration for later geometric arrangements of ceramic tiles. The surviving drawings include an extensive series executed in St Mark's Cathedral, Venice, in the summer of 1861. A later series in 1863 cover the famous medieval tiles and mosaics in situ in the abbeys of Yorkshire. George Maw took an active interest in archaeology and published papers on aspects of Roman mosaics. Thus the manufacturing output of the firm, certainly until it became a limited liability company in 1888, was based on a background of sound scholarship by an informed and educated family. The eclectic nature of Victorian tile designs, responding to the pressures for a whole variety of decorative styles, meant using every available source of design idea. The works built up an impressive library which included such obvious source material as *The Grammar of Ornament* (compiled by Owen Jones and published in 1856), as well as more obscure titles such as *booke of Sundry Draughtes principally serving for glaziers*, which was an 1848 copy by Henry Shaw of a 1615 book which showed lead strip glazing patterns for windows. From pencil annotations to the patterns, it is clear that this book provided ideas for geometric tile arrangements – a clear demonstration of the Victorian application of a visual form of lateral thinking.

Like many educated and reasonably wealthy Victorians of their age, George and Arthur Maw were polymathic in their interests which undoubtedly contributed to

A chromolithographed plate of Egyptian patterns. This is one of the eight plates devoted to Egyptian decoration in Owen Jones's Grammar of Ornament. Published in 1856, this inspirational volume was widely used by tile designers.

the vigour and enterprise of the firm. George Maw's early interests in agriculture were allied to a passion for botany. His particular love was the genus *Crocus*, examples of which he cultivated in his garden at Benthall Hall, Shropshire. In 1886 he published a fine monograph on *Crocus* which he illustrated himself. In an unpublished letter Ruskin described the drawings as 'most exquisite.... and quite beyond criticism'. Maw travelled widely on botanical expeditions, including one trip with Dr (later Sir) Joseph Hooker in 1871 to the High Atlas in the south of Morocco, a mountain range never previously explored by European botanists. His botanical interests inevitably affected the firm's designs for tiles, which included a series of printed tiles depicting British wild flowers in the crisp style of botanical illustration.

Another aspect of George Maw's scientific interests was the then undeveloped subject of geology. He collected specimens of clay from many parts of Britain and fired and tested them, writing up the results for the Museum of Practical Geology in London. A further extension of his geological interests into tile-making promoted the introduction of a series of tiles decorated with trilobites and fossil tree roots from the Coal Measures rocks. The culmination of George Maw's interests in clays, ceramics and botany came with his patent for ceramic plant labels which could be lettered up at the works to customers' needs using a low-fired black enamel which made them imperishable. These labels were incidentally invaluable for the labelling of wine cellars too!

Arthur Maw was concerned with many facets of the technical development of tile-making, being the author of most of the nearly 20 patents which the company granted. He also wrote an authoritative account of encaustic tile-making which appeared in the ninth edition of the *Encyclopaedia Britannica*. Meanwhile, a drawing signed 'Maw & Co, Benthall Works, Dec 15th 1859' in his hand shows the use of

Watercolour design for a roof (right) using elaborately shaped and coloured tiles. Signed 'Maw & Co, Benthall Works, Dec 15th 1859', a simplified version of this design with coloured rectangular roofing tiles in a geometric pattern was used on the cottages (left) adjacent to Arthur Maw's home in Ironbridge, Shropshire.

highly decorative tiles for a roof, including very ornate ridge tiles. Other similar drawings dated 1861 have been attributed to M Digby Wyatt and it seems likely that the two may have collaborated prior to the 1862 London Exhibition. A simplified version was implemented on one side of the roof of a group of cottages adjacent to Severn House in Ironbridge where Arthur Maw lived for many years. The zig-zag, criss-cross colours are a rare experiment in English architectural polychromy and reminiscent of the colourful roofs in the Burgundy area of France. It is interesting that the decorated side of the roof is overlooked by some of the main windows of Severn House; the other side is quite invisible, remaining out of sight and probably out of mind!

The contribution of the Maw family to the cause of art manufacture in the 1850s and 1860s must be compounded by that of the dozens of other manufacturers working in the same field both in Britain and Europe (but not as yet in the United States). The combined output of tile factories at this time was enormous and *The Building News* of 15 February 1867 echoed the general astonishment at their impact by saying, 'When we speak of ornamental tiles we now make use of what is almost a household word, and yet it is not more than thirty years ago that a tile meant simply a roofing tile, and the most imaginative fancy could connect the word with nothing more ornamental than the blue and white lining to the cool dairy, with the history of the prodigal son fairly set forth, or perchance the old Dutch fireplace with Aesop's fables most morally rendered.'

The popularization of tiles was due to a number of factors, all of which were vital to the success of the art industry. Early in the tile revival Herbert Minton had shown considerable flair for presenting his firm in the right circles by demonstrating tile pressing in 1843, not only to the Society of Arts in London but also at a soirée organized by the Marquess of Northampton as President of the British Association. This was described as 'a brilliant gathering', at which were present Prince Albert, the Duke of Wellington, Sir Robert Peel (who was Prime Minister at the time), a number of bishops and about 30 foreign princes. Prince Albert's interest was such that Minton prepared a description of the process and a drawing of the press, which he presented only four days later. The 'promotion' seems to have paid off since the following year, in 1844, a geometric and encaustic tile pavement was made for Osborne House, the new royal residence on the Isle of Wight.

In 1860, two years after Herbert Minton's death, it was Maws' turn to promote its expanding tile-making empire. During a visit to Shropshire, 160 delegates from the British Archaeological Association inspected the tile works and were liberally entertained at George Maw's home, Benthall Hall, where a majestic new tessellated pavement had been laid. In his speech of welcome, reported in full in the *Art Journal*, Maw was able to boast that:

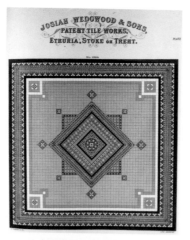

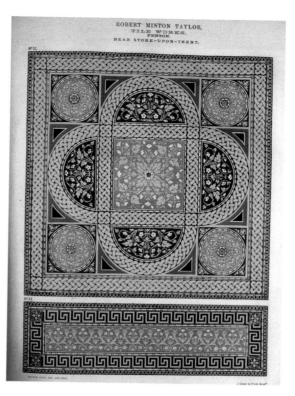

Printed catalogue covers and pages from a variety of tile manufacturers. These are (clockwise from top left): Maw & Co (wall tiles), Josiah Wedgwood, Robert Minton Taylor, Maw & Co (floor tiles) and Craven Dunnill & Co.

a considerable proportion [of his factory's production] are sent to America, India and the Colonies. Amongst the principal works we have executed, or have in hand, abroad, I may mention the pavements of the entrance hall of the new University of Toronto; also nearly the whole of the ground floor and upper corridor of Osgoode Hall, Toronto, laid by our own man sent out for the purpose; the entrance hall of the Hong Kong Club; deck house and other parts of the steam-yacht 'Said', for the Pasha of Egypt, laid by our own men; Jessore Church, Bengal; ground floor in New General Post-office, Calcutta; and the Cathedral of Spanish Town, Jamaica.

Whilst building up a good reputation and gaining prestige were important factors in attracting clients, they needed to be backed up by the production of printed catalogues of tile designs. Companies issuing catalogues after about 1850 were able to take advantage of the new process of colour lithography which presented their tiles in the most effective way possible. Large format catalogue pages depicted not only individual designs but also suggestions for layouts for floor pavements and wall linings. Important buildings were shown and famous people to whom tiles had been supplied were invariably quoted with pride and medals and awards were often used to decorate the heads of the pages. Maws' new catalogue of 1867 included some pages which had undergone no less than 12 printings. *The Building News* declared it 'a triumph of steam printing' which 'shows not only the vast variety of tiles

The highly decorative cover of a tile catalogue produced by Mansfield Brothers in c. 1880. The striking image of the works has much in common with the Craven Dunnill cover opposite and shows three large bottle ovens as well as five smaller ones, together with a railway siding and wagons.

English tile manufacturers at the American exhibitions.
Below left. The Maw & Co stand at the Chicago World Fair of 1893 was designed by Charles Henry Temple.
Below right. The display of Minton Hollins & Co at the Centennial Exhibition, Philadelphia, 1876.

which are in use or may be used for a variety of purposes, but it indicates the great enterprise combined with art knowledge which the firm possesses.'

When catalogues from different firms and countries are compared, a similarity of patterns and presentation can be discerned. Commercial rivalry and even plagiarism were an inevitable part of an art industry and a number of instances have been found of manufacturers keeping copies of each other's catalogues. By 1873 *The Builder* was commenting that 'tile designs run too much in a groove; they are arranged upon certain main types, which seem to recurr [sic] again and again'.

Another significant form of promotion for the art industries which recurred throughout the second half of the nineteenth century was the exhibition. In Britain the 1851 Great Exhibition to the Industry of All Nations at the Crystal Palace established a high profile for art industries, and exhibitions along similar lines were to follow in venues around the industrialized world for the rest of the century. Significant though the 1851 Exhibition was in so many ways, it came too early to provide a showcase for the fully fledged revival of tiles. Nevertheless Herbert Minton showed examples of his new colour-printed tiles and his new series with opaque enamels, known as 'majolica' tiles, was used to great effect in the Alhambra Court.

There were rather more tiles to see at the next of the international exhibitions, which was held in London in 1862. Maws had been actively developing their own brightly coloured and strongly patterned majolica tiles and these were presented at the exhibition on a stand devised by George Maw with 'a collective series of architectural productions illustrating the clay manufacturers of the Shropshire Coal Field'. One of the principal features was a chimney-piece of majolica tiles set in

Left. The coat of arms of Sir Henry Cole
and a lettered frieze form part of the
ceramic decoration of the central
Refreshment Room at the Victoria and
Albert Museum, London, whilst (below) a
mosaic portrait of Cole in an elaborate
ceramic frame was placed on the West
Staircase in 1878.

stone, which was designed by M Digby Wyatt. Both manufacturer and designer
received prize medals and excellent coverage, with illustrations, in the architectural
and building trades press. Such occasions provided an important 'shop window' for
the products of this fruitful collaboration between art and industry.

By the time of the Paris International Exhibition in 1867 the manufacture and use
of tiles was in full swing and a considerable area was given over to those from French
and English manufacturers. Contemporary critics admired these tiles for both their
decorative and functional qualities. M Digby Wyatt foresaw the time when tiles 'will
be rapidly extended in every direction into civil structures of every description, from
national museums to ladies' boudoirs'.

As far as museums were concerned, tiles were already a feature of both
collections and buildings. The Department of Practical Art in South Kensington,
which was established in 1852, had purchased a number of items from the displays at
the Great Exhibition the previous year. These were used to establish a small museum
which was essentially the embryo of today's Victoria and Albert Museum. The
purchases included a number of Minton tiles intended 'for use of students and
manufacturers' and the role of the museum in design education for industrial
production was seen as highly important. This role continued as, over the next 25
years, the museum's permanent buildings evolved, incorporating large quantities of
decorative ceramics. Tiles, terracotta and mosaics were all employed, along with
mural painting, and students at the South Kensington Schools (forerunner of the
Royal College of Art) were able to gain practical experience on site. The ceramic
staircase with its 68 tiled risers and 'Della Robbia' panels and friezes was followed by
the Ceramic Gallery itself. Its designer, James Gamble, produced a gallery with ten
majolica-clad columns around the drums of which were the names of distinguished
potters in the giant ceramic letters of a pictorial alphabet designed by Godfrey Sykes.

Above. The tiles for the columns of the
Victoria and Albert's central Refreshment
Room were specially made by Minton
Hollins in Stoke-on-Trent, as were the
elaborate letters making up the frieze which
was designed by Godfrey Sykes. This
photograph shows the room in use.
Right. The West (or Ceramic) Staircase at
the *Victoria and Albert Museum*, designed
by F W Moody. The tile panels represent
literature, music and art and between each
step is a tiled riser.

The Grill Room at the Victoria and Albert
Museum was designed by Sir Edward
Poynter. The predominantly blue and white
tiles in a Dutch style are set into dark
walnut panelling. The smaller panels below
feature mythological subjects, whilst above
are large figurative tile panels in elaborate
'frames' representing the months and
seasons of the year. The panels were the
work of the pupils in the museum's art
schools.

Similar columns were used in the central Refreshment Room, where the stipulation for washable materials made glazed ceramics the obvious choice. The finale to this spectacular demonstration of art and industry came with the Grill Room which was designed by Edward Poynter. The large tiles forming the lower dado were set in polished dark walnut, while above the seasons and months of the year were depicted. A class of female students was used to hand-paint these tiles, which were predominantly blue and white.

The development of the Royal Scottish Museum in Chambers Street, Edinburgh, followed similar, though slightly later, lines. The great hall was a huge elegant bird-cage of iron and glass with a tiled floor (which was removed in 1971). Beyond the main entrance hall the floor of an arcade was set aside for the major manufacturers of tiles and mosaic who were invited to submit examples of their best designs, which were to be laid for the enlightenment of visitors. These sample pavements still survive and are a vivid reminder of the museum's very active role in promoting design in the art industries of the day.

Whilst the controlling centre of design education was certainly in South Kensington, the teaching of students went on throughout Britain in the newly established schools of art, some of which were in the centres of tile production such as Stoke-on-Trent (the Burslem School of Art) and Coalbrookdale in the Ironbridge Gorge. Manufacturers supported their local schools, no doubt seeing the value of an educated work force. Talents flowed in both directions; thus in 1880 Owen Gibbons took up the position of Headmaster at the Coalbrookdale School, having spent his student days contributing to the internal decoration schemes of the South Kensington Museum. Whilst teaching at Coalbrookdale, he not only wrote a textbook on design but also prepared tile designs for Maws on a freelance basis, thus providing a further illustration of the strong links between art and design education and industrial manufacture.

The printed sources of visual reference material available to both tile designers and students increased rapidly in the 1850s and 1860s, helped, as with trade catalogues, by the availability of good colour printing. One of the earliest and perhaps the most influential was Owen Jones's *Grammar of Ornament*, first published in 1856. Its colour plates provided a huge resource of decorative ideas for manufactured goods of many types, not least for tiles. Although Jones was adamant that the historical and exotic styles should be sources of inspiration, rather than used for imitation, it is clear that his encyclopedic reference work was used for direct artistic plagiarism. The well-thumbed copy which survived at Maws until the late 1960s is fondly remembered by Arthur Maw's granddaughter as a source of ideas for family Christmas cards in the early years of this century. Jones's work was paralleled in several European countries and notable for its similar layout and content is *L'Ornament Polychrome* which was

Above. The Royal Scottish Museum in Edinburgh, built between 1861 and 1874, used plain geometric tiles for the floor of its main hall whilst leaving the adjacent arcade for the display of sample pavements by leading tile manufacturers.
Below. An exercise for a tile design based on a snowdrop by a student at the Coalbrookdale School of Art, c. 1880.
Opposite. Sketches for the decoration of a private concert room by John W Bradburn for the 1884 National Competition.

compiled by A C Racinet and first published in France in 1872.

As far as the design process for industrially produced tiles was concerned, many manufacturers established their own design offices, employing locally trained talent and researching and reproducing historical designs themselves. Nevertheless most of them were also shrewd enough to see the advantages of commissioning designs from renowned architects and designers whose names (and reputations) were given prominence in the printed catalogues.

Conversely, many architects were reliant on the design abilities and sensibilities of the large manufacturers. A few architects, such as Pugin and Burges, took a detailed interest and an active role in the tile designs and layouts in the buildings for which they were responsible. But many did not and it is important not to underestimate the design departments which the larger manufacturers ran alongside their production units. In many schemes it was they, rather than the architect, who were responsible for the detailed choice of layout, design and colour. They provided an important subsidiary tier of creativity underneath the general supervision of the architect and brought industrial experience and economic resourcefulness to the aesthetic task of using tiles in architecture.

During the second half of the nineteenth century the ideals of the emerging Arts and Crafts Movement inevitably conflicted with those of the art manufacturers, often resulting in heated debate. In a series which appeared in the *Art Journal* of 1874 entitled 'On the Progress of our Art-Industries' Professor Archer took a more optimistic view of industry, declaring that 'There are those who take the onesided view that the manufacturing spirit of the age is killing the small Art-spirit which still exists. Such persons are not aware of the good that is being effected by our Art-workers; who, whilst they are bound to meet the instant requirements of trade are nevertheless day by day improving their work.' He went on to praise Messrs Maw, describing George as 'a gentleman who possesses highly cultivated taste'. He concluded by referring to Maws' other great excursion into ceramics in the form of art pottery, remarking that 'with so strong a love for their art, and so thorough a knowledge of its technicalities, it was all but impossible for Messrs Maw to avoid trying their hands on general pottery' and 'that has been done with excellent taste'. Other tile manufacturers in Britain (such as Burmantofts, Pilkington and Craven Dunnill) and later in the USA (Grueby) ventured into art pottery, often with some success. Their commercial knowledge, together with their practical experience of clay bodies and glazes, gave them an established technical expertise which the smaller artisan potter lacked. The balance between art and industry must have been quite fine and a report on the 1888 Art and Crafts Exhibition in London noted that 'Mr De Morgan must be given the premier place amongst our English potters of today, his mastery of blues, greens and purple reds yielding results which only one other English house approaches, and it must be acknowledged that Messrs Mawe [sic] are running him very hard for first place.'

Opposite. Student designs by J W Bradburn for a pattern based on the bramble.
Right. A watercolour by J W Bradburn illustrating how a plant form can be stylized to produce a repeating tile design.
Below. An original design dated 1883 by J W Bradburn for printed dado tiles. The drawing illustrates the way in which the patterned six-inch tiles were intended to be used with a decorative border and incorporated corners and a moulded skirting tile.

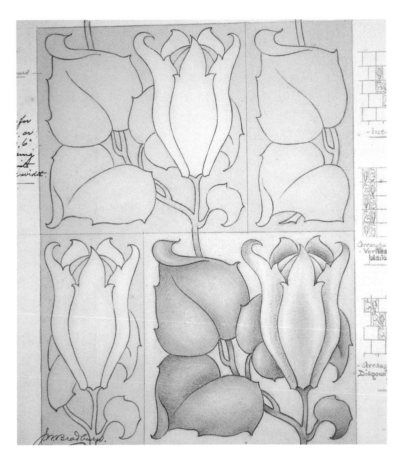

The Gothic Revival

The magnificent tiled floor of the Chapter House at Westminster Abbey, laid between 1255 and 1258, was protected by wooden flooring after the Dissolution. In 1841 the tiled floor was studied and drawn in detail, arousing great interest. The central group of four tiles depicts the Royal Arms of Henry III, flanked by centaurs and griffins.

The revival and use of the Gothic style in nineteenth-century architecture is a story of epic proportions which has attracted the attention of many writers and historians. Like other stylistic revivals, it was fuelled by a variety of cultural attitudes; these ranged from a yearning for medieval antiquarianism to the desire for an expression of nationalism through architectural style. But, above all, the Gothic Revival helped to meet the need for a sense of religious experience in churches in which ritual and liturgy were paramount.

The nineteenth-century environment, whether religious or secular, was the sum total of a collection of visual and decorative elements of great diversity and emotional power which were composed of such materials as stained glass, ironwork, stone carving, wall-painting and stencilling and, of course, ceramic tiles. What is of interest is not simply the contribution which tiles made to the Gothic Revival, but also the effect of the Revival on the rebirth of the inlaid, or as it became known, encaustic floor tile in the 1830s and its subsequent development into a major industry. In Britain, and to a lesser extent in France and Germany, huge family companies developed to meet the demand and many thousands of people were employed in making tiles.

The increase in church building in the late 1840s and 1850s was remarkable. For instance, by the middle of 1846, some 400 new churches were under construction in

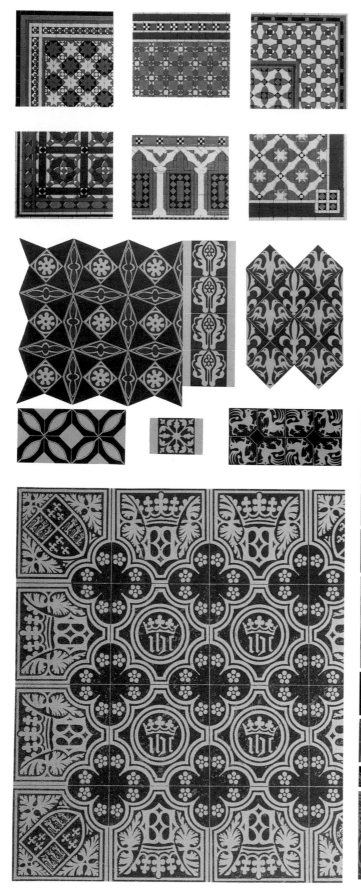

Medieval tile designs were promoted by published colour plates of ancient examples. These included Henry Shaw's 1852 plate of Gloucester Cathedral (left below), a French record of the choir pavement at the *Abbaye De Vivoin* (left centre) and a page of designs from the *Middle Ages* from L'Ornament Polychrome, published in France in 1872 (below).

The published patterns influenced designers, such as Matthew Digby Wyatt (left) and manufacturers, such as Maw & Co (opposite).

Britain, almost all of them employing some variant of the Gothic style and therefore candidates for decorative encaustic floor tiles. From a commercial viewpoint alone, the opportunities were tremendous. No one saw this more clearly than the tile manufacturer Herbert Minton of Stoke-on-Trent whose ability to work with leading Gothic Revival architects, especially Pugin, helped him to establish a reputation which ensured almost a monopoly of his company's tiles in churches by the time of his death in 1858. The Lichfield Diocesan Church Calendar of the following year lists well over 150 new and restored churches in that English Diocese alone which had been paved with Minton tiles.

Whilst Herbert Minton had been the pioneer of large-scale encaustic tile-making, other rival companies such as Maws and Godwins soon became established and contributed to the boom. In 1880 *The Builder* quoted figures for church-building in Manchester which are a reminder of the huge potential market for tiles: between 1848 (when the Manchester Diocese was formed) and 1879 no less than 220 new or replacement churches had been erected. Such was the output of the new encaustic tile industry that it is estimated that more than half the churches in Britain are paved, at least in part, with Victorian tiles.

It is perhaps ironic that it was industrially mass-produced floor tiles that went to meet the demand which had been created, at least in part, by a desire to emulate handmade tiles of the medieval period. For many architects and church restorers the medieval originals, though often by now worn, crumbling or smothered with box pews, had a powerful attraction. The quality of their designs was certainly remarkable and a recognition of this has now extended beyond Britain. For instance, Anne Berendsen, a Dutch tile historian, commented in her *Tiles: A General History* (published in 1967), that English medieval floor tiles 'are of a quality so much superior to those of the Continent ... Their finer execution, sparkling fantasy and richness of decorative detail, their splendid display of heraldry and, above all, the evocative power of their figures, place them on a very much higher artistic level.' It was particularly these qualities which antiquarian-minded architects sought to reintroduce through the Gothic Revival.

The appreciation of medieval tiles had already begun during the second half of the eighteenth century (see the first chapter). Tiles were actually only one part of the rapidly growing scholarly interest in medieval history and antiquities. The resulting archaeological investigation of medieval sites provided further material evidence of the decorative arts of the period. Archaeological discoveries, such as the medieval kilns and tiles at Malvern Priory, Worcestershire, in 1833, stimulated the Worcester architect Harvey Eginton to seek modern copies from the local firm of Chamberlain.

Shortly afterwards, in 1840, a decisive boost to the accurate remaking of medieval tile designs came when the Societies of the Inner and Middle Temple decided that

The Chapter House of Westminster Abbey was restored by Sir George Gilbert Scott between 1866 and 1872, during which time Minton made some replacement tiles whose inlaid patterns are much less worn than the medieval originals. The four-tile design makes up a Gothic rose window pattern of strong architectural character.

Temple Church in London should be properly restored, after several partial and imperfect restorations. During the course of the new restoration, the floor was excavated and traces of the original medieval tiles were found. It was decided to replace these with modern versions and, in order to ascertain something of the layout of the originals, the decision was taken to investigate the medieval tiled floor of the Chapter House at Westminster Abbey (which was of a similar date). The Chapter House tiles had not been seen for many years and had been covered with a boarded floor whilst the room was used for the storage of government documents.

The new tiles at Temple Church were made in Stoke-on-Trent by Herbert Minton and the publicity surrounding them certainly set the scene for a spectacular decade of success for his firm. Minton's tiles were hailed by Sydney Smirke (one of the architects responsible for the restoration of Temple Church) as 'a new manufacture of

Opposite. Colour lithograph of the interior of Temple Church, London, shortly after its restoration in 1841. Following damage to the building during World War II, the surviving early Minton floor tiles were relaid in groups in the triforium (above).

Floor tiles designed by AWN Pugin and made by Minton, from St Augustine's Church, Ramsgate, Kent. Above. South porch. Centre. Pugin chantry chapel (with Pugin's monogram). Below. Altar floor in Pugin chantry chapel.

great beauty, that has been brought into existence by the recent revival of the taste for ancient ecclesiastical architecture'. The designs made for Temple Church appeared in Minton's first printed catalogue of 1842.

The revealing of the Westminster Abbey Chapter House tiles created great interest in antiquarian circles and their designs were to have a significant influence on the new manufacturers. Their impact was facilitated by the work of John Gough Nichols who published the first of a series of illustrations in 1841 entitled 'Examples of inlaid Gothic tiles'. His work combined scholarship with practicality and was intended as 'a means of directing the attention of Architects to that mode of pavement for Churches ... which is most appropriate and accordant with ancient example'. Nichols's work was followed by the publication of numerous illustrations and descriptions of medieval tiles over the next 20 years which provided a scholarly point of reference for both tile manufacturers and church architects.

Important though antiquarian inspiration was, the use of tiles in Gothic Revival churches was much more fundamental than simply introducing copies of medieval work. The tiles, like other materials in the building, contributed to the new ecclesiological ideals in which architecture was used creatively to express spirituality. The new emphasis on ritual rather than preaching removed cluttered galleries and ranks of box pews, opening up aisles where tile pavements could draw the eye and mind eastwards to chancel, altar and the sacraments. Here rich encaustic tiles, sometimes using as many as eight inlaid colours, floored the new religious focal point whilst tiled dados and reredos in some cases adorned the walls.

The orchestration of materials and their use in the building (or restoration) of a church was the job of the architect. Pre-eminent in Britain and playing a pioneering role in the Gothic Revival was Augustus Welby Northmore Pugin (1812-52). His energetic and almost fanatical interest in reviving medieval styles of building and their associated ritual included an interest in encaustic tiles, which he placed 'near the head of those church ornaments which, next to stained glass, and when used in a wholehearted way, most charm the eye'. His biographer, Benjamin Ferrey, writing in 1861, said that 'among the various objects occupying Pugin's attention, not one received a greater share than the revival of encaustic tiles'. Pugin, who developed close personal links with Herbert Minton and produced designs for him to manufacture, used tiles in most of his churches. These include an important group in North Staffordshire, constructed for Roman Catholic clients, of which St Giles, Cheadle (1841-6) is perhaps the finest. Here his patron, the Earl of Shrewsbury, backed by considerable family wealth, gave Pugin the opportunity to use his creative talents.

In 1844 Pugin built a house for himself, 'The Grange', on the cliffs at Ramsgate, Kent, overlooking the English Channel. Next door he built, with his own money, St

Augustine's Church with its attendant cloister, sacristy and school. Here he relished the prospect of being both 'paymaster and architect' and made significant use of tiles. The choice and arrangement of floor tiles was as important as the designs on the individual tiles themselves and the tiled floors at St Augustine's demonstrate Pugin's mastery in both these areas.

Characteristically Pugin's church floor layouts used the simplest tiles, which were often alternate black and red plain quarry tiles laid diagonally for the nave. Moving eastwards, there is a growing crescendo of pattern and complexity which culminates in the full glory of the sanctuary floor before the altar. In the south transept at St Augustine's is a chantry where Pugin is buried, the floor being chequered with specially designed tiles bearing his arms and monogram.

Among the many nineteenth-century British architects who worked in the Gothic style, William Butterfield (1814-1900) stands out as someone who used coloured materials, such as tiles, in a strong, almost wilful, way to differentiate between the structural features of churches. His love of polychromy and striking use of contrasting materials, such as red brick and white stone (of which Keble College, Oxford [1867-83] is an example) is remembered by many as the 'streaky bacon style'. The same original treatment in distinctive geometric patterns characterizes his use of tiles inside churches, on both floors and walls.

A 1989 survey of Butterfield's work by the tile historians Philip and Dorothy Brown attests to substantial use of tiles in 75 of the 102 churches included in Paul Thompson's gazetteer of Butterfield buildings. They describe his distinctive tile arrangements as 'often interesting, even exciting, and still sometimes disturbing'. Plain tiles (without any pattern) were often used sparingly, but to great effect. Dull red unglazed tiles may complement grey stone in a reredos or, as a narrow band, may carry the eye across a cool expanse of light stone or whitewashed wall, helping to define spatial relationships. One of Butterfield's favourite devices was a bright yellow zig-zag of glazed plain tiles streaking across a pavement and the Browns found these still visible in 26 churches.

Butterfield's polychromatic effects, derived from the intrinsic colours of structural materials such as stone, bricks and tiles, can be seen particularly well in All Saints Church, Margaret Street, London, which was commissioned as a model church in 1849 by the Cambridge Camden Society (later the Ecclesiological Society), which urged that churches should adopt 'real' materials. The pavement of the church is one of Butterfield's finest and illustrates the way in which tiles can provide the link between church design and ritual and liturgical symbolism. The whole sequence is eloquently described by Thompson thus:

The nave floor provides a bold simple prelude, a deep red background with a big white stone diaper and black checks, and clever triangle variations along the aisle. In the chancel the background becomes

The nave floor at All Saints Church, Margaret Street, London. In the foreground are patterned encaustic and geometric tiles by Minton. The geometric patterns of the tiling complement the coloured marbles of Butterfield's 1858 pulpit. On the north wall of the nave, beyond the pulpit, can be seen two of the five tile panels depicting biblical scenes and figures. These were designed by Butterfield in 1873, painted by Alexander Gibbs and manufactured by Henry Poole and Sons.

*a sparkling white, with broad red stripes and diapers and triangles of black and soft green. In front of
the altar rails there are white, red and black zigzags at the sides and in the centre big diamond patterns
lined with soft fossil grey marble, filled with yellow patterned tiles and a maze of tiny white triangles.
The sanctuary floor is again more complex; big strips and diapers of fossil grey against a red
background forming diamonds filled with patterned yellow, or black and white and red and green; and
on the final step patterned tiles in blue and yellow and white and red tracery.*

Although the Gothic Revival and its associated use of tiles is seen most fully in
Britain, the style did have some impact in France and also in Germany. British tile
manufacturers appear to have made almost no contribution to continental markets,
despite the fact that the designs and applications of encaustic tiles were in many cases
very similar. Instead, continental manufacturing companies developed from the 1840s
onwards to meet the needs of the individual countries.

In France the firm of Boulenger was established at Auneuil near Beauvais in 1848
and one of its founding brothers, Jean-Baptiste Aimé Boulenger (1825-87), took
encaustic tile-making to extraordinary heights. He undertook work for the great
French architect and church restorer Viollet-le-Duc and this alliance between
manufacturer and architect is perhaps comparable to the Minton and Pugin
relationship in Britain. Encaustic tiles made by Boulenger were used in churches
throughout France and even found their way into Britain, being used at the Napoleon
III Mortuary Chapel which was designed by Henry Clutton and built onto St Mary's
Church, Chislehurst. Boulenger was charged with making special tiles for the chapel,
of which the most distinctive are those with the letter 'N' for Napoleon surmounted
by the Imperial Crown and those bearing the image of the Napoleonic Eagle. In
Belgium the large firm of Boch Frères was established by Victor and Eugène Boch at
La Louviere in 1844. Even more important for the Gothic Revival was the factory they
built just over the French border at Maubeuge which specialized in encaustic tiles and

pavement quarries. German Gothic Revival tiles, which like those being made in Britain followed medieval precedents, were a speciality of Villeroy and Boch at Mettlach.

The design of tiles for churches was one area where tile manufacturers and architects built up and maintained strong mutual links. The Minton/Pugin collaboration of the 1840s was followed by others where designs for tiles were initiated by both manufacturer and architect. For instance, in the 1860s Maw and Co were manufacturing floor tile designs which they had commissioned from leading architects such as M Digby Wyatt, J P Seddon and G E Street. The reverse process operated too and records of architect-commissioned specials from Maw and Co exist for a number of church floors.

In some cases special designs were the result of the discovery of fragments of original medieval tiles which had been revealed when churches were undergoing restoration. This copying of archaeological material was seen as a way of maintaining a link with the original Gothic past. The following description of the restoration of Lichfield Cathedral (1857-61) is typical of a situation which was also occurring in many churches elsewhere:

On the soil under the surface being disturbed, fragments of tile work were discovered here and there all over the building. A very clever workman, one John Hamlet, collected these fragments, and made out several patterns of tiles, which in early days had plainly formed part of the pavement. These patterns were drawn out in colours and placed in the hands of Messrs Minton; and the beautiful floor in the centre Choir Aisle between the Stalls is composed in the main of tiles made after the patterns thus happily brought to light and reproduced.

Gilbert Scott (who was the architect responsible for the restoration of Lichfield)

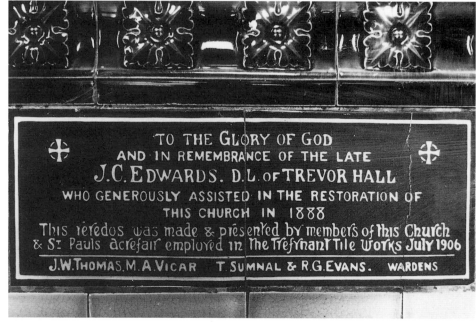

The tiled reredos at St John the Evangelist Church, Rhosymedre, Clwyd. The tiles were made at the local Trefynant tile works in 1906 and were presented in memory of its former owner, Mr JC Edwards.

in a paper which he read to the Royal Institute of British Architects in 1862 formalized this conservation approach. He developed a set of rules and suggestions entitled 'On the Conservation of Ancient Architectural Monuments and Remains', which declared that whilst floors must be levelled and freed from damp, monumental slabs and old tiles should be left. He regretted those situations in which 'the memorials of the dead have perished and the works of Mr Minton (to which they have fallen victims) have scornfully ousted those of his teachers'.

With so many examples of original medieval designs available as archaeological specimens or coloured plates in published works, it is perhaps not surprising that manufacturers in Britain and the continent relied heavily on them as a source of design ideas to meet a market that was essentially revivalist in character. Certain designs were adopted, with minor variants, by almost all manufacturers across Europe. One example is the fleur-de-lys, symbol of the Virgin Mary, which was very widely used in churches. In Britain alone 22 variants have been recorded on tiles from British manufacturers. Only very rarely do contemporary Victorian images appear on church floor tiles. One striking exception is the floor designed by J P Seddon for his controversial restoration of Llanbadarn Fawr church near Aberystwyth, Wales. Here Duplex burner oil lamps are depicted on the floor tiles - an image directly derived from Victorian technology rather than taken from any medieval precedent.

Although many of the actual designs were authentic, the overall appearance of a new church pavement was very different to that of worn and dull medieval tiles. There were criticisms that Victorian manufacturers were copying these designs 'with a certain over-neatness and prettyness', and concern too over the use of shiny surface glazes which created 'a look of uncomfortable lubricity which was particularly offensive'. To counteract this, some manufacturers went to great lengths to make their tiles deliberately rugged and unmechanical in appearance, thereby appealing to architects whose interest in the Gothic style was tempered with an Arts and Crafts philosophy. Craven Dunnills of Jackfield created their 'Ancient' range (which may even have been artificially distressed) to meet this need and the rough 'orange peel' texture of the tiles made by Godwins of Lugwardine, Hereford, found favour with both Gilbert Scott and G E Street.

In many cases architects and restorers were able to utilize the standard designs and arrangements offered by manufacturers in their coloured catalogues. The result, sometimes, is a certain predictability in the use of tiles in Victorian churches. The ubiquitous nature of encaustic tiles and other Victorian furnishings in English churches is celebrated in John Betjeman's poem which begins:

> The Church's Restoration
> In eighteen-eighty-three
> Has left for contemplation

The tiled dado in the sanctuary of Rhosymedre church, Clwyd, using both relief-moulded (for grapes and chalice panel) and encaustic tiles (for foliage and IHS designs).

Not what there used to be.

Later in the poem he laments the Victorian incumbent who:

Gave the new addition,

Pull'd down the dull old aisle,

To pave the sweet transition

He gave th' encaustic tile.

Realization of the problems posed by too many patterned tiles came early on in the Revival. In his 'Essay on Church Furniture and Decoration' (published in 1845) Rev Edward Cutts concluded that:

the leading fault has been the mistaken idea, which has prevailed in designs for stained glass also, and in many other things, that the greater the quantity of rich work (or colour or material) the richer the effect would be: whereas, to produce a rich effect, rich work (or colour or material) must be judiciously set amidst a foil of plainer work. In a window the coloured glass must be relieved with an abundant quantity of white and yellow; in a pavement the inlaid pattern tiles should be relieved with a sufficient intermixture of plain tiles.

The mistake of using too many patterned tiles was partly avoided by a more detailed study of medieval pavements. Here, the basic arrangement was often a criss-cross of plain bands enclosing groups of four, nine or 16 decorated tiles. Copying this helped to rationalize the overall visual appearance and, on a more economic note, reduced the number of the more expensive inlaid tile required. Several architects contributed pavement designs to manufacturers' catalogues, as did Lord Alwyne Compton, Bishop of Ely, for Maw and Co. His pavements, which made only limited use of patterned tiles, were considered by Gilbert Scott to be better than Pugin's.

Church floor layouts combining tiles with stone and marble were quite common, particularly in the larger churches and cathedrals. At Lichfield Cathedral, for instance, Gilbert Scott's 1860 design for the floor of the restored choir and presbytery combined a superb display of geometric and richly patterned encaustic tiles (donated by Colin Minton Campbell as a memorial to his uncle, Herbert Minton) with polished strips of Derbyshire limestone and four roundels of incised marble inlaid with black mastic. Tiles used with other materials, such as brass, glass and cast-iron (particularly for heating grids), provided further decorative opportunities for the church architect. Brass insets into tiles stayed bright with the polishing effect of feet, whilst semi-spherical glass insets (as used to brilliant effect in the sanctuary pavement of the church of the Holy Innocents, Highnam, Gloucestershire) collected and reflected light with a jewel-like quality.

The majority of the tiles used in Gothic Revival buildings were floor tiles. But wall tiles were employed for dados in chancels and there were also opportunities for the creation of biblical texts through the use of letter tiles which were supplied in several sizes and faces (including both Gothic and Roman) by the large manufacturers.

Encaustic tiles were used as commemorative and memorial tablets, offering durability and a wider range of colours and decoration than could be achieved with stone.

Above. This memorial tile to Bishop Selwyn of New Zealand and Lichfield (1809-78) was originally one of a group of similar tiles on the internal walls of St Michael's Church, Derby.

Opposite above. Commemorating the French Boulenger family, this tile was set in the elaborately tiled porch at their local church of Auneuil, near Beauvais. Opposite below. The Boulenger family tomb at Cauvigny records on circular encaustic tiles details of each member buried there. This one is for the founder of the tile works, Aimé Jean Baptiste (1825-87), who was also known as Jean-Baptiste Aimé.

The New Palace of Westminster provided the supreme secular demonstration of the Gothic Revival. Minton encaustic tiles were laid as elaborate decorative pavements in many parts of the building.

Opposite. View of the Peers' Lobby, with floor tiles dating from 1847, looking towards the Chamber of the House of Lords. This page, reading from left to right: top row. St Stephen's Hall, coat of arms of Edward III, one of the founding Knights of the Collegiate Chapel of St Stephen, on the site on which the Victorian St Stephen's Hall was built; Peers' Lobby, three lions passant-regardant. These lions, symbolizing England, appear widely throughout the building. Second row. Peers' Lobby, monogram of Victoria Regina; Central Lobby, part of a circular border with national emblems, here depicting Ireland's golden harp and shamrock leaves. Third row. Central Lobby, monogram of Victoria Regina flanked by Tudor roses; Peers' Lobby, lion passant-guardant. Fourth row. Members' Entrance, the crowned R denotes Richard II and this design alternates with white harts chained and ducally gorged; St Stephen's Hall, the coat of arms of Edward the Confessor with five martlets. Bottom row. Central Lobby, the thistle representing Scotland; Royal Gallery, part of a border bearing the Latin inscription 'Domine salvam fac Reginum' ('God Save the Queen').

Examples of the Ten Commandments, the Apostles' Creed and passages from the Scriptures can be found treated in this way. Letter tiles were similarly used on the risers of steps, such as those between chancel and altar, where their hard ceramic nature has proved much more durable than painting on stone or plaster. Wall tiling to the sanctuary was frequently combined with a ceramic reredos which offered scope for hand-painted or modelled work of the highest quality.

As also happened during the medieval period, tiles were occasionally used in the nineteenth century to elaborate various forms of church memorial. These tiles range from the 12-inch-square encaustic tiles which bear details of the deceased and are set diagonally into church walls to the heraldic and other devices created in tile form and set into stone graveyard monuments. One of the most striking and extensive uses of tiles for funerary monuments can be found in Northern France. Members of the French tile-making family of Boulenger are buried at Cauvigny, 25 km south-east of Beauvais, in a classical structure with a round-arched entrance, topped with a pediment and entirely covered in encaustic tiles in sombre buff, white and black. Special tiles record details of those buried there; the inside of the tomb is tiled throughout and includes a small encaustic-tiled altar.

The preoccupation so far with ecclesiastical examples of the use of tiles in the Gothic Revival ignores one important landmark in the development of the style for public buildings in Britain. Many of the buildings erected in the early part of the nineteenth century had been in a Greek Revival style (such as Smirke's British Museum) but a desire for change was in the air. On the night of 16 October 1834 a serious fire broke out which destroyed most of the old Palace of Westminster. This single event was to change the architectural climate of public building and ultimately foster the Gothic style as a symbol for the nation. The ensuing competition for a replacement was won by Charles Barry whose design included a brilliant series of drawings executed with the help of A W N Pugin. Through his church buildings Pugin was already well known as a pioneer enthusiast for the use of encaustic floor tiles. The decision to incorporate them in the New Palace of Westminster seems to have been taken by 1843 when *The Builder* reported the Commissioner of Fine Arts as having pronounced 'that the floors of the several Halls, Galleries and Corridors should be formed in encaustic tiles, bearing heraldic devices and other enrichments in colours laid in margins and compartments in combination with polished British marbles'. The following year an exhibition of decorative art suitable for the embellishment of the interiors was held which included ideas for paving in various styles and materials. Among the ideas featured was mosaic paving by Owen Jones, ornamental tiles by Copeland and Garrett, an ornamental pavement by Minton and Co and tiles by Chamberlains of Worcester. The first tiles were laid early in 1847 on the floor of the Lords' Lobby and consisted of 'encaustic tiles by Minton, of lions on a

Encaustic tiles form colourful insets in the tomb of William Joseph Vavasour who died on 11 January 1860. His tomb is at Hazlewood Castle, near Tadcaster in West Yorkshire.

Watercolour of the Crypt Chapel at the Palace of Westminster, as envisaged by Edward Middleton Barry, son of Charles Barry.

red ground, and initials on a blue ground alternately formed in squares by black marble margins; and in the centre is a red and white rose in coloured marbles on a blue ground'. At the same time red and blue encaustic tiles bearing the Lions of England and the Royal monogram were installed in the fireplaces in the Prince's Chamber.

Installation of tiles continued in subsequent years until one of the most complex and extensive series of Victorian encaustic tile pavements found anywhere in the world had been built up. A contemporary guide book praised the floor of the Central Lobby with its Latin inscription which translates as 'Except the Lord Keep the house their labour is lost that built it' and declared that 'there is no lack of power in our present manufacturers when their abilities are really called out to vie with the most elaborate and artistic effects of decoration of this kind in former times'. Pugin wrote to Herbert Minton in 1852 describing his products as 'vastly superior to any ancient work' and 'the best tiles in the world, and I think that my patterns and your workmanship go ahead of anything'. This jingoistic celebration of tiles and Gothic architecture was entirely appropriate to the time and place; the same spirit found more provincial expression in the various new town halls being erected, particularly those in northern England (see the sixth chapter).

In an even more diluted form, the Gothic Revival spread to North America too. Until the 1880s such tiles as were to be used for Gothic Revival churches were imported from both Britain and France. For example, the floor tiles used in the cloisters of Trinity Church, Boston (now removed), and probably those surviving on the floor of the west vestibule were imported from Boch Frères and Co of Maubeuge, France. The use of English and French encaustic tiles in Toronto, Canada, particularly in St James' Anglican Cathedral (1850-3), is probably largely due to the influence of the architect Frederick William Cumberland who was born and studied architecture in England. By the time he settled in Toronto in 1847 he would have been well-acquainted with the work of Gothic Revival architects such as Pugin and Butterfield and with their use of tiles. A similar pattern of direct importation from several British manufacturers can be seen in the fine floors of the Church of St John the Evangelist, Montreal.

The New World, however, lacked the direct stimulus of the European medieval tradition and in both architecture and the related use of tiles any development of the Gothic style was relatively limited. Instead, the USA in particular looked towards its own developing tile industry, and the tiles later used in church buildings there have a distinctly Arts and Crafts flavour. Particularly impressive are the floor tiles made at the Pewabic Pottery of Detroit, Michigan, which were designed by Miss Mary Chase Perry. These tiles decorate the floors of the cathedral church of St Paul, Detroit (installed 1910), and are fresh and original, yet still complement the thirteenth-century English Gothic style adopted for the building by its architect Ralph Adams Cram, of Cram, Goodhue and Ferguson, New York. Tiles of a similar character are used in the chancel, sanctuary and ambulatory of the immense Cathedral Church of St John the Divine in New York City.

Whilst Arts and Crafts tiles were gently pointing the way to new directions for the Gothic Revival in North America, something very novel and totally different was afoot back in Europe. Between 1894 and 1899 Paris was to witness the building of a new church which, whilst maintaining the superficial appearance of traditional Gothic, was actually constructed of reinforced concrete. This highly experimental building incorporated ceramic 'tiles' as a form of decoration internally and externally and thus took both the use of tiles and the Gothic Revival into a brand new era.

The church was Saint-Jean de Montmartre and its architect was Anatole de Baudot (1834-1915). Baudot had been a pupil of Viollet-le-Duc and remained faithful to his influence, although he also believed strongly in the progress of science and technology. His lively conception of architecture included the notion that 'what was logical in the Gothic period remains so but conversely if one can resolve a problem in a more satisfactory way in 1890 than in 1250, then one should apply the latter solution'. Baudot resolved the decorative problem of unadorned concrete by combining ceramics with reinforced cement. Coloured and glazed stoneware ceramic roundels and triangles supplied by Bigot were fixed to the cement before it set. These jewel-like ceramics ornament the curves of the main entrance porch, enliven the brick façade with fine coloured strands and underline the interlacing of the simple curved tracery of the windows. Inside the church, the same ceramic decoration is used to ornament the balustrade of the gallery and to decorate the altar.

Later reinforced concrete churches in France, such as Le Raincy (1922-3) by the Perret brothers adopted concrete in its pure state with no ceramic facings. The use of applied ceramics (essentially circular tiles) on the concrete of Saint-Jean de Montmartre represents both an interesting intermediate stage in the development of concrete as a material for churches and a final swansong for the 60-year partnership which tiles enjoyed with the Gothic Revival.

The tiles from the Royal Gallery at the New Palace of Westminster were made by Minton in 1847 to designs by AWN Pugin. These tiles separate and define the words of a Latin inscription and their design demonstrates Pugin's skill in using flat patterns derived from medieval sources. His book, Floriated Ornament, which reflects this enthusiasm, was published two years later in 1849.

Cool, Clean and Hygienic

The merits of ceramic tiles in terms of coolness will be immediately apparent to anyone who has leant against the tiled dados in the Alhambra Palace on a baking hot southern Spanish day or sought refuge from the midday sun in a tile-lined courtyard in Portugal. This traditional quality of coolness, understood for centuries in many Mediterranean countries, is essentially a product of the tiles themselves. Their ceramic body is hard and, coupled very often with a smooth, shiny glazed surface, has the same effect in appearance and touch as natural marble and stone.

In the nineteenth century the traditional purpose of wall tiling as a means of keeping buildings cool was extended in other important directions – tiles as a means of keeping buildings both clean and hygienic. In some instances tiles were also used for their light-reflecting qualities and even as a fireproof lining for ceilings and vaultings. The growth of the population had resulted in overcrowding and associated insanitary conditions and, as concern for public health and hygiene rose, the hard, smooth glazed surfaces of mass-produced tiles grew in popularity. Their availability in an almost infinite range of shades and patterns was essentially secondary in many architectural applications. It is the very functional aspect of tiles which provides the link between an extraordinary array of building types which range from the Royal Dairy through butchers' and fishmongers' shops to municipal swimming baths and public lavatories.

The Royal Dairy at Frogmore, Windsor, with its highly decorated walls and floor tiles and ceramic fountains, was the nineteenth-century epitome of a cool, clean and hygienic environment.

Above. Minton's new majolica glazes were used on a frieze of relief-decorated panels depicting rural activities, which runs around the walls of the Royal Dairy, Windsor.
Opposite. Whilst marble was used for the settling slabs, the floor was covered with patterned tiles which were both attractive and functional, with their slip-resistant surface.

The merit of lining dairy walls with glazed tiles had already been appreciated in the eighteenth century (see the first chapter). Prince Albert, in designing the dairy attached to the home farm at Frogmore, Windsor, took the use of tiles to new levels of functional and decorative importance. Although built near the end of his life (construction began in 1858), this project was under the Prince Consort's close personal direction with John Thomas working as executive architect. Prince Albert would have been personally familiar with the use of tiles in interiors through their applications at Osborne House.

Prince Albert's model dairy consists of a two-storey residence, offices and, beyond a courtyard, the sumptuous tiled creamery which is 12 metres (40 feet) long and over 6 metres (20 feet) wide. The tiling was supplied by Minton and gives the immediate impression of being far more varied and exuberant than Wedgwood's earlier efforts. It exploits the rich solid colours of the new 'majolica' glazes which were then being successfully developed by Minton for use on pottery as well as tiles. Beneath a sloping painted timber roof supported on six columns, a ceramic frieze runs around the entire room, bearing profile portraits in white relief of all the royal children. These are interspersed by bold relief sea horses in white against pale blue. In contrast, the windows and wall niches are framed with block printed border tiles of five different patterns. With some justification the *Illustrated London News* of 27 July 1861 referred to the interior as a 'perfect gem of taste and art'.

The completion of the Royal Dairy,
Windsor, was reported in the Illustrated
London News of 27 July, 1861. The
account, which was accompanied by this
wood engraving, referred to the interior as a
'perfect gem of taste and art'.

In functional terms the various applications of tiles and ceramics go further. The
tiles provide a wall lining down to the level of the white marble slabs which run the
length of the room and carry the large ceramic basins for separating the cream. The
superiority of tiles over flaking whitewashed walls gave them more than aesthetic
appeal to a generation that was fascinated by the relationship between art and
science. Meanwhile, tiles on the ceiling helped with ventilation. The square recessed
panels are actually pierced ceramic tiles of the kind developed by Minton for the
Pugin stove exhibited at the 1851 exhibition. Here their function was to extract the
warmed air which rose to the ceiling and was replaced by cool air through the
windows which had two linked sets of opening casements, together with metal
screens to prevent the entry of insects. Tiles on the floor are equally functional. At
first glance their lacy white-on-buff repeating pattern looks simply pretty. In fact, the
white glaze is recessed into the buff body of the tile, thereby not only protecting it
from wear but also creating a Victorian non-slip floor for an environment which was
often wet underfoot.

The royal approval for tiled dairies led to emulations elsewhere by the aristocracy.
One such is the octagonal example built in 1870 for the Duke of Hamilton on his
Easton Estate in Suffolk. His family crest was incorporated into the tiled floor, along
with an octagonal marble fountain; the tiles on the walls feature vertical panels of
flowers and birds in low-relief white slip on a plain buff ground. This was a

mechanical version, devised by Maws, of the French *pâte-sur-pâte* (paste on paste) technique used for decorating porcelain. The dairy, though highly decorative, was, like the Royal Dairy at Frogmore, still used for butter- and cheese-making and the estate staff came there to collect their daily milk.

Later in the nineteenth century the estate 'model dairy' moved out to new commercial pastures to become a venue for Victorian family outings. One of the most interesting pioneers was College Farm at Finchley, North London, whose buildings, erected in 1882, were a showpiece for the newly formed Express Dairy Company. The ornamental dairy building was originally thatch-roofed for coolness and the walls inside were lined with Minton tiles, chosen appropriately from their 'rustic figures' series. Tiles were used elsewhere too, including inside the building where cows were on view to the public; areas of plain white hexagonal tiles edged with a border were often used in stables and animal houses as a wall lining behind the feeding mangers. At College Farm the floor too was laid with a 'tasteful but inexpensive aisle of Minton tiles, which look clean and pleasant'. These words, from a contemporary visitor, sum up the essential qualities of tiles as clean and good-looking architectural materials suitable to be used in the vicinity of livestock.

The qualities of cleanliness and good looks can be further extended when tiles are used in conjunction with water, particularly when the water is in motion, as in a fountain. The sense of coolness is heightened and a mood of freshness and sparkle is created. Tiles provide an ideal material for the basins of fountains; their glazed surfaces offer a far greater range of colours than natural stone or even marble could achieve. In Britain their use in this way was relatively uncommon, although Queen Victoria used blue, pale green and white geometrical tiles in the basins of the ornamental fountains on the terraces at Osborne House.

In southern Europe fountains frequently took the more traditional form of drip fountains which were built into a vertical wall surface and surrounded by decorative tiling. By the end of the nineteenth century such fountains had become popular in the warmer parts of the United States and California-based manufacturers such as Batchelder-Wilson Co. developed a wide range of designs. The orifice from which the water emerged was usually made the primary decorative element in a 12-inch-square tile and often featured the open mouth and head of a fish, frog or other aquatic creature.

The adaptation of the tiled wall fountain to a drinking fountain was a particularly strong feature of American tiling. The opportunity for decoration on the tiled area of the wall behind the water dispenser and bowl was rarely missed. But an even more distinctively American adaptation of ceramics to fountains was the art tile soda fountain. This was the invention of John Gardner Low whose Art Tile Works of Cambridge, Massachusetts, was one of the landmarks in nineteenth-century

Below. The octagonal tiled dairy at Easton, Suffolk, was built in 1870 for the Duke of Hamilton.
Bottom. A tiled drinking fountain made for the Federal Title and Trust Company, Beaver Falls, Pennsylvania, USA.

Opposite. A La Mère De Famille, a Parisian delicatessen. The interior, which dates from around 1900, includes a geometric tiled floor and a border with the name of the shop in bold letter tiles.

Above. The late nineteenth-century interior of Aux Cinq Poissons, one of the oldest fishmongers in Paris, with tiles from the Sarreguemines studio. The panel on the left depicts a coastline in Brittany with a fisherman whose catch is proudly displayed on the shore. The rear panel shows a variety of fish, crustacea and seaweeds, set against a seascape with rocks, sailing ships and a medieval castle.

American tile history. America had introduced soda water refreshment early in the nineteenth century and at the 1876 Centennial Exhibition in Philadelphia Low is thought to have seen large soda water stands of marble. About 1883 he began several years of study on the advantages of the tile soda fountain with the result that on 27 August 1888 he submitted his detailed plan to the Commissioner of Patents in Washington. He claimed that 'baked clay, which can be readily modelled in shape and glazed in any desirable colour, presents a material vastly better than marble, both for beauty and use of working' and devised a form of structure 'which is well adapted for incrustation with glazed or enamelled tiles'. Low's patent was granted a year later and his tile soda fountain exemplifies his conception of an object which is both useful and beautiful – a duality in which ceramic tiles excelled.

The growth of food retailing from urban-based shops offered great scope for the application of tiles to shop premises (and indeed it continues to do so today). In Britain some of the earliest examples are butchers' shops dating from the 1870s but within a decade the fashion for tiling had also spread to fishmongers, game dealers and dairies. The latter had, by now, become high street shops where milk and dairy products were sold, representing a change in function from the earlier rural dairies but continuing the century-old tradition of using tiles for cool, clean interiors.

Functional though the tiles were, they usually contributed a great deal to the architectural decoration of the shops too. On the outside, moulded relief tiles or faience would often form pilasters flanking doorways or windows and various forms of ceramic lettering might be used on the facia or the stall riser (the solid area below the shop window). Pictorial panels, either underglaze-painted or tube-lined, were frequently deployed as visual features inside, offering something of the size and grandeur of an oil painting (sometimes complete with ceramic frame) but able to

Tile panels, often decorated with farm scenes and animals, were a common feature of butchers' and dairy shops in Britain. Clockwise from top left. Detail of a tiled frieze from a butcher's shop, *Attercliffe, Sheffield*. Tube-lined panel by T&R Boote, c. 1913, from the former dairy shop at 93 London Street, Reading. Tiled panel from the entrance to a butcher's shop, Congleton, Cheshire. Butcher's shop, Fishguard, Dyfed. Milkmaid panel from London Street, Reading.

Opposite above. Tiled stall riser from the front of a butcher's shop in Wymondham, Norfolk.

Opposite below. Tube-lined panels from 93 London Street, Reading.

Above. Sainsbury's grocery shop at 143 High Street, Guildford, Surrey, on its opening day in 1906. Wall tiling and ceramic mosaic floors by Minton Hollins were used by Sainsbury's to create a consistent image for their branches. Opposite. The tiled meat hall of Harrods, Knightsbridge, London, was designed by WJ Neatby and completed in 1902.

withstand constant washing down. The subjects were often pastoral, highlighting cattle, sheep, pigs and hens and in many cases breeds that are now extremely rare - an interesting example of the history of farm animals being recorded in contemporary decorative schemes.

Many of the early British grocery chain stores used tiles to establish their own distinctive house styles. Sainsbury's appear to have used wall tiling in their shops from the very founding of the firm in 1869. A 1930s drawing of the back wall of their first shop at 173 Drury Lane, London (demolished in 1958), shows panels of hexagonal tiles similar to those used in the stables of the aristocracy. In 1882 the first of their branches opened (at London Road, Croydon) in the form which was to become familiar across the country. Both walls and counter fronts were tiled in rectangular panels and the floor was laid in patterned ceramic mosaic - all supplied by Minton Hollins from Stoke-on-Trent.

The most elaborate scheme for retail premises in Britain was probably that designed by W J Neatby for Harrods Meat Hall, which was completed in 1902. The 'medieval' hunting scenes, incorporated into an Art Nouveau setting, were made by Doultons and are well known. The scheme attracted praise from a German magazine in 1903, not just for the artistic tile decoration but for the fact that 'everything that is not glass or marble is clad in glazed pottery tiles'. This ensured that 'even on the hottest summer days the space is comfortable to stay in' and the author concluded that 'architecturally and decoratively alike, this provision hall is a triumph of original modern style and in the application of sound principles'.

The same duality of stylish decoration and practical principles about tiling can be seen in the new municipally provided services made possible by a piped water supply system. Indeed tiles, in a very functional capacity, began to make a contribution to the lives of the great working class mass of the population in

Victorian Britain. An Act of Parliament in 1864 heralded the desirability 'for the Health, Comfort and Welfare of the Inhabitants of Towns and populous Districts to encourage the Establishment therein of public Baths and Wash-Houses'. Municipally inspired philanthropy brought architectural opportunities where tiles and huge quantities of glazed bricks could serve as clean and hard-wearing materials in the cause of human hygiene.

The provision of public baths grew considerably towards the end of the nineteenth century and the Duke of Westminster captured the mood of civic concern for cleanliness in the collect written in 1894 for the opening of Woolwich Public Baths, London. It began 'O God, who has taught us by thy servant John Wesley that cleanliness is next to Godliness, we thank thee for the public spirit which has caused these Baths to be erected in our midst...'

As the concept of leisure grew, the emphasis gradually moved away from bath cubicles catering for people without baths at home to public swimming baths. Swimming baths provided opportunities for long runs of decorative tiled dados and the introduction of Russian or Vapour Baths and Turkish Baths gave scope for exotic tile schemes which exhibit the thoroughly practical qualities of cleanliness and hygiene.

Increasingly, bath schemes came under the aegis of the corporation engineer rather than the architect and this, together with a growing preference for plainer tiling schemes after 1900, served to restrain the ceramic decoration of baths. The contract specification for Madeley Street Baths in Hull, issued in 1909, made it clear that 'the designs of the tiles submitted are to be suitable for a building of this class and a tile of a neat good design and excellent quality will be preferred to showy floral patterned tiles'. This is an interesting instance of florid decoration for its own sake being rejected in favour of a more mature 'fitness for purpose' philosophy characteristic of the early twentieth century .

A concern with cleanliness and public hygiene was closely related to developments in sanitation. The provision of a foul drainage system in the middle of the nineteenth century served to make tile manufacturer Henry Doulton a rich man through the sale of salt-glazed sewer pipes. Public lavatories were an integral part of the provision for sanitation, although their utilitarian use of tiles, often in plain colours, did much to promote the view that Victorian tiling was 'lavatorial'.

Nineteenth-century concern for health and hygiene created a further area of architectural expansion through hospital building and improvements. Once again, glazed wall tiles played an important part in making sure the buildings were easily cleaned and free from infection. Large quantities were used as dados in corridors and operating theatres were entirely lined with them. New provision was made for children's wards and here tile picture panels took on both a decorative and utilitarian

Minton Hollins relief-moulded tiles from Sainsbury's Brondesbury branch, Kilburn, north London, which opened in 1888.

role. The Hospital Committee Report for 1912 from Paddington Green Children's Hospital argued that they served three useful purposes, which were 'to brighten and decorate the walls of the waiting room, to interest and distract the children from their sufferings: and also (the panels being washable) to reduce the cost of the annual cleaning'.

John Greene's aptly named survey of these schemes, *Brightening the Long Days*, documents over 70 hospitals in Britain which had tile pictures and the fashion spread to the other countries of the British Empire too, with examples known at Poona in India and in two New Zealand hospitals. Doultons emerged as the leading supplier of these panels and in 1904 celebrated the company's contribution in a booklet entitled *Pictures in Pottery*. The reader is left in no doubt as to the value of:

the kindly idea of enlivening the walls with suitable decorative panels, to in some degree brighten and cheer the enforced stay of the weary sufferers in the wards, and to bring fresh thoughts of nature and happiness to their tired minds. Who that has seen a Babies Ward, bright with the merry pictures

Above. A handpainted panel from Hooper and Sons' fish shop, Southsea, Hampshire, by Carters of Poole (c. 1910).
Right. 'Old King Cole' tile panel from the Children's Ward of St Hilda's Hospital, Hartlepool, which opened in 1927. This panel was painted by Edward W Ball, one of Maw & Co's most talented tile artists.

CINDERELLA AND THE GLASS SHOE.

of nursery stories on its glistening walls, with the cheerful nurses eagerly telling off some infantile jingle to the tiny little patients, can forget the beauty of the picture, and its promise of many a bright recollection in the future for the little ones restored to health?

Doulton's best-known tile artists were Margaret Thompson, William Rowe and John H McLennan and the quality of their work is generally outstanding. Nursery rhymes and fairy tales predominated as themes for hospital tile pictures but soothing country scenes such as 'Feeding the Poultry' and 'Apple Gathering' were considered suitable too. The largest concentration of pictures is in the Royal Victoria Infirmary, Newcastle-upon-Tyne, which was built between 1900 and 1906. The four children's wards were decorated with 60 Doulton tile pictures, of which 55 remain on view and are still enjoyed by present-day children and adults. Every conceivable nursery rhyme and story is featured, sometimes taking up more than one panel, so that 'Tom, the Piper's Son' stealing a pig is accompanied by a second panel where, after being beaten, 'Tom went Roaring Down the Street'. In most hospitals long vertical-format pictures were used on the narrow wall area, breaking the regular rhythm of the windows, whilst square or landscape-format panels allowed different subjects to be accommodated on the larger areas of plain wall at the ends of the wards.

The subjects of hospital tile pictures were sometimes extended beyond the juvenile japes of Humpty Dumpty to the realms of history and contemporary events. The 'Coronation Ward' of Cardiff Royal Infirmary (formerly known as King Edward

Tile panel from the John Nixon Ward of Cardiff Royal Infirmary, c. 1912. The panel was designed by Philip H Newman and made by WB Simpson and Sons Ltd of London. The hospital originally had 36 tile panels, including a series depicting Welsh history.

VII Hospital) which opened in 1912, included panels depicting the Coronation of King George V (June 1911) and the Investiture of HRH Edward, Prince of Wales, at Caernarfon Castle (July 1911), together with other panels illustrative of Welsh history.

One of the most interesting new opportunities for the architectural use of tiles arrived with the steam locomotive. This great leviathan was a powerful but dirty beast and for its associated buildings the glazed surfaces of ceramic tiles, bricks and faience offered an immediate advantage over stone, which rapidly became grimy. The developing railway networks of Britain, followed by those of Europe and then the United States, brought in their wake a completely new building type and thus a new architectural challenge – the railway passenger station. The first examples, from the 1830s, were modest structures which were almost domestic in scale. At this point the great renaissance in the manufacture and use of tiles was still a decade or more away and the early stations lack tiles completely. By the time later stations were built, architects had succeeded in creating buildings which were more monumental and more original than those of the early pioneers and it was at this stage that tiles and architectural ceramics began to make an important contribution. The railway station as a building type spread around the world and with it the use of decorative tiles. These tiles were robust and colourful and could be used by architects to help make rail travel a memorable experience and to promote the visual image of their railway company clients.

An early example of this use of tiles, dating from 1865, survives at Shrub Hill Station, Worcester, where two linked 'pavilions' providing waiting room accommodation have been constructed entirely from cast-iron and tiles. The tiles are in panels set flush with the cast-iron framing, which was made by the local Vulcan Foundry. Whilst being highly colourful, the designs on the tiles are also eclectic, ranging from the Greek key pattern through a frieze of cornucopia to a number of designs derived from the Alhambra. A small proportion of the tiles are unglazed and these have now absorbed over 100 years of railway grime, highlighting the superiority of glazed surfaces in such surroundings. Even today the tiles make a strong visual impact and their exotic designs, evoking thoughts of distant places, create a perfect prelude to a journey.

Of more immediate assistance to the railway traveller were the thoughtful maps of the north-east of England railway network. With their moulded brown frames, these large tiled maps, which were built into the walls of stations, have often proved more durable than the rail routes themselves and the 1890s system is now preserved quite literally on tablets of clay!

An illustration of the worldwide spread from Britain of both railways and ceramic building materials is provided by Dunedin Railway Station on the South Island of New Zealand. This impressive Edwardian building in Flemish Renaissance style was

Above. The faience for the booking office and the mosaic tiled floor at Dunedin railway station, New Zealand, were supplied by Doultons, England, in 1907 Below. Tile panels set into glazed brickwork at Haarlem Railway Station, Holland, 1904.
Opposite. Tiled map of the North Eastern Railway, c. 1895, at Scarborough station, Yorkshire. This is one of a number of identical maps used throughout the network and made by Craven Dunnills.

completed in 1907. The interior demonstrates the ability of one of Britain's leading ceramic manufacturers to meet the needs of architect and client thousands of miles away. Many firms devised telegraphic code words for each of their hundreds of designs which were printed in special 'colonial' editions of catalogues, thus enabling architects and manufacturers to communicate easily. The scheme supplied for Dunedin by Doultons covered both walls and floors in shades of cream, ochre and blue. The adaptability of ceramics was demonstrated by the ornately modelled ticket windows and the frieze of cherubs and foliate scrolls. The floor consisted of 725,760 small, square ceramic tiles which were made up into panels featuring the emblem of the New Zealand railways, as well as appropriate imagery such as railway wheels, wagons and signals with a centrepiece bearing a British steam locomotive.

Perhaps the most complete and co-ordinated ceramic railway station is, appropriately, in Holland where tile-makers, builders and architects adapted their centuries-old skills for making and using tiles to new buildings with comparative ease. Haarlem Station was completely re-built in 1904 under the direction of the architect D A N Margadant. His striking permutations of glazed bricks, tile panels and dark brown woodwork produced a crisp and functional building with an Arts and Crafts flavour mixed with elements of Art Nouveau. The ceramic experience begins as the prospective passenger enters the station from the street into a lofty entrance hall. High up over each side are two gigantic panels consisting of around 800 tiles each. The contrast in the subject-matter of the two panels, which are painted in greeny-brown monochrome, could hardly be more extreme. On one side a team of horses is drawing a plough whilst opposite sinewy blacksmiths are working iron, a reminder that the railway served both town and country. The panels are the work of the artists D P de Ruiter and J Y van Rossum, who were leading ceramic painters with the Rozenburg firm in The Hague. A tile-lined tunnel leads off the station foyer and a series of steps gives access to the platforms above. Here ceramic materials serve a number of different functions. The white-glazed bricks of the station buildings reflect light and look clean. But their starkness is relieved by bands of blue-glazed brick which act as string courses to pull the different parts together. The decorative tile panels incorporated in the glazed brickwork serve as an entertaining and sophisticated system of visual identification with, for instance, the station clerk's office being indicated by crossed quill pens and a bottle of ink. Such use of pictograms is early and a valuable feature for a building which by its nature must cope with foreign visitors. There is no attempt at Haarlem to use tiles for their own sake. Thus in the elaborate refreshment rooms wood predominates, creating a warm and homely feeling which is entirely appropriate. But in the lavatories, which lie off the back of the restaurant, tiles come into their own again for their hygienic qualities. Yet a dismal lavatorial look has been successfully avoided by the use of a bold, stencilled design for the dado. This design, which is known as 'peacock's eye', was carried out by the Rozenburg artist D P de Ruiter. Considered overall, Haarlem Station is a building where tiles lighten, decorate, inform and entertain with equal success and efficiency.

As nineteenth-century buildings became larger and more densely grouped together, so the multi-functional value of tiles became apparent. Their glazed surfaces not only helped spaces such as basements, internal courtyards and narrow passages to look and stay clean but in addition, because of their reflectivity, increased the amount of natural light reaching these potentially gloomy places. Joseph Bolt, in an address to the Liverpool Architectural Society in 1880, noted that in the Liverpool and London Chambers building 'the lighting of the inner court was very deficient until all the available wall space had been covered, on my suggestion, with glazed white tiles, being, I believe the first occasion on which they had been used so extensively for such a purpose'.

The mass use of plain tiling developed even further in the USA. Here a form of tile lining to large internal vaulted spaces was devised whereby the tiles not only presented a clean and light-reflecting surface but were also structural and fireproof. The pedigree of this form of tiled vaulting originated in the ages-old Mediterranean system of erecting thin masonry vaults, a technique which was brought to perfection in the Catalonia region of Spain. In the 1880s this technique was taken across the Atlantic by Rafael Guastavino and his son (of the same name), where it flourished under new conditions. After a period of initial disbelief, this form of tiled vaulting (which became known as Guastavino) became popular with American architects and was used in numerous public buildings such as Carnegie Hall in New York City. It involved the use of bonded layers of tiles and was ideal for all manner of buildings, ranging from churches to railway stations, since it created a lightweight and fireproof vault which needed the minimum of propping during construction. Being composed of fired clay tiles and cement, the vaulting is completely non-combustible

The Oyster Bar on the lower level of Grand Central Station in New York, 1913. This elegant dining space is defined by Guastavino vaulting which uses cool, clean ivory tiles.

and is resistant to the spread of fire. The tiles protect their mortar from the destructive effect of heat. In their promotional activities the Guastavinos emphasized this aspect and in July 1889 they established a corporation which called itself the Guastavino Fireproof Construction Company. The great Chicago fire of 1871 and the growing concern for fireproofing and safety codes that characterized the architectural and building professions for the rest of the century undoubtedly benefited the Guastavinos, who seem to have maintained an absolute monopoly.

The use of Guastavino vaulting extended to underground railways in America too. New York City's first subway line opened in 1904 and the original City Hall Station was given special architectural treatment because of the role it played in serving the centre of the city's government. Instead of the straightforward 'tunnel', City Hall Station was constructed with a series of Guastavino vaults along its length, giving it a special character. The station has been closed since 1945 and, although a Landmark building, it remains unseen by the travelling public. The white matt tiles of the vaulting, arranged in herringbone pattern, contrasted with the green and brown glazed tiles at the edges of the vault. Meanwhile blue and white lettered plaques bore the name of the station which one contemporary writer likened to 'a cool little vaulted city of cream and blue earthenware like a German beer stein'.

Below. The lightweight, fireproof tiled vaulting of City Hall Station under construction in 1902. The curved wooden supports were removed after the layers of tiles had been set.
Bottom. The herringbone Guastavino tiling of City Hall subway station, New York City, taken from an old postcard. Designed by Heins and La Farge, the station opened in 1904.
Opposite. The impressive entrance to City Hall subway station, unseen by the travelling public since 1945.

City Hall
Subway Station,
New York.

Tiles and the Home

Using tiles in the home, especially for bathrooms and kitchens, has now become so commonplace that many people would regard them as indispensable. In countries with a long tradition of making and using tiles, such as Holland and Spain, their use around the home has helped to reflect the status of its occupants. Indeed in Spain 'to have a house without tiles' became a proverbial expression for poverty.

Industrial mass production of tiles and their improved distribution enabled the homes of all sectors of nineteenth-century society, whether situated in a traditional tile-making area or not, to benefit from a ceramic material that could be both cheap and beautiful. This does not imply that all homes were equal – but that tiles in one form or another might, from this time onwards, be found in homes throughout Europe.

Ingenuity in the application of tiles in the home knew no bounds. In 1878 the *Pottery and Glass Trades Review* posed the question 'To what use cannot tiles be put?'. It would seem that there was none for it proceeded to answer with 'Corridors and chair-mouldings, door-frames and windows are set with them; hearths outlined or made wholly from them, doors inlaid, and staircases decorated ... summerhouses are gay with them, for the tile is always fresh and cool-looking in its bright designs, while nothing is warmer for winter rooms than the dark earth-coloured ones.' These comments serve to reflect precisely the state of the industry, as well as the enthusiasm

At Home – A Portrait by Walter Crane, 1872. The use of tiles in the fireplace surround is typical of the period. They were both practical and pretty.

of its customers and their willingness to use tiles to introduce variety and decoration into the home.

From primitive times the hearth and fireplace have been the focal point of the home and it is here that tiles have so successfully combined their decorative contribution to architecture with the purely practical job of providing a fireproof wall lining. Coal-burning fireplaces were one of the most significant sites for the domestic use of tiles from the 1860s until World War 1. Since the beginning of the nineteenth century cast-iron had been increasingly used for fireplace surrounds. It was cheap and could be cast in moulds which allowed the mass production of elaborate ornamentation but it lacked colour. By the 1850s there was a growing trend to incorporate tiles in side or top panels, as well as in the hearth. The benefits of tiled hearths were recognized by the new *Journal of Design and Manufacturers* which, in a series of hints for the decoration and furnishing of dwellings in 1850, recommended that 'where the tenant has to put a new grate in his dining room, by all means let him take the trouble of seeing Mr Sylvester's last new pattern, with its radiating hearth of Minton encaustic tiles'. On a purely practical note the writer emphasized that a tiled hearth 'radiates into the room, making a most comfortable and natural spot for warming the feet upon, without exciting the good housewife's ire that you are damaging the polish on her best fender'.

The cast-iron surround served as a convenient frame for tiles and the fireplace became a miniature gallery of pictures around the fire. In most cases the tiles were set in plaster and bolted into frames from the back, making them difficult to change.

Opposite. A majestic and unusual fireplace made by the Martin Brothers Pottery in 1891 for the billiards room of Alexander Henderson's Oxfordshire house, Buscot Park.

Above. Ceramic serendipity. A fireplace in a cottage in Broseley, Shropshire, created from an extraordinary assortment of tiles by a worker at the local tile works.

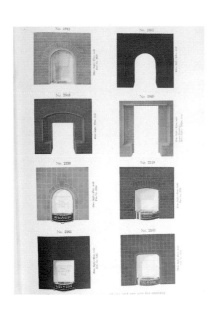

Tiled fireplaces adopted a wide variety of forms and styles, reflecting the eclectic nature of nineteenth-century interior design.

Opposite top left. Cast-iron grate with tile side panels, from the O'Brien Thomas catalogue, 1891.

Opposite centre left. Tiles and cast iron, from the O'Brien Thomas catalogue, 1891.

Opposite bottom left. Moulded fireplace by Maw & Co in the Renaissance style, c. 1870.

Opposite right. Plainer slabbed fireplace surrounds, dating from after 1900.

This page, far left. A page of plain slabbed fireplace surrounds, dating from around 1900.

Left. Fireplace designed by CFA Voysey, c. 1908, for Capel House, New Broad Street, London, using tiles from Medmenham Pottery.

Below left. Moulded fireplace by Maw & Co in the Art Nouveau style, c. 1900.

Below right. Heavy moulded ceramic fireplace, complete with tiled hearth and ceramic fender, from Arthur Maw's home in Ironbridge, c. 1870.

However, the Coalbrookdale Company took fireplace tiles into the realms of fashion accessories by means of a patent slip-out tile frame for their cast-iron fireplaces. Thus tiles around the fireplace could reflect the latest trends in design or even the seasons of the year.

The seasonal problem of how to treat the tiled fireplace during the summer was tackled by Lucy Crane (Walter Crane's sister) in her *Art and the Formation of Taste*, which was published in 1882. Recognizing that an unused open fireplace was 'a great black hole in our homes', she advocated that the hearth should be tiled in plain strong colours such as red, brown or green, sensibly avoiding tiles with a pattern on them 'as the ashes obscure and spoil the effect of the design'. She felt that the vogue for filling the grate with heaps of shavings garlanded with artificial flowers or a Japanese umbrella was uncomfortable and inappropriate, preferring instead that it be 'a separate and detached object, capable of being removed and in its place in the summer filled with plants...'

The growing mass market for fireplace tiles led to the establishment of a number of new tile factories in Britain, France, Holland and Germany, notably between 1860 and 1880. A kaleidoscopic riot of decorated tiles was produced which ranged from expensive hand-painted examples to cheap relief-moulded and transfer-printed designs. This ensured that whatever the function or scale of a room, be it grand dining-room or maid's bedroom, fireplace tiles were available of a suitable nature and at an appropriate cost. Decorative motifs from every corner of the world and from all periods of history were copied, adapted, developed or sometimes debased in conditions of intense commercial competition. Some iron foundries developed special links with the tile manufacturers and were even responsible for registering the designs in their own name. Although the majority of fireplace tiles were mass-produced, the sheer quantity of designs from which to choose helped to give each fireplace an individual character.

Block- or transfer-printed tiles were particularly common and one of the most important designers in Britain associated with this technique was John Moyr Smith. After a childhood and early training in Scotland, he moved south to make his name as a designer and illustrator. His best-known tile designs were produced by both Mintons China Works and Minton Hollins in large quantities and exported to the USA and the countries of the British Empire. They were considered very appropriate around the late Victorian domestic hearth, being both morally improving and educational. Literary series abounded such as 'Scenes from Shakespeare', 'Tennyson's Idylls', 'Scott's Waverley Novels' and 'Pilgrim's Progress'.

The fireside academy was extended by such obvious themes as months and seasons of the year and days of the week and Maw and Co produced 12 birds, using Bewick's engravings of British birds. A series of 12 'trades' brought out in the 1880s

Above. The aesthetic contribution of ceramic tiles to the domestic hearth could be complemented by art pottery from the same manufacturer; in this case it was Maw & Co.

Opposite. This painting of a homely scene by Henry Treffry Dunn shows delft tiles around the fireplace. The two men are Theodore Watts Dunton and Dante Gabriel Rossetti.

included such now-vanished characters as 'The Navvy' and 'The Hooper'. But for sheer fun Wedgwood must surely take the prize with their series entitled 'An Eventful Day's Fishing'. The designs included 'Think I Shall Have a Rise Here' (bull charging fisherman), 'In a Fix' (fisherman with line tangled in branches) and 'Those Horrid Boys' (fisherman watching swimming party). Nursery fireplaces offered opportunities to use nursery rhymes and improving narrative subjects such as Aesop's fables. Some designers, such as Walter Crane and Kate Greenaway, were equally at home designing for tiles or children's books.

The captivating nature of fireside pictures on tiles has been immortalized in the poetry of the great American Henry Wadsworth Longfellow. He arrived in Cambridge, Massachusetts, in 1837 and rented rooms on the upper floor of the Craigie Mansion, which was built in 1759 and which had English printed tiles from Liverpool around three fireplaces. In 1843 Longfellow married and his father-in-law purchased the house for the couple. In due course, their six children were born there. It is not difficult when reading his poem *To a Child* to imagine Longfellow sitting in front of a roaring fire in the rear bedroom holding one of the children on his lap and looking at the tiles around the fireplace opening.

> *Dear child! how radiant on thy mother's knee,*
> *With merry-making eyes and jocund smiles,*
> *Thou gazest at the painted tiles,*
> *Whose figures grace,*
> *With many a grotesque form and face,*
> *The ancient chimney of thy nursery*
> *The lady with the gay macaw,*
> *The dancing girl, the grave bashaw*
> *With bearded lip and chin;*
> *And, leaning idly o'er his gate,*
> *Beneath the imperial fan of state,*
> *The Chinese mandarin.*

All these improbable characters are featured around the fireplace and Longfellow could be granted poetic licence for describing them as painted rather than printed!

Poetry inspired by tiles later changed to tiles inspired by poetry. In 1874 Longfellow published his poem *The Hanging of the Crane*. The crane here refers to the iron device used to suspend a cooking pot over the fire and *pendre la crémailliere* (to hang the crane) is a French expression for a house warming. The poem muses on a series of domestic scenes throughout the life of a typical couple; young lovers alone, the arrival of children, the sorrows of their eventual departure and the joys of a golden wedding day. Within a couple of years Maw and Co had translated the poem into a series of relief-decorated fireplace tiles, probably with an eye on the American

Freestanding tile stoves were a distinctive
feature of Swedish living rooms. Their
decoration was frequently integrated into
the overall design of the room.
Above. Sturhof, Sweden.
Left. Tullgarn, Sweden.

Nineteenth-century tiles and iron.
Opposite left. Ceramic stove designed by
AWN Pugin for the Medieval Court at the
Great Exhibition, 1851. The ironwork is
by Hardman of Birmingham, the majolica
pierced tiles by Minton.
Opposite right top and centre. Cast-iron
radiator covers by the Coalbrookdale
Company, c. 1870, incorporating Maws'
pierced tiles.
Opposite right bottom. Triangular corner
stove in the Appliqué Room of the Schloss
Favorite in Germany.
Right. The Grill Room at the Victoria and
Albert Museum, London. The iron and
brass grill, designed by Sir Edward Poynter
in 1866, is set off by a surround of blue
and white tiles decorated with sunflowers.

export market.

Freestanding ceramic stoves, often in iron frames, continued to be popular in Europe throughout the nineteenth century, employed as a means of heating domestic rooms as well as for cooking. But the fashion never really caught on in Britain. This was despite a very spectacular and architectural example in the form of the tile and iron stove designed by A W N Pugin for the Great Exhibition in 1851. This was a prominent feature at the centre of the Medieval Court, with its tall iron finials standing more than 3 metres (9.8 feet) high. The ornate ironwork was made by Hardman of Birmingham whilst the tiles, not surprisingly, were made by Minton in Stoke-on-Trent. The tiles were perforated to allow warm air to escape and their considerable thickness, with deeply incised relief decoration, aided heat radiation, following the principle of German stove tiles. After the exhibition the stove vanished and, despite its prominence, it did not spawn a new era of tiled stoves in Britain.

Twenty years later, however, decorative cast-iron covers for hot water radiators made an appearance and in some instances they used perforated tiles similar to Pugin's stove tiles. Even later, some new stylish perforated tiles were made and used in the USA as grilles for heating and ventilating systems. Particularly interesting are the designs showing leaping deer and archers by Leon V Solon, an outstanding tile designer who was awarded the Gold Medal for Applied Arts by the American Institute of Architects. Interestingly, he had emigrated from England where his father, Marc Louis Solon, had worked for many years for Mintons.

In contrast, stoves were quite popular as a form of heating in American homes and the 'art tile' industry, which by the 1890s had established itself in centres such as Boston and Trenton, found a ready outlet for their sentimental products for stoves. The cause of ceramic stoves was taken up vigorously by Caryl Coleman in a series of articles in *The Decorator and Furnisher* in 1882. He predicted that 'the day is not far distant when stoves in this country will be made entirely of tiles and the frightful nickel-plated iron monsters, so ugly in form and weak beyond expression in ornament, will be banished forever from our homes'.

The pictorial qualities of tiles, so important around the domestic hearth, ensured that they found use too as inlays for furniture of wood, bamboo and cast-iron. The tradition of incorporating plaques and tiles had begun in France during the eighteenth century when products from the Royal Sèvres Porcelain Factory were used by French furniture-makers in grand commodes and writing desks. English furniture-makers, including Thomas Sheraton, were able to take advantage of the new jasperware cameos, medallions and plaques being produced by the enterprising Josiah Wedgwood, though once again these products were primarily for the rich.

As mass-produced tiles became more widely available, their applications for furniture were increasingly recognized. *The Builder* of 1843, writing on tiles, made the

Hvitträsk, near Kirkkonummi, Finland, was built in 1902 by Eliel Saarinen and his young architect partners as their home and studio. This tiled stove, following a Scandinavian tradition, formed part of an interior which made effective and modern use of straightforward materials.

rather prophetic comment: 'very ornamental, too, they would prove for hearth and mantel-pieces & they might be applied for dairies, conservatories, and even some articles of domestic furniture'. Thirty years later, however, after a plethora of cheap tiled washstands, rather gaunt planters and flimsy tables beset with tiles, the same magazine declared that 'the free introduction of tiles in wooden furniture must be deprecated; the materials do not harmonise at all'.

In 1878 the *Pottery and Glass Trades Review* was even more emphatic in its denunciation of the modern trend in cheap, tiled furniture, pleading 'from one occasion spare me - the freak which lets a band of tile-work into walnut bedsteads and bureaus. It is hard to say, too, why they should not be used in furniture, where porcelain plaques are quite at home. Perhaps the idea of bringing together wood warranted not to last twenty years with careful usage, and tile which will last till the Ptolemies come again is not correct'.

Oak and satinwood were not favoured for use in conjunction with Victorian tiles but ebony was considered suitable since 'in hardness, and the brilliant polish it takes, [it] approaches more to the character of the tile texture'. It was used very effectively by furniture designer Charles Bevan who produced two ebony showpieces for the 1872 International Exhibition in London, both of which are now in the collections of the Victoria and Albert Museum.

The hallways of Victorian middle-class homes quickly became adorned with tiled furniture in a variety of forms, often standing on tiled floors. The hall chair lost its personal family insignia and the back panel was inset instead with one, or a pair, of six-inch tiles decorated with scenes from Shakespeare or early English history,

Opposite. Corner of a sumptuously tiled bathroom, complete with fireplace, at Gledhow Hall, Leeds. The tiles and faience were supplied by Burmantofts of Leeds for the owner, Mr J Kitson Junior. This lavish scheme was illustrated in The Builder of 18 July 1885.

Above left. A bathroom at 8 Addison Road, ·London, with a simple tiled dado consisting of a veritable menagerie of De Morgan animals and birds.

Above right. Tiled inserts to a cast-iron wash basin stand. Taken from the O'Brien Thomas catalogue, 1891.

Kitchen tiling in the nineteenth century was restrained and functional.
Opposite. A child-sized version – the kitchen of the Swiss Cottage at Osborne House, Isle of Wight, was built by Queen Victoria and Prince Albert in 1853 for the royal children.
Above. The Victorian kitchen at Tredegar House, Newport, Gwent, has wall tiling supplied by Maw & Co.

thereby evoking at least a general sense of historical pedigree. Likewise, the wooden, cast-iron or bamboo hall stand often had a row of decorative tiles and the aspidistra could be neatly housed in a square brass-framed jardinière set with tiles. The advice of the *Furniture Gazette* of 26 April 1879 that 'we recommend our cabinet making firms to introduce tiles wherever they can consistently do so' certainly seems to have been heeded. And the tile manufacturers responded with catalogue pages headed 'Tiles for cabinet work' or 'Faience furniture inlays'.

The most widespread use of tiles in furniture was in the ubiquitous washstand which, before piped water supplies and drainage, was a feature of almost every bedroom. The quality of both the timber and the tiles covered a huge spectrum, ranging from imported hardwoods with a fine polish to cheap, grained pine and from costly handpainted or tube-lined tiles to cheap transfer prints. Regardless of material 'the tiles at the back are in every respect to be preferred to any other expedient for keeping the wall free from splashes, and they help not a little to enhance the effect of the whole' (*Furniture Gazette*, 19 July 1879).

Although printed tiles were very widely used in washstands for a mass market, they came in for some harsh contemporary criticism. Lewis Day, writing in *The Artist* in 1887, declared that 'the ordinary run of printed tiles are eminently inartistic in their total effect, obviously cheap, and to the cultivated eye, proportionately nasty'. Ironically the same words might be applied to many of the bathroom tiles made and used today!

In the nineteenth century the tiled bathroom was essentially a feature of richer houses which had the luxury of piped water and drainage, although these features were becoming commonplace towards the end of the century. Some remarkable

schemes were devised, using a rich and wide variety of tiles. At Lord Armstrong's country house, Cragside in Northumberland, a large plunge bath set in the floor was itself lined with Dutch blue and white tiles depicting knights on horseback. More unusually, the tiles were incorporated into a mahogany frame which acted as a splash-back behind the bath. Even more imposing were the hooded baths with their shower cabinets cased in carved mahogany and tiles. Fish, dolphins, seaweed and seashells were popular motifs for bathroom tiles and complemented stained-glass windows, solid brass taps and a plethora of controls, all of these features designed to display the owner's undoubted wealth, taste and approval of modern sanitary standards.

It was in the kitchens of the nineteenth century that the use of tiles showed perhaps the most restraint and thereby the greatest contrast with the present day. Many smaller kitchens served as communal living spaces and the walls were often simply brick-lined. Such tiles as there were would have been incorporated into the back of the kitchen range. Their utilitarian function was paramount and they were worlds apart from the late twentieth-century tiled Aga backs with their personalized idyllic scenes. Larger Victorian kitchens did have tiled walls, which were often plain or at most decorated with a combination of white or cream octagons with smaller squares of blue or brown at the corners. These kitchens were busy, impersonal places staffed with a hierarchy of domestics, in which elaborate tile schemes would have been inappropriate. Those decorated tiles which were used sometimes took the form of stern admonitions, such as 'Waste not want not' and 'A place for everything and everything in its place'.

For any visitor to a house the first room encountered inside the front door was the hall and the widespread application of geometric-shaped tiles for hall floors became one of the most characteristic tiling features of the century. It should be borne in mind, however, that geometric patterns are not the sole preserve of nineteenth-century tiles and throughout history numerous variations have been rendered in all kinds of materials, particularly marbles and stone, and especially in Italy. Thus in Batty Langley's book *The City and Country Builder's and Workman's Treasury of Designs*, published in London in 1745, there are several pages of plates showing geometric designs which would be equally applicable to floors, decorated plaster ceilings or even marquetry.

A knowledge of geometry and the properties of its basic shapes was commonplace in the nineteenth century. Schools of Art in Britain included the subject as an integral part of their courses and the Department of Science and Art in London supplied them with examples of solid geometry in plaster for practical drawing work by students. Numerous text books on the subject were available, including one by Thomas Bradley who held the post of 'professor of geometrical drawing' at Kings College London.

Plain coloured tiles of simple geometric shapes were cheap and easy to manufacture and could be arranged in a huge number of different permutations, from the simple to the very elaborate. Occasionally patterned tiles were included to personalize grander floors, for example (below right) the cross foxes emblem of the Williams-Wynn family at Wynnstay, Ruabon, Clwyd.

Geometric tiles were widely used for the front pathways and steps of terraced houses and villas, especially in urban areas in Britain. The practice was continued in California (opposite top left) where an additional Spanish influence introduced greater colour.

The use of geometric-shaped floor tiles offered a number of practical advantages. One of the attractions was the huge number of different permutations of pattern that was possible. J C Loudon, in his *Cottage, Farm and Villa Architecture* (1836), demonstrated that even the humble rectangular shape of a paving brick can achieve a decorative effect when two colours are used in combination, illustrating no fewer than 13 possibilities. Tile manufacturers made available diamonds, squares, rectangles, triangles, lozenges, hexagons and octagons which, with the added option of a dozen or more different colours, offered almost infinite scope to pattern-making. Most manufacturers suggested a series of standard arrangements in their catalogues and some also included a diagram of geometric shapes 'showing the mutual relation of the various forms and sizes of Tiles and Tesserae... for the assistance of Architects and others who wish to arrange their own Designs'. Such geometric tiles were machine-pressed from dust clay and usually fired high enough to produce a very hard and vitrified product. This firing process has been the secret of their long life in many of the houses where they still exist in daily use. To many Victorian designers, including Christopher Dresser, geometric pattern was equated with a sense of order rather than any idea of fashion and even today these patterns have a timeless quality.

A turn-of-the-century tiled house name above the doorway of 'Villa Elisabeth' in Ghent, Belgium.

J C Loudon's praise for the new geometric and encaustic tiles for halls and passages in the 1830s was followed by that of others, including Matthew Digby Wyatt. Yet the most noticeable advocate was Charles Eastlake who, in his *Hints on Household Taste* (which was published in Britain but was even more influential in America), left readers in no doubt as to the practical and aesthetic virtues of tiles:

There can be little doubt that the best mode of treating a hall-floor, whether in town or country, is to pave it with encaustic tiles. This branch of art-manufacture is one of the most hopeful, in regard to taste, now carried on in this country. It has not only reached great technical perfection as far as material and colour are concerned, but, aided by the designs supplied by many architects of acknowledged skill, it has gradually become a means of decoration which, for beauty of effect, durability, and cheapness, has scarcely a parallel.

Eastlake's advice, less often heeded, was extended to the walls too, suggesting that 'an inlay of encaustic tiles, to a height, say, of three or four feet from the ground, would form an excellent lining for a hall or ground floor passage'.

Geometric tiles also found widespread application on the approach to the house, as well as in its porch and hall. From the 1880s to the outbreak of World War 1, thousands of pathways were laid outside Victorian and Edwardian villas and terraces in Britain. Older houses were also treated to new tiles – as can be seen in London's Bloomsbury and Belgravia. The starkest and most striking geometric designs were created by using only black and white tiles, a practice which was particularly popular in the sophisticated streets of West London. Other regional variations did occur and the tilework designer Mr Ambrose Wood noted that 'in North Wales light-coloured tiles consisting of drab, salmon, chocolate, white and sage, in fairly rich colour combinations' were more frequently selected. His explanation, thoroughly pragmatic, was that 'the roads there are largely of limestone formation; hence the light-coloured dust and footmarks when wet do not so easily disfigure the pavement'.

Hard-wearing though they undoubtedly were, tiled pathways and halls had their critics. Arts and Crafts architect Philip Webb observed that 'any kind of glazed tile is disagreeable to walk on, and more so from the nails on country shoes'. The practice of glazing floor tiles had developed very much to meet an ecclesiastical market (see the third chapter). For domestic use matt, unglazed finishes were preferable and several manufacturers experimented with different textures to reduce the risk of slipping.

Practical considerations in designing geometric tile pavements for the home included the need to 'avoid making any combination which appears – "spiky" as anything of that kind makes one feel unpleasant when treading upon it'. It seems that some of the design lessons brought home by the 1851 Exhibition, with its carpets resembling three-dimensional tropical rain forests, had been learnt by manufacturers to good effect. Rather less restraint was displayed by speculative builders in the almost riotous combinations of colours and patterns of tiles used to line the lower parts of outer porches, which were frequently visible from the street. Tiny terraced railway workers' houses in towns like Crewe still demonstrate the ability of builders to use cheap, mass-produced tiles to create identity and a shared sense of style.

Another particularly interesting example of this democratization of decoration can be seen in many of the surviving entrance staircases to the tenement buildings in Glasgow's West End (known to Glaswegians as Wally Closes). Tiled wall linings provided a hard-wearing surface for the communal spaces and from about 1904 to 1910 a recognizable Glasgow style became evident, frequently using sub-Mackintosh Art Nouveau designs. Many of these tiles were designed by the Glasgow firm of J Duncan and they were executed in the tube-lined technique. Continuous tile borders, sometimes running up three flights of communal stairs, depicted such local scenes as paddle steamers on the Clyde going 'doon the watter' to day trip destinations such as the resort of Rothesay on the Isle of Bute.

The practice of incorporating decorative tiles into the external brickwork of houses was used in quite distinct ways, which varied according to the prevailing style and circumstance. Mid-nineteenth-century houses built in Britain in a vaguely Gothic style lent themselves to decoration, with diapers of tiles sometimes set in stone mouldings. String courses of tiles were used to give horizontal emphasis and pointed arch gables were often set with tiles. There was something of an unexpected alliance between Ruskinian architectural philosophy and the use of machine-made tiles for decoration which shows itself in the work of Birmingham architect John Henry

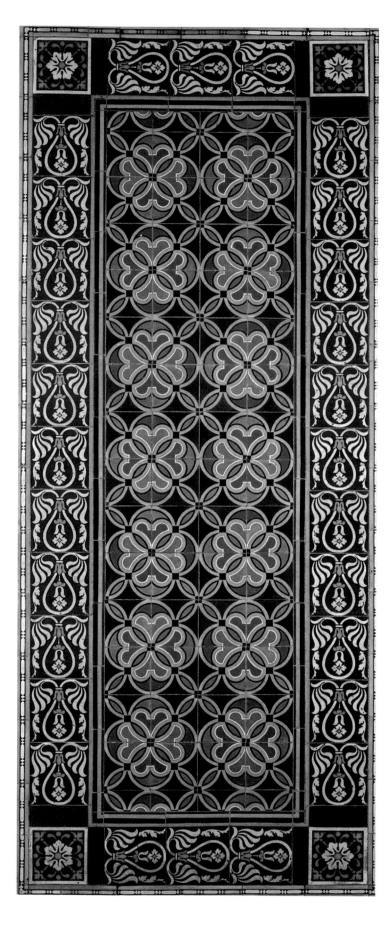

The extensive patronage of Minton's encaustic tiles by Queen Victoria and Prince Albert, at their home on the Isle of Wight, led to their widespread use for hallways by the 1860s. These examples, which include a Latin greeting, are in the Marble Corridor at Osborne House.

Chamberlain. He absorbed Ruskin's enthusiasm for polychromy but argued that broad surfaces should be treated simply and that bright, contrasting colours should be reserved for smaller parts. Thus he used encaustic and geometric tiles as small punctuating roundels or string courses in two of his major buildings, Birmingham School of Art and 'Highbury', the impressive home he built for the politician (and no relation) Joseph Chamberlain. Despite the factory origins of the tiles, the designs, which closely followed medieval interpretations of natural foliage and fleur-de-lys, made them acceptable.

Later in the century, tiles set into the brick and stonework of domestic houses became allied with a very different aesthetic movement. Holland, which pioneered the use of tiles for house names in the sixteenth century, made a comeback at the end of the nineteenth with tile panels in the 'Jugendstil' (or Art Nouveau) style providing lavish external decoration on houses, particularly in Amsterdam. These panels mainly appear above doorways or windows and are often recessed into brickwork.

Unlike Ruskinian Gothic, these tile decorations are only rarely integrated into the overall architecture of the house which is usually far less flamboyant than the tiles themselves. The tile decoration relies not on self-contained repeated design elements of quatrefoil or fleur-de-lys but instead on large panels exuberant with pelicans, peacocks or pansies. Their decorative impact is heightened by their relatively staid brickwork settings and is thus even more apparent to the passer-by. Public art is created from private domestic architecture. Similar use of tile panels occurs in other European countries notably Belgium (Ghent) and the border area of northern France.

Across the Atlantic in Philadelphia houses with tiled fronts were known in the 1850s. *The Builder* of 20 December 1851 described them as being of white clay with surfaces of glass and vivid colours. The tradition continued into the twentieth century on the exterior of apartment blocks, often with considerable success. The tiles frequently introduce colour, pattern and sometimes even humour to a building type which can otherwise be large and almost anonymous.

Doorways to houses in Holland, France and Belgium made use of Art Nouveau-style tiles and sometimes ceramic keystones. Below. Detail of a house in Amsterdam. Bottom. A tiled door surround and keystone, Saint Amand les Eaux, France. Opposite. The tradition continued in the twentieth century in the USA with exterior ceramic decoration to apartment block entrances. This example is in Cambridge, Massachusetts.

The Architecture of Illusion and Grandeur

 rchitectural decoration in all its many forms and styles has the power to raise a building from the mundane status of a simple structure to a palace of delight with new meanings and values; few materials aid this process more than richly coloured and highly glazed ceramic tiles. In the nineteenth century tile manufacturers joined forces with architects to produce a memorable series of buildings which transported their users out of a grey, industrial everyday world to a ceramic-clad utopia. In this way public houses became glittering palaces tiled inside and out; billiard rooms, theatres and aquaria emerged as tiled second cousins to the Alhambra; town halls and civic buildings used tiled walls, floors and even ceilings to foster an imposing municipal grandeur and in shops and commercial premises the consumer began to be wooed by tiled pictures and lettering. The 30 years between 1880 and 1910 yielded some of the richest and most remarkable tiling schemes yet seen and represent a significant contribution to late nineteenth-century cultural achievement. With more than a hint of self congratulation C T Davis, author of one of the standard British textbooks on manufacturing bricks, tiles and terracotta, was able to write in 1895 that 'the higher the culture of a people, the greater their use of tiles'.

Of all the various decorative styles available for exploitation through the use of ceramic tiles, the Moorish or Alhambra style was particularly successful in capturing imaginations in Britain as well as parts of Europe and the USA. Its unfamiliarity was

From 1865 onwards William Burges worked with the third Marquess of Bute, transforming Cardiff Castle into a building of a romantic, fairytale quality. Tiles played a part in creating the illusion and were used, for example, in the summer smoking room where the tiled floor is centred on a map of the ancient world surrounded by circles of spouting whales, huntsmen and horses. Around the walls, in a very different style, are painted tile panels depicting legends of the zodiac.

doubtless an attraction but the publication of Owen Jones's sumptuous books on the Alhambra in the 1840s, with their bright and novel colour plates (see the first chapter), helped to bring home to architects and others the extraordinarily emotive atmosphere which rich decoration combined with bright colours could evoke. It also provided manufacturers of items such as tiles and decorative plaster with a detailed and accurate source of patterns to copy. Yet despite the thoroughness and accuracy of Jones's work and the well-intentioned efforts of the tile manufacturers who followed his published examples, there was often only a fine dividing line in these exotic decorative schemes between the sublime and the monstrous. Ruskin, for example, thought the ornamentation of the Alhambra 'detestable... it is a late building, a work of the Spanish dynasty in its last decline, and its ornamentation is fit for nothing but to be transferred to patterns of carpets or bindings of books'. He classed 'Alhambras and common Moorish ornament...under the head of Doggerel ornamentation'.

Nevertheless, the Moorish style proved a considerable attraction to those with illusions of exotic splendour, not least to a London cotton merchant who needed to build on a billiard room. Alexander Collie was the owner of 12, Kensington Palace Gardens, and in 1864 he commissioned Matthew Digby Wyatt to make extensive alterations to this fairly sober house, which had been built in 1845. Collie had recently purchased the remarkable majolica-tiled fireplace with which Maw and Co and Wyatt had won prizes at the 1862 London International Exhibition. The fireplace, 'which very tastefully adapted the style of the Alhambra', was incorporated into the scheme

Above. Matthew Digby Wyatt (1820-77) was known for, amongst other achievements, his Moorish tile designs.
Right. Digby Wyatt's fireplace, designed for the 1862 International Exhibition in London and set with Maws' majolica tiles, was incorporated in 1864 into the tiled Moroccan billiard room at 12, Kensington Palace Gardens.
Opposite. The Arab Hall at Leighton House, London (1877-9), was designed by George Aitchison to accommodate Lord Leighton's large collection of Middle Eastern tiles.

for the new billiard room and Maws supplied a ceramic dado in a similar style. *The Survey of London* describes the room as 'a rich and glittering invention in the Moresque style'. The tiled dado was broken only by the fireplace, doorways and the upright wooden seating typical of the male-dominated Victorian billiard room. The table itself stood on a solid rectangle of floor marked out by tiles, whilst the surround was strip-boarded for the comfort of the players. A colonnade of lavishly gilded Moorish arches around the upper half of the room framed mirrors which multiplied the magnificence of the space.

Other rooms in the Islamic style followed elsewhere. Some were the result of a wish to perpetuate the memory of distant travels, such as the Moorish smoking room at Rhinefield House, Hampshire, which was commissioned by Mrs L W Munro as a reminder of her honeymoon in 1888. Others were designed to incorporate precious objects acquired during travels in the Near East, such as the Arab Hall at Leighton House, London, designed by George Aitchison between 1877 and 1879. William De Morgan was responsible for arranging the tiles, which were mainly Syrian and Iznik wares of the late sixteenth and seventeenth centuries collected by the artist Frederick Leighton. Many of the tile sets were incomplete and De Morgan had to do some clever infilling with his own tiles.

The Moorish style (and related Iznik and Persian styles) were favoured in France too at this time. Matthew Digby Wyatt's Moorish majolica tiles displayed at the 1862 International Exhibition in London were paralleled elsewhere in the same exhibition by the French ceramic exhibits designed by Theodore Deck. His rich turquoise blue and translucent emerald green glaze colours were much admired. French architects and designers had already been introduced to the delights of Middle Eastern decoration through a handsome volume of etchings entitled *Recueil de dessins pour l'Art et l'Industrie*, which was published by de Beaumont and Collinot in 1859. This formed the basis for a later series of volumes of colour lithographs called *Encyclopedie des Arts Decoratifs de l'Orient*, which were published in Paris between 1871 and 1883 and found their way into the reference libraries of several British tile manufacturers.

The transmission of the Moorish style, aided by printed sources, reached Italy too. In the hills of Valdarno near Florence, stands the extraordinary Alhambraesque castle of Sanmezzano, transformed from a small villa by the Marquis Ferdinando Panciatichi Ximenes d'Aragona. Work began no later than 1853 and Panciatichi almost certainly knew of Owen Jones's influential books, copies of which were in the Fondo Palatino of the Biblioteca Nazionale. Work continued on the building until 1873, resulting in a Moorish palace in Tuscany which displays a lavish use of highly coloured mosaics, tiles and stucco. The series of rooms includes the Hall of the Peacocks with its tiled dado in geometric pattern and the Hall of Spanish Plates with a ceiling where dozens of ceramic plates are set in a geometric embroidery of

The exotically patterned walls of the Arab Hall at Leighton House contrast with the plain turquoise tiles seen on the main staircase in the distance. Lord Leighton declared that his new Hall was 'a little addition for the sake of something beautiful to look at from time to time'.

The Villa of Sanmezzano in Tuscany was
transformed between 1853 and 1873 with
tiles, mosaic, glass and stucco into an
improbable Moorish palace.
Opposite. The Hall of Lilies
Below. The Hall of Peacocks.

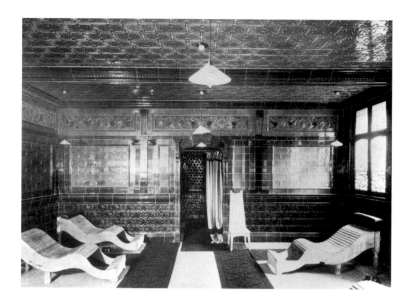

decorative stucco. The building superficially exploits the decorative syntax of the Moorish style but in its use of tile pattern it falls far short of the subtlety of the Alhambra.

The creation of illusion by the use of exotic tile work was particularly important in the numerous Turkish Baths which opened in Britain in the late nineteenth century. Despite their popularity then, their origins go back to at least 1679 when bathing 'in the Turkish mode' in London involved rooms lined with Dutch tiles. Oriental Baths opened in Leeds in 1866 which were designed by the architect of its Town Hall, Cuthbert Brodrick. They were in a robust Moorish style using a range of ceramic building materials including red, blue and black bricks, encaustic tiles and terracotta which *The Builder* in 1862 had praised as 'materials which no climate will touch or destroy' and which offered architects 'opportunities for exercising every facility they possess'. The Leeds baths suffered the indignity of being refaced in the Gothic style in 1882 and demolished in 1969. A more fortunate survivor is the former Nevills New Turkish Baths off Old Broad Street in London. The architect for this below-ground complex (which now serves admirably as a Turkish restaurant) was G Harold Elphick who in 1894 employed the large tile-making firm of Craven Dunnill to produce several ranges of shaped tiles which helped to destroy the gridded monotony of square tiles and get closer to the Moorish originals. The commercial success of Turkish Baths was certainly helped by the lavish use of tiling in exotic schemes, which seem to have titillated the desires of the users. Robert Allsop, in his textbook *The Turkish Bath: its Design and Construction* (published in 1890), declared that 'with the public the best bath will be the most elaborate and most flashily decorated, and the moth-and-candle principle comes into play'. His own view of an attractive bath was 'one in which the visitor will feel interest in the design', adding that 'artistic decorations have here a commercial value'.

With all their glittering industrially produced tiles, late nineteenth-century Turkish Baths may have satisfied contemporary customers but they probably bore little resemblance to the originals in eastern countries. Allsop's textbook laments that

Above. The tiled walls and ceiling of the Turkish Baths of the Imperial Hydro Hotel, Blackpool. The tiles were supplied by Burmantofts of Leeds in c. 1900 and the architect was James B Broadbent. Opposite. The Criterion Theatre on Piccadilly Circus, London, was designed by Thomas Verity between 1870 and 1874. The upper part of the walls employs a light and delicate scheme of hand-painted tile panels by WB Simpson & Sons, and mirrors which complement and reflect the painted ceiling. The lower dado is of more robust relief-moulded tiles supplied from the Maw & Co catalogue.

Public house tiling schemes from a Craven Dunnill album of record photographs, c. 1895. From top: interior of Dog and Duck, Aston, Birmingham; exterior of Dog and Duck; Church Hotel, Eccles, Manchester; Ordsall Hotel, Manchester.

'here is a branch of architectural design absolutely unstudied. Few architects visit the East, and none enter the baths there, either in Egypt, Turkey or Morocco. The ordeal of the true oriental shampooing doubtless deters the few who might be curious about these buildings.'

The ability of tiling schemes to uplift patrons and transport them away from reality was utilized in other nineteenth-century buildings devoted to pleasure, such as theatres. Thus at the Criterion Theatre, London, high-relief tiles of the 1870s line the walls of the stairways as part of a sophisticated classical scheme of decoration, whereas at the later His Majesty's Theatre, Aberdeen, by Frank Matcham a maroon tiled dado with a flowery Art Nouveau frieze is used behind the circle. Perhaps the ultimate in esoteric tiled pleasure buildings were the seaside subterranean aquaria built in the 1870s at Brighton and Scarborough by E Birch of London. Scarborough's powerful colonnades of Moorish arches in brickwork were offset by tiled dados and floors, the latter incorporating encaustic tiles of shells, seaweed, starfish and dolphins, alas all now gone.

Nineteenth-century America shared Britain's interest in the decorative styles of the Near East, learning about them mostly from European publications since few people had actually been there. However, an important link emerged in the figure of Jacob Wrey Mould (1825-86) who was Owen Jones's most talented pupil. Whilst articled to him, he accompanied Jones on visits to the Alhambra and worked on several of Jones's most influential books. In 1853 he moved to New York, taking 'his master's ability to combine vigorous eclectic designs with bright polychromy'. His work (with others) in the development of Central Park, New York, reaches a climax with the use of the tiles on the ceiling of Bethesda Terrace, which was constructed between 1859 and 1864. The ceiling is over a pedestrian arcade located beneath the park's main transverse road at 72nd Street. It is composed of a grid of iron beams enclosing large squares of colourful encaustic tiles. The tiles were designed by Mould but made in England by Minton and they incorporate a narrow slot into which a brass key fits to enable them to be used, almost uniquely, on a ceiling. The tiled ceiling, together with the colourful painted wall decoration and the elaborately carved stonework of the exterior, makes the terrace the architectural focal point of its picturesque setting.

Whilst British-trained designers and British-manufactured tiles may have crossed the Atlantic successfully, one distinctive group of Victorian buildings have resolutely remained in place to act as something of a national icon. Practically unique to Britain (and to judge from replicas overseas, much-admired everywhere else) are the ornate and highly decorated public houses of the late Victorian and Edwardian eras. Here ceramic tiles joined forces with etched, cut and coloured glass, cast-iron, brass, mahogany and moulded plaster to assault the aesthetic senses and draw customers in from the murky streets to drink in surroundings which were almost theatrical in their opulence and splendour. In *The Northumbrian Pub* Dr Lynn Pearson describes these institutions as sensual beasts, arguing that 'these were not ordinary buildings, but buildings designed to tease the senses'. As she rightly points out, they were not built for fun but with the serious commercial intent of extracting money from the drinking masses.

Earlier public houses were not nearly so alluring. Often they were simple ale houses, domestic in scale and character and distinguishable from adjacent houses only because of some lettering on the front and a gas lamp over the door. The move away from small-scale pubs brewing their own beer was partly caused by the increasing dominance of the brewery as the owner and supplier of beer to a whole series of public houses. The result was a sense of competition between rival brewers and from 1880 to 1900 there was a great deal of remodelling or rebuilding. Architects boldly accentuated corner sites and ruthlessly exploited a whole portfolio of motifs to make their pubs instantly recognizable. Tiles and a wide range of architectural ceramics, including faience and terracotta, were frequently used to achieve this effect externally, along with architectural features such as clock towers and huge hanging lamps. *The Victualling Trades Review* was able to report in 1896 that 'the embellishment and decoration of our hotels, restaurants, bars and public houses has been almost entirely revolutionised during the last decade. Instead of dark, low-roofed, and often insanitary premises, we find elegant, airy, light apartments whose decorations, being "things of beauty" may be presumed to be, to the customers and owners alike, "joys for ever"'. Tiles were equally popular inside the pub and they, together with all the

Later nineteenth-century public house interiors used colourful, shiny materials such as tiles, glass and mirrors to create opulent and alluring drinking palaces. *Opposite.* Built as the Palsgrove Hotel in 1883 to a design by G Cuthbert, this impressive interior, with tiles by Doulton, now houses a branch of Lloyds Bank in the Strand, London.
Right. The Salisbury, Haringay, London.
Below. The King's Head, Tooting, London.

decorative materials, represented an 'era of mass production, allowing more people to enjoy an illusion of riches at a realistic price'. The manufacturers of these decorative materials, including the tile manufacturers, produced elaborate catalogues which enabled architects to assemble an interior design from standard elements. Indeed Mark Girouard, in his *Victorian Pubs*, has described the pub architects of London as 'commercial hacks'.

Far from resulting in dull standardization, this off-the-peg approach to architectural decoration has, in skilful hands, produced some memorable buildings. Amongst the best are the series of pubs built in Birmingham between 1896 and 1904 under the supervision of the architectural practice of James and Lister Lea. These architects evolved a formula for pubs but delegated a good deal of the detailing of both tiling and terracotta to the manufacturers themselves. If the skills and judgment of the tile fixer are also seen as factors, we can see that the final appearance of these buildings is the result of far more than just the architects' contribution. From the surviving documentation on pub tiling schemes it is clear that the drawing offices of many of the larger tile manufacturers were well equipped to devise and execute detailed designs and tiling schemes.

From the 1880s onwards, tiled picture panels made a significant contribution to the interiors of public houses, coffee houses, dining-rooms and cafés in Britain and Europe. With roots in Portugal and Holland which went back to the seventeenth century, these picture panels, which could cover several square metres, were the highest form of the tile decorator's art and were in many cases signed and dated. They defy easy analysis in terms of their contribution to architecture. In one sense they are pieces of fine art; the creative expression of usually a single artist which happens to have been rendered on a group of ceramic tiles rather than on a canvas or a piece of paper. Considered thus, just like a picture hung on the wall, the tile picture is no more than decoration for architecture. But, because the tiles making up the picture are an integral part of the wall surface of the building and are permanent, their subject-matter, execution and positioning in relation to architectural elements is as much architecture as fine art.

Moulded frames in high relief were a feature of many British nineteenth-century tile pictures employed in architectural settings and the use of sombre glaze colours for the frames, such as dark brown or bottle green, was quite characteristic. The pictures themselves were generally the most decorative part of a completely tiled interior with the walls featuring a tiled dado and ceiling cornice with plainer, lighter tiles between into which the tile pictures were set. The subject-matter varied enormously but the bright and sparkling images (so much more robust than oils on canvas) added a touch of class to any establishment.

Diners at Edinburgh's Café Royal were edified by the portrayal on tiles of six great

Elaborate architectural schemes for the exteriors of public houses could be built up from repetitive and often standard units of tiles and faience. Both the Crown Liquor Saloon, Belfast (right) and the Warrington Hotel, Maida Vale, London (below) used tiles from Craven Dunnills of Jackfield, Shropshire.

Overleaf. Le Cochon à l'Oreille is a very complete example of a late nineteenth-century café in Les Halles, the old market district of Paris. The walls are decorated with pictorial tile panels showing scenes from the local area and are from the Sarreguemines studio.

Le VENTRE de PARIS a pu émigrer
son COEUR reste aux HALLES

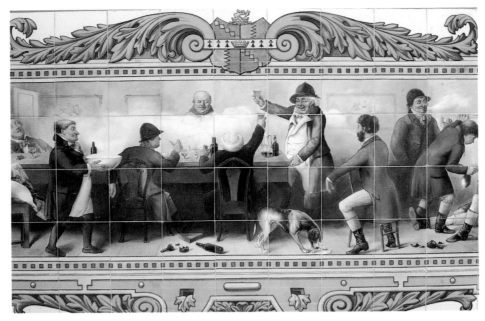

discoveries, which ranged from William Caxton's moveable type to Stephenson's
steam power. The panels, by Doulton artists, were installed in 1900 and a further two
were used in the adjacent Oyster Bar, displaying suitably maritime subjects - the first
Cunard liner 'Umbria' and a Liverpool paddle steamer. Mirrors and fine mahogany
woodwork added to the general illusion of style and quality. A remarkably similar
decorative formula was used in several turn-of-the-century Parisian cafés. At La Potée
des Halles, for instance, the walls above the tables and bar feature tile panels
ornamented with allegories of beer and coffee, represented by female figures who
are encouraging customers to drink up and re-order. Nearby, at Le Cochon à l'Oreille,
the large tile panels are of a more documentary nature and depict boisterous scenes
from the colourful old market district of Paris.

*Opposite. La Potée des Halles, Paris. This
bistro interior of around 1900 still has its
decorative tiles by the Sarreguemines
studio. The tile panels, which are flanked
by mirrors, are allegories of beer and coffee,
represented by female figures encouraging
customers to drink up and re-order.
Above. Hogarthian scenes from the Grand
Hotel, Colmore Row, Birmingham, where
the subjects as well as the tiles themselves
are glazed over!*

   Though now re-sited, the five tile pictures from the former dining-room of the
Grand Hotel, Colmore Row, Birmingham, give an idea of the artistic subtlety which
could be achieved. The subjects of the pictures were all appropriate to their setting
and the tiles were supplied by Minton Hollins of Stoke-on-Trent. The largest picture,
with an elaborate tile 'frame', depicts the traditional dinner and celebrations after a
fox hunt with a group of huntsmen in various states of inebriation seated around a
table. A brilliantly executed haze of tobacco smoke hangs over the whole scene and,
whilst the hounds forage for scraps on the floor, an attempt is made to revive a
slumped figure in one corner by tickling him with the 'brush' or tail of the fox.
Colour and humour were vividly captured by the artist, W P Simpson. He was
employed by Minton Hollins to produce large panels for special orders and his talent
for such work was much admired by the *Pottery Gazette* in 1897. The other four panels
are by Albert Slater and depict pheasants foraging for food, partridges in a cornfield
landscape, a sly fox making off with a duck and a Highland scene of a dog with a dead
stag – ceramic foretastes of the delicious game dishes awaiting the diner!

   Tile pictures are in general less common in the United States but one very
impressive series was produced by the Atlantic Terra Cotta Company for the Marine

The interiors of the magnificent Foreign and Commonwealth Office in Whitehall, London, are the work of two separate architects who both used tiles but in different ways. The old India Office interiors, designed by Matthew Digby Wyatt, culminate around the Durbar Court (1866). Here Wyatt used coved tiled ceilings to the loggia (right) and a balcony in Maws' new majolica glazes. George Gilbert Scott's Foreign Office interiors, built between 1861 and 1868, included stately classical corridors with geometric tiled floors (opposite) and ceilings supported by iron beams and quadrant-shaped brackets which were infilled with majolica tiles. In the Locarno Conference Room (above) the ceramic roundels bear the emblems of different countries.

Grill of the McAlpin Hotel in New York. The 14 large panels were set in highly
decorative, heavily moulded frames with segmental arched heads. Each panel
depicted a particular aspect of New York's maritime history, designed by Fred Dana
Marsh. The result was a strongly co-ordinated scheme in which tiles and architectural
ceramics played a leading role in developing a theme for the interior decoration.

Flamboyant and alluring though such nineteenth-century tiled eating and
drinking places might have been, the same ceramic materials were also put to use in
a much more sober cause – the architectural pursuit of civic grandeur. Arguably the
most monumental and memorable buildings of nineteenth-century Britain were
those built to serve government at both a national and a local level. In London the
New Palace of Westminster, the Foreign Office and the Law Courts demonstrated
through their architectural expression the increasing influence of government on
everyday life. Meanwhile, the rapid rise of the industrial cities in the Midlands and
the North of England spawned a rash of new town halls and the civic responsibilities
which these buildings housed in turn gave architectural birth to municipal libraries,
museums and other public buildings. The range of materials employed in these
costly and prestigious projects was vast and included ceramic tiles in many cases.

If the New Palace of Westminster put encaustic tiles in the limelight in the
context of a Gothic Revival building (see the third chapter), the next act to steal the
show was certainly the tile pavement of the neo-classical St George's Hall in
Liverpool. When the building opened in 1854 it was heralded by the *Illustrated London
News* as 'a perennial monument of the energy and public spirit, in the nineteenth
century, of the people of Liverpool; a place which, of all the cities and towns in the
British Empire is surpassed only by the metropolis in magnitude, wealth and
importance; and which, in the quick yet solid growth of its commercial greatness,
surpasses even the metropolis itself'.

The story of the building's development is complex, going back to 1836 when
Liverpool no doubt felt the need to compete with Birmingham in mastery of the
municipal league table. A scheme for a concert hall was combined with another for
Assize Courts and the competition was won by the young Harvey Lonsdale Elmes
who put forward a neo-classical design which was both knowledgeable and
powerful. Work started in 1841 but sadly Elmes died of consumption in 1847, leaving
Robert Rawlinson (the engineer for the building), together with the Corporation
Surveyor, to keep the project going. At this stage it seems unlikely that tiles were
envisaged as part of the decorative scheme for the building and in September 1851 *The
Builder* announced that 'the floor of the (great) hall is to be laid with Yorkshire flags,
like the corridors and entrances'.

The introduction of the encaustic tile pavement to the scheme seems to have
come through the increasing involvement of C R Cockerell, who was appointed

*The interiors of St George's Hall, Liverpool,
represent the ultimate in the architectural
pursuit of civic grandeur. A Minton
encaustic tile pavement was used in the
Great Hall (below) and beneath the organ
gallery a circular tiled floor surrounds the
crest of the Prince of Wales (opposite).*

architect in 1851. Cockerell altered Elmes's decorative scheme for the Great Hall and commissioned the tile pavement from Minton.

The Great Hall is 51.5 metres (169 feet) long (including the recesses at either end) and 22.5 metres (74 feet) wide (including the balconies). The tile pavement occupies most of this area in a sunken form with a walkway all round and it has been estimated that over 30,000 tiles were used. The design of the floor has not been attributed, although Alfred Stevens has been credited with the design of the figurative borders. The overall design consists of a large central circle flanked by two smaller circles, each of which are surrounded by four still smaller circles. The largest circle contains the royal coat of arms surrounded by a laurel wreath within a 16-pointed star. This is surrounded by bands of classical ornament and a vigorous figurative border which depicts Neptune with tritons, sea nymphs, boys on dolphins and tridents – an appropriate design for a major seaport whose coat of arms are borne in the smaller circles flanking the central one. In the smallest circles are the Star of St George, the Rose, the Thistle and the Shamrock, the emblems of England, Scotland and Ireland respectively. Beneath the organ gallery is a fine circular panel bearing the crest of the Prince of Wales. When the lights of the chandeliers illuminate the great tile pavement and the Father Willis organ swells majestically, it is difficult to disagree with Norman Shaw's verdict on St George's Hall as 'a building for all times, one of the great edifices of the world'.

Ironically most of those who have praised the building over the years have never seen the tiled floor of the Great Hall, for a decision was taken in the 1860s to cover the central well with a wooden floor to make it more suitable for dancing. This floor has only been taken up on a few occasions during the twentieth century. Whilst it has deprived many of the spectacle of the tiles, the wooden floor has undoubtedly preserved them in a pristine state. The difference in wear between the tiles in the sunken section and those on the walkway, which has never been protected, is very striking.

Liverpool's architectural triumph found challengers in many other towns and cities who also sought to express their municipal pride through the construction of prestigious buildings. Leeds Town Hall (1853-8) by Cuthbert Brodrick is a further move away from pure neo-classicism and the entrance hall is paved with Minton tiles bearing designs which use six or seven different colours and are known as 'civic encaustics'. The completion of the building was an opportunity for celebration on an astonishing scale and a chance for the newly grown city to measure itself against its neighbours and claim its new status. Queen Victoria, with Prince Albert, made her first royal visit to the city for the occasion, thus marking an important step forward for Leeds. The visit, on 7 September 1858, was commemorated by the decoration in tiles of a classical pedimented archway in Beckett Park, Leeds. The date and purpose

of the visit were recorded using Minton letter tiles across the frieze.

By the 1860s British town halls had largely adopted the Gothic style, allowing tiles to make an even greater contribution to municipal prestige. Manchester Town Hall, commenced in 1868 and designed by Alfred Waterhouse, has walls lined with terracotta and tiles, both of which materials Waterhouse was renowned for using in major commissions. Nearby Rochdale makes even greater use of tiles in its town hall, which was designed by W H Crossland and opened in 1871. The main entrance under the *porte cochère* and balcony opens into a spacious rectangular hall which was originally known as the Exchange. The whole of the floor area is tiled with Minton tiles, laid out in a distinguished arrangement designed by Heaton, Butler and Bayne. The pavement is punctuated by eight massive columns of polished red and grey Aberdeen and Peterhead granite which support the fine vaulted ceiling of red and white Mansfield stone. These columns lead to the staircase, which in turn gives access to the great hall, and they form a natural grid for 15 panels of tiles decorated with either the Royal Arms or those of the County of Lancaster or the Borough of Rochdale. An unfortunate and very permanent ceramic spelling mistake occurred during manufacture when the legend 'Crede signo' ('Believe in the sign') with the Borough of Rochdale Arms was rendered as 'Credo signo' ('I believe in the sign').

As the powers of the local authorities were extended in nineteenth-century Britain, so new public buildings were erected to provide services. This expanding area

Above. Town halls provided opportunities for elaborate heraldic designs in encaustic tiles. In Rochdale Town Hall, opened in 1871, the Minton floor tiles display the Royal Arms.

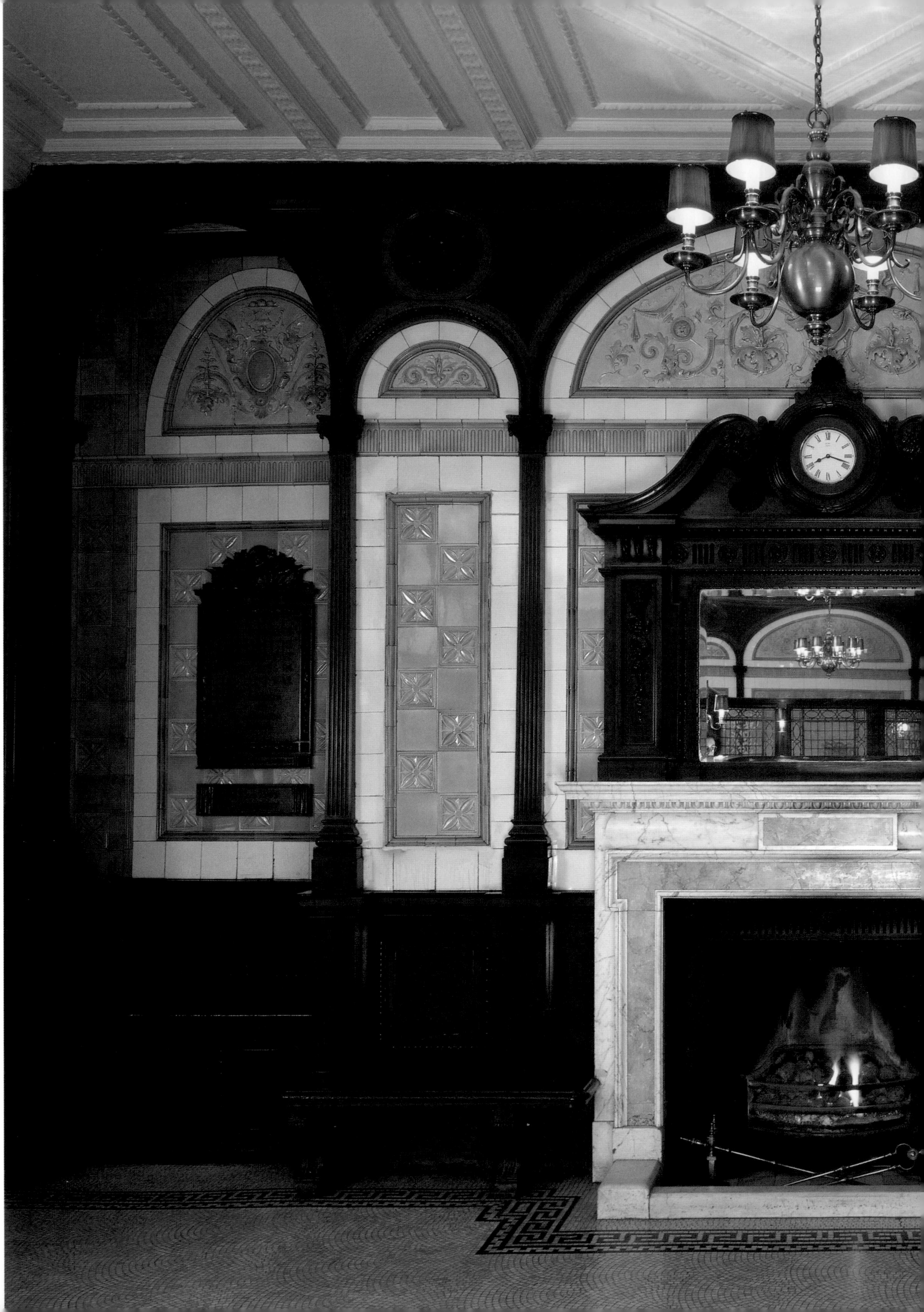

The interior of the Union Discount Bank at Cornhill in the City of London, c. 1900, was one of several major tiling schemes for banks and insurance offices by the architect J MacVicar Anderson. The tiles and architectural faience used here, and in most of his other schemes, are by Burmantofts of Leeds.

The Bibliothèque Nationale in Paris was built in the 1860s by Henri Labrouste. The interior was designed to be both impressive and fireproof. The shallow iron domes of the main reading room are inset with Copeland's ceramic panels and central skylights.

of architecture, which included such diverse building types as museums and art galleries, libraries, sewage pumping stations, municipal gas and water offices, offered further opportunities for the use of decorative tiles.

The dazzling effect of completely tiled walls and floors was sometimes topped with an additional ingredient – a ceramic tiled ceiling. An important pioneer in this somewhat improbable use of tiles in public buildings (which required efficient fixing methods to counteract the effect of gravity!) appeared in France. Henri Labrouste's magnificent reading room for the Bibliothèque Nationale in Paris, completed in 1868, has nine domes supported on slender iron columns, each dome being lined with curved slabs (ie large tiles) with relief decoration in white on a soft carmine ground. The tiles were supplied, not by a French manufacturer, but by Copelands of Stoke-on-Trent in the English Potteries. George Augustus Sala, who saw the building in 1868, related the story of its origins:

That the ceiling of these domes should be composed of earthenware slabs was, I believe, part of the primary design, and continental Europe was explored, and explored in vain, for potters willing to undertake a task so colossal. But Dresden hung back; the Dutchmen confessed that such tiles were beyond their ken; the Chinamen who covered the porcelain Tower of Nankin were not forthcoming; and even Sèvres shrank from what the Americans would term such an almighty big thing. At length the Messrs Copeland expressed their willingness to grapple with the difficulty...

Sala's verdict on the ceiling that 'the effect of the whole is wonderfully light, graceful and airy' remains true today but, despite this, the French architect's use of English tiles to line domes did not catch on and it has not been followed elsewhere. Instead, later tiled ceilings, found occasionally in banking halls, tend to be flat with screw-fixed high relief moulding used to support large ceramic slabs.

Britain's ability to export tiles for use in impressive public buildings can be seen in North America too. The American Federal Capitol, on its prominent site in Washington DC, had developed rapidly from the late eighteenth century onwards and, at the time when the building of the New Palace of Westminster was well under way in London, the new House and Senate wings on Capitol Hill were conceived. The differences between the two systems of government did not prevent a choice of Minton's encaustic tiles for parts of the expanding Capitol Buildings and in 1855 an extensive floor for the House of Representatives was made by Minton in Stoke-on-Trent and shipped out to the USA. This prestigious project not only provided confirmation of Minton's tile-making supremacy in his own country but also established encaustic tiles from England as a suitable and worthy flooring material for the most important public building ('the people's building') in the USA. Later in the 1850s, tiles were supplied for the Brumidi Corridors in the Capitol where they are still in situ. These bold and strongly coloured neo-classical pavements contrast with the oil and fresco work of Constantino Brumidi with its birds, animals, flowers and fruit interlaced with scrollwork.

For the next 20 years Britain enjoyed an unrivalled period of tile export to the USA and Canada. This phase coincided with the popularity in America of the High Victorian Gothic style in which a colourful use and combination of materials, including tiles, made an important architectural contribution to public buildings. The Philadelphia architect, Frank Furness (1839-1912), was a leading figure and his design (with George Hewitt) for the Pennsylvania Academy of the Fine Arts (1872-6) included the use of English encaustic tiles for the ground floor of the staircase well, together with a striking blue and white tiled dado.

By the 1880s the American tile industry was beginning to respond to the demand at home for tiles on a large scale and in later grand public buildings in American cities these domestic products soon displaced European imports. A good example is provided by the Pension Building in Washington DC. In 1881 Congress authorized the construction of a fireproof building for the Pension Bureau and General Montgomery C Meigs was placed in charge. He evolved a plan whereby all the offices were placed around the perimeter of a great central hall in a brick rectangular building inspired by the Palazzo Farnese in Rome. In his annual report of 1885 Meigs explained his choice of clay tiles for the Great Hall floor. He stated that traffic was so heavy in the public area of the building that wooden floors would not hold up; moreover, there was a need to wash these floors easily. Funds were appropriated in 1886 and the tiles installed were specified as 'six-inch octagon tiles, with squares in the corners, in solid plain colours – gray, drab, and chocolate brown'. These tiles were not imported but home-produced by the American Encaustic Tile Co of Zanesville, Ohio, and

examples still survive on the second-floor corridor. The vast open space of the Great Hall became the venue for Presidential Inaugural Balls and, prior to the one held in 1901, a large tile panel bearing the presidential seal was installed on the floor between the giant Corinthian columns that separate the west and central courts.

However grand nineteenth-century public buildings might become, there still remained the very practical problem of finding your way around them and here tiles often played an important role. Most public buildings, such as government offices, had a proliferation of corridors giving access to individual offices or rooms on each floor. These corridors were frequently tiled with plain-coloured floor tiles arranged in a geometric pattern and invariably bound on either side of the corridor by a border. Various devices of tile layout were used to punctuate these endless spaces, thereby reducing visual boredom and making the spaces intelligible to the user of the building. Thus the thresholds to the doorways usually have a separate rectangle of tiles and sometimes a pattern of tiles; long corridors are broken into tiling 'bays' which correspond with the rhythm of the building and decorative panels are used to emphasize crossings and junctions.

The use of tiles and tiling patterns to establish geographical identity became even more important as underground railways developed in which passengers had no contact with normal landmarks. The construction of New York's subway system began in 1900 and from the outset ceramic tiles, plaques (see the seventh chapter) and mosaic material were used, not only to embellish stations but to establish their identity.

Opposite and above right. A pedimented faience ticket booth and tiled dado by Maws provided an impressive prelude to a journey from Russell Square station on the London Underground.
Above left. Tiles and mosaic at 51st Street subway station, New York City.

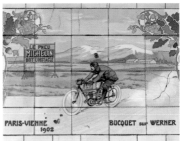

Very extensive use of tiles underground was continued on three of London's tube lines which opened in 1906-7 and went down much deeper than the New York subway. It has been estimated that over 30,000 square metres of tilework (some 1.5 million tiles) were used on 94 platforms and access passages at 43 stations. Decorated tiles or relief plaques, as used in the New York subway, were absent from this earliest phase of London tube tiling. Instead, distinctive geometric patterns were created by the use of 9 inch by 3 inch glazed tiles in various colours. The scheme is attributed to Leslie W Green who was architect to the three underground railway companies and, although at first glance the design seemed simple and rather uniform, it did allow each station a unique variation of pattern and colour as well as its name in 38-centimetre- (15-inch-) high chocolate-brown lettering. The tilework ran the entire length of the circular platform tunnel and reached a height of about 2.25 metres (7 feet 6 inches), above which was painted plasterwork. Vertical tiled bands extended above the wall tiling at intervals, giving the station tunnel a barrel-like appearance. Their positions were carefully predetermined and a double set of tiled rings was placed on either side of the exit passageways and station name panels, no doubt to draw the passengers' attention to these locations. Only fragments of these earliest decorative tile schemes survive. Later, London Transport, under the guidance of its general manager Frank Pick, was to achieve very high standards of functional design and corporate identity in which ceramic tiles played an important part (see the eighth chapter).

The artist, designer and pioneer socialist Walter Crane was an eloquent proponent of the role which decorative architecture might play in enriching people's lives. In a lecture series in 1896 entitled 'Art and Life and the Building and Decoration of Cities' he argued that, 'The decoration of public buildings should be the highest form of popular art as it was in the Middle Ages, when a town-hall, or a church, was no bad equivalent for a public library stored with legends and symbols - historic as

Opposite. The formal, classical grandeur of Barry's Reform Club, Pall Mall, London (1837-41), is enhanced by a later tiled floor in a similar style.
Above. The 34 tile panels at the Michelin building in London (1911) are a key ceramic component in one of the best-ever examples of 'advertising' architecture. The larger picture shows Charles Terront who rode for three days and nights to win the epic 1891 Paris to Brest cycle race on the first Michelin pneumatic tyres.

they were, which impressed themselves upon the unlettered, through the vivid language of design.'

By the end of the nineteenth century this philosophy could be seen not just in town halls and civic buildings but also in a wide range of commercial buildings. As the power of the consumer grew, shops, banks, arcades and commercial headquarters employed tiles to promote themselves through a form of 'advertising' architecture.

Few buildings can match the witty, attention-seeking exuberance of the Michelin building in London's Fulham Road. The French tyre company had set up depots in London as early as 1904 but it was not until 1910 that a suitable site for a much larger centre was found in Fulham Road. The building, which opened in January 1911, was designed by François Epinasse, an engineer on the staff of Michelin at their Clermont-Ferrand headquarters in France. Its reinforced concrete structure on the Hennebique system was, however, masked by ceramic materials. The entire front of the building and parts of the side elevations were clad in white, blue, yellow and green 'Marmo' tiles made by the Leeds Fireclay Company. The basic style of the building followed contemporary Edwardian practice but the decorative elements were replaced by the symbols of the company and the product, creating a permanent and audacious piece of architectural public relations. Thus, plaques, capitals, spandrels and tympani feature wheels surrounded by rubber plants, leaves and berries, tyres and the company's name and monogram.

However, the outstanding feature of the building is the 34 tile panels depicting scenes from the early days of motoring. These were made by the Paris firm of Gilardoni Fils et Cie to designs by E Montaut. Fascinated by cars and their performance, Montaut's designs evocatively capture the first days of high-speed road travel. There is an intense drama which has gripped the public imagination ever since the building opened. The cars seem alive, speeding through the countryside, curving round bends, drivers with hands clenched on the wheel and scarves flying. Tyres may wear but the tiles here (and in similar buildings elsewhere) have proved to be a robust, effective and endearing ingredient of architectural image-building.

The entrance hall of the Michelin building in London. The tile panels around the walls celebrate Michelin's involvement in the history of early motor racing. The witty mosaic floor with its Latin motto 'Nunc Est Bibendum' ('Now is the time to drink') shows Bibendum raising a champagne glass of sharp objects demonstrating the repairability of Michelin pneumatic tyres.

The Craft Tradition

 espite the enormous changes which industrialization brought to tile-making in the nineteenth century, there was, in most countries, a parallel and continuing output of tiles by small companies or individuals with an interest in ceramic craft skills and a commitment to artistic creativity. Whilst in terms of output their sum total of production was small, they nevertheless made a significant contribution to architecture and the decorative arts and in many cases exerted an influence on both architects and large commercial tile-makers. Often their tiles found favour with architects of a similar philosophy, resulting in fruitful working relationships which produced some memorable tiling schemes. These can be found in Britain and many European countries and provide an interesting contrast to the predictable appearance of mass-produced tiles in some situations. But it was in the United States that craft tile-makers really came into their own, establishing at the end of the nineteenth century a tradition that continued and flourished and in many cases produced tiled architecture of a quality that has only recently become recognized.

Of the many writers and practitioners of an Arts and Crafts philosophy, pride of place and credit as a pioneer must go to William Morris (1834-96). His great influence is not so much through the tiles which he or his firm designed and decorated as through his books and lectures and the effect these have had on his own and subsequent generations. However, hand-painted tiles were one of the earliest

Gaudi's extraordinary creativity with ceramic materials, in square or broken pieces, represents an antidote to conventional industrial tiling from the nineteenth century. Opposite. A mosaic medallion from the ceiling of the hall of columns, Güell Park, Barcelona.

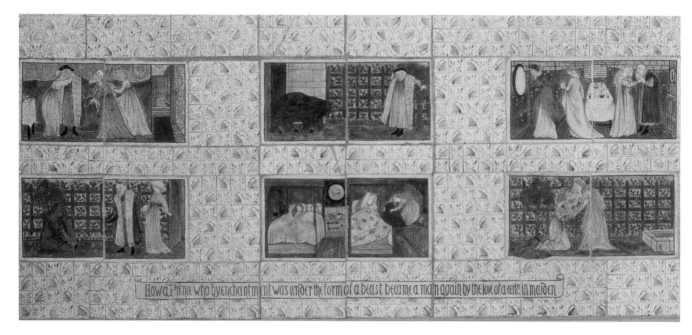

How a Prince who by enchantment was under the form of a beast became a man again by the look of a certe in maiden

products of Morris, Marshall, Faulkner & Co, which was founded in 1861. The first tiles to be decorated were for the Red House, Morris's own home which was built for him by the architect Philip Webb. The only means of firing the tiles was a stained-glass kiln which restricted the decorators to using low-temperature-firing enamels on top of bought-in glazed tiles. Such decoration is very vulnerable to wear and the weather and this, coupled with a lack of understanding of ceramic chemistry, has been suggested as the reason for the poor survival of Morris tiles. For example, some Morris tile panels which were installed in St Peter's Church, Bournemouth, Dorset, in the 1870s had to be replaced in 1899 because the glaze had turned to powder and the designs had totally disappeared. Perhaps the most ambitious and best-preserved series of Morris tiles in their architectural setting are those over a fireplace in the Old Hall of Queen's College, Cambridge. These tiles include a series of 12 designs depicting the months of the year through their respective labours, a theme also well worked by many of the large industrial tile producers. Thus June is illustrated with a figure sharpening a scythe for mowing and December with a man slitting the neck of a hog. The figures are surrounded by Morris's 'swan' design, a typical Morris chequered pattern of alternating swans and foliage.

Paul Thompson's study of Morris's work describes his tiling as 'watercolours on a white background, the design crossing the joints between the tiles as if they were irrelevant'. The soft character of the designs was the result of the use of delicate brushwork as opposed to the harder form of mechanical printing which Morris took exception to, even when only used as an outline guide to painting. Thompson reached the rather harsh verdict that 'had Morris been less prejudiced in favour of

Above. Overmantel tile panel depicting the story of Beauty and the Beast. Designed by Edward Burne-Jones and painted by Lucy Faulkner, this panel comes from Birket Foster's house at Witley, Surrey (1862). Opposite. Portrait of William De Morgan (1839-1917) by his wife Evelyn. He is seen holding an example of his art pottery and part of a charger can be glimpsed behind.

hand work, he might have seen that tiles were most obviously suited to bold patterns and colours, arranged in abstract geometric mosaics'.

If Morris's own tiles were not a huge success either in design or execution, this failing was more than compensated for by his firm acting as a major outlet for the more skilfully executed tiles of his great friend William De Morgan (1839-1917). Morris first met De Morgan whilst the latter was a painter. At about this time De Morgan transferred his artistic interests to stained glass and carried out occasional design work for Morris & Co, including tiles. His father was a Professor of Mathematics at University College, London, and he shared his father's scientific approach to work and life, taking a keen interest in chemistry. In 1869 he began experimenting with lustres on ceramic tiles and from then on until the 1890s he was fully occupied with designing and making tiles and pottery and experimenting with glazes. When De Morgan found that Morris's strong personality was inhibiting his design work, he established his own studios successively at Chelsea, Merton Abbey and Sands End, Fulham. His tile designs, which number over a thousand, were derived from a variety of sources including Iznik pottery and feature vivid patterns of leaves and flowers, birds, monsters, ships and animals. Their lasting and universal appeal can be judged by their application in the late twentieth century to the gift trade, appearing on such objects as PVC tote bags and wrapping paper.

De Morgan's tiles were not cheap, restricting their use to the more wealthy clients of architects and thereby posing the same egalitarian dilemma which Morris faced with his own wallpapers and textiles. Jon Catleugh's book on De Morgan tiles has shown that plain tiles from a large manufacturer such as Maws were about a third of the price of De Morgan's and that Walter Crane's popular and stylish printed designs were available for less than a quarter of the Arts and Crafts painted alternative. Interestingly, De Morgan tiles were used extensively in two fireplaces at Adcote, Shropshire, a new country residence designed by Norman Shaw for that most industrial of iron founding families, the Darbys of Coalbrookdale.

The same year, 1879, saw De Morgan's first contribution to naval architecture with a commission to design the tiles for Tsar Alexander II of Russia's yacht 'Livadia'. Sadly there is no record of the extent of his work on this extraordinary ship, which was described by *The Times* as 'a sea palace erected on the back of a huge steel turbot'. Between 1882 and 1900 De Morgan supplied tiles for 12 ships built by P & O, many in the form of panels for use in smoking-rooms. The important link with P & O seems to have come through their architect, T E Collcutt. De Morgan's other important collaborator was Halsey Ricardo, with whom he entered into a partnership for ten years from 1888. Ricardo was a great champion of the use of colour in architecture and his most important architectural statement, using some of De Morgan's tiles, was the house he designed in 1904 at Addison Road, London, for Sir Ernest Debenham.

Opposite. Halsey Ricardo's enthusiasm for colour in architecture was put into practice with the tile decoration by De Morgan for Sir Ernest Debenham's house at 8, Addison Road, London.
Below. A design for wall decoration in hand-painted tiles by William De Morgan.

De Morgan's tiles and their designs have received a great deal of attention over the years and they are now much prized by collectors. This emphasis has tended to take attention away from other contemporary Arts and Crafts tile-makers whose architectural contributions were important too. Amongst these, the Medmenham Pottery is of particular interest. Its patron and founder was the wealthy soap magnate, R W Hudson, who lived at Danesfield House near Marlow in the Buckinghamshire Chilterns. In 1897 pottery workshops and kilns were erected at Marlow Common in an attempt to foster rural craft and for a few years, subsidized by Hudson, the enterprise was an epitome of the Arts and Crafts philosophy. Its printed catalogue set out the aim of the operation as 'producing architectural pottery and tiles possessing individuality in design and execution'. In order to achieve this aim, it was felt that 'we must place ourselves in conditions approximating to those of the old potteries whose ware delighted and inspired us. We therefore established our pottery right away in the country. We use our Marlow materials as much as possible and employ village workpeople.'

Such worthy, if romantic, ideals and the financial backing of a wealthy industrialist

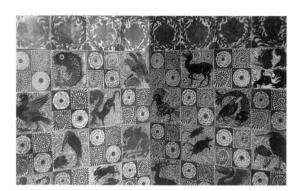  

would not have achieved the quality of the Medmenham tiles without the technical and artistic contribution of Conrad Dressler, who became the pottery's director. Dressler had come from the Della Robbia Pottery in Birkenhead and was an accomplished sculptor. The handmade look and feel of the Medmenham tiles attracted the attention of architects such as C F A Voysey and Norman Shaw. Despite this, Dressler became disillusioned and by his own admission 'had to allow some of the ideals with which he started to fall seeming into desuetude. The hope of finding native talent that could be brought into line with the work turned out has not been fulfilled.'

Dressler moved on to invent his tunnel oven, which displaced traditional bottle ovens and changed the skyline of tile and pottery towns around the world. There is not much to show of his ceramic work whilst at Medmenham but one surviving Irish building is distinguished by his vigorous sculpture in clay. This is Sunlight Chambers, built by Lever Brothers (soap manufacturers and rivals to Hudson!) in 1901 as their Irish head office. As part of their education and advertising philosophy the company decided to commission a series of 12 ceramic panels for the building, to be placed over the ground and first-floor windows. These panels illustrate the extraction of raw materials for soap, the manufacturing processes, and merchants buying and selling oils and scents. The everyday use of soap is represented by women visiting washing troughs and using scrubbing boards. It is slightly ironic that one major soap-maker should have used the products of a craft tile works supported by a rival soap-maker.

The story of English Arts and Crafts tile- and pottery-making experiments is considerably enlivened by a ferment of creativity involving outlandish characters and bizarre designs. For sheer determination it is hard to beat the efforts of Sir Edmund Elton at his ancestral home, Clevedon Court, in Somerset. This 'English country baronet and two boot boys' (as he described his pottery) received his original

Above left. De Morgan ruby lustre tiles set around the dining-room fireplace at Adcote, Shropshire. The house was designed by R Norman Shaw and completed in 1879.
Above centre. Tiled dado to the staircase and landing at Cragside, Northumberland, which was designed by R Norman Shaw. The tiles probably came from Medmenham Pottery.
Above right. Two Medmenham Pottery tiles from the firm's showroom in Soho Square, London.
Opposite. Two panels from a triptych made by Della Robbia Pottery, Birkenhead, for the Memorial Church, Wallasey. They are signed by Harold Rathbone and dated 1899.

inspiration to make ceramic pictures in different-coloured clays whilst watching men at work in the local brickworks. His initial venture was a total failure but he went on to produce a range of extraordinary pots whose aristocratic pedigree no doubt helped sales in the USA, including those sold through Tiffanys. His surviving contribution to tiled architecture is the clock tower he presented to the town of Clevedon to mark Queen Victoria's Diamond Jubilee in 1897. It is decorated with two courses of tiles which show the birds of the air, the beasts of the field and the fishes under the sea. Similar animal, bird and fish themes predominate in the extraordinary work of the three Martin brothers of Southall, West London. Although best known for their pottery, especially their grotesque bird caricatures serving as tobacco jars, they also produced tiles and architectural pieces. The same rather sombre glazes were used and the best surviving example of their tilework is the massive fireplace made for the billiard room at Buscot Park, Oxfordshire (see illustration in the fifth chapter).

The craft producers of tiles in Britain in the 1890s were characterized by their diversity rather than the size of their output. They may have shared a common Arts and Crafts philosophy but individual expression ensured a rich spectrum of designs which architects and potential clients must have found quite confusing. However, one feature of the Arts and Crafts Movement which helped to present the producers in a more coherent way was the Art and Crafts Exhibition Society. In the matter of exhibitions, England was the first in the field and the Society mounted its first show of artistic handicrafts, for which William De Morgan was a committee member, in 1888. Yet despite this early and positive lead the Arts and Crafts Movement, certainly in the field of tiles and architectural ceramics, was destined to make far less impact in Britain than in the United States.

The tide of expansion in industrial tile-making in the USA from the 1880s onwards was quickly followed by the growing influence of a group of dynamic and creative individuals with a more craft-based approach to making and using tiles. The reasons for their success are complex. Some were recent immigrants from Europe, who brought with them ceramic traditions for which they were able to find new expression in the stimulating artistic climate of the 'New World'. Their products were not, however, mere imitations – they established new styles and sought new uses for tiles in a surge of democratic creativity. The leadership provided by certain key pioneering figures certainly helped to spread the word.

Pre-eminent among these was the remarkable Henry Chapman Mercer (1856-1930) and his Moravian Pottery and Tile Works at Doylestown, Pennsylvania. A former Harvard scholar and man of independent means, at the age of 40 Mercer was able to count himself among America's leading archaeologists. However, a year later he had abandoned archaeology and begun the experiments which were soon to make him one of the most original and successful tile-makers in America.

Uniquely among American tile-makers, Mercer had received no professional training in art or the business of ceramic manufacture but he set about discovering all that he could in a characteristically scholarly and systematic fashion. His labours were rewarded since in no less than two years he had successfully produced striking new designs and glaze effects and devised methods of hand fabrication that produced tiles cheaply enough for them to compete nationally with the machine-made varieties. In the same way and in contrast to many of his ceramic contemporaries in America and Europe, Mercer consistently operated his hand-crafted tile operation at a profit.

Mercer's tiles were most distinctive; his techniques of manufacture, coupled with his fertile imagination, produced some very remarkable products. His flat-surfaced, plain tiles which were suitable for use on floors, walls or as surrounds for decorative tiles, were stamped out of hand-rolled slabs of clay in geometric shapes. His decorated relief tiles were hand-pressed from moulds and then hand-glazed. All this hand-work gave delightful variations in colour, tone and texture to the overall effect of Mercer's finished schemes.

For the bulk of his work he employed two other techniques for producing tiles; one he called 'mosaic' although it is closer in concept to stained-glass design than to traditional *tesserae* mosaic. The second he called 'mural brocade'. This was only suitable for use on walls or ceilings as these tiles were in effect sculpted. Mercer extracted the main elements of the design from their background, selecting figures, animals, flowers and so on which lent themselves to sculptural representation. Each element was then treated as a separate entity and was cut in silhouette, modelled in deep relief and often pierced through completely. These tiles took advantage of the extra dimension of mortar and had to be set into concrete or plaster in such a way that the mortar could become the background field. Some of the richest examples of Mercer's mural brocade tiles were used in the unique house that he built for himself at Doylestown. Fonthill, an ambitious project, was a personal architectural expression of Mercer's great interest in concrete and was to be his home for the rest of his life. The house was built using reinforced concrete which was poured in situ, a pioneering technique that he had already experimented with in the successful construction of his

The handmade tiles of the American Henry Chapman Mercer were distinctive and original.
Opposite above. Glazed brocade tile of a bee from the garage terrace room at Mercer's house, Fonthill, Doylestown, Pennsylvania.
Opposite centre. Floor tiles made by Mercer for Wellington House, Syracuse, New York, a house designed by Ward Wellington Ward.
Opposite below. A Mercer mural at Avery Coonley School, Downer's Grove, Illinois. This panel, which depicts the Western hemisphere, was set opposite another of the Eastern hemisphere, the two linked by a sailing ship. The scheme symbolized education uniting the world.
Above left. Mercer's 'Fire' and 'Rain' tiles at Wellington House, Syracuse, New York.
Above right. Detail of a fireplace by Mercer at Saugerties Public Library, New York. Seven panels depict Irving's 'Rip Van Winkle' story. Here Rip falls into a long sleep.

technique that he had already experimented with in the successful construction of his mission-style cloister pottery works. It resulted in some exceptionally unusual spaces and interesting surface finishes in conjunction with his tiles.

It took Mercer some four years to build Fonthill and a further two years, from 1914-16, to build his third major concrete building, now the Mercer Museum, Doylestown, which he used to house the 20,000 tools he had gathered in less than 20 years. This collection remains today much as Mercer left it – a systematic study of the American pioneer hand tools which he saw as a clear link between ancient and modern man.

Mercer represents the ultimate American Arts and Crafts tile-maker. He and his followers despised machine-made 'art tiles' as 'mathematical chromatic blends, and up-to-date eruptive marblings encircling the openings of fireplaces, or glittering upon soda water fountains'. Even when they used the impressions of natural materials such as leaves and plant forms, industrial 'art tiles' were considered cold and inhuman.

One of the major centres of 'art tile' production was Boston where in 1877 the Low family had established what was to become a large and successful industrial enterprise. Ironically, it was through an apprenticeship at Lows that one of Mercer's most important Arts and Crafts contemporaries, William H Grueby (1867-1925), came to ceramics. Grueby was later greatly impressed by the work of the French potter, Auguste Delaherche, whose matt-glazed art pottery was a feature of the 1893 World's Fair in Chicago. He established the Grueby Faience Co in Boston in 1894 and produced a variety of tiles and larger architectural faience, of which soft colours and matt glazes were a hallmark.

The bold counter-relief decoration of Grueby's floor tiles, employed without the use of coloured clay inlays, was similar to that of Mercer's and very different in character from the smooth machine-made tiles generally available. These unusual relief qualities led to a novel use of these tiles as a form of architectural 'signposting'. When the Perkins Institution and Massachusetts School for the Blind was completed in 1913, its architect R Clipson Sturgis adopted Grueby tile features to assist the youthful blind occupants. These included paths and corridors with distinctive patterning and accentuated crowning at junctions to assist with maintaining an accurate sense of direction. Special raised pattern tiles of various familiar animal forms were used where dados met doorways, giving a point of reference and a feature of interest for the blind child.

A significant figure who stood in the mid-ground between American Arts and Crafts tile-makers and mass producers is Herman Carl Mueller (1854-1941) who in his later years struck up a friendship with Mercer. He came from Germany where he had attended the Nuremburg School of Industrial Arts. He must have been thoroughly familiar with German stove tile-makers in the area and this knowledge was to reveal itself later in the character and style of his ceramic work. He left Germany in 1878

Opposite. Mercer's 'St George and the Dragon' mosaic in the fireplace of an American private house.

settling initially at Cincinnati where his skills as a sculptor were put to use modelling for an art pottery. He went on to work at the American Encaustic Tile Co at Zanesville but eventually started his own company, Mueller Mosaic, in Trenton, New Jersey. Like any commercial concern this company had to make sales to survive and he was unable to indulge in art for its own sake, like Mercer or Mary Chase Perry of Pewabic Pottery in Detroit. Nevertheless he firmly held and practised the belief that artists should play an important role in producing commercial ceramics. He felt strongly that ceramics should be totally integrated with their architectural environment and, operating as he did with one foot in the Arts and Crafts camp and the other in commercial production, was in a unique position to demonstrate by example the strengths of both.

The relative success of craft tile-makers in the United States compared with Britain can be partly explained by the presence of the large, affluent middle-class society of the late nineteenth and early twentieth centuries, which was busily engaged in American home-building. Architects, designers and makers set out to meet the demand from the large number of people who wanted to implement William Morris's standards of honest workmanship. Furniture, rugs, door latches and of course tiles, all of which bore the reassuring signs of human involvement, were sought after to fulfil the domestic Arts and Crafts ideal. The American use of Arts and Crafts tiles in the home is seen nowhere better than in the buildings designed by Ward Wellington Ward (1875-1932). Ward moved from New York City in 1908 to Syracuse and during the next 18 years he designed over 200 private houses in central New York State, putting into practice Arts and Crafts approaches in a region which was already an important centre within the movement and which already held key figures such as Gustav Stickley and his Craftsman Studios. Ward and other Arts and Crafts architects used the tiles from Henry Chapman Mercer of Doylestown, Pennsylvania, extensively.

Indeed Ward is credited with using Mercer's tiles in more domestic buildings than any other single architect in America. He achieved a harmony between setting and ornament in his architecture through his sensitive uses of tiles, stained glass and other materials. The focus of his living-rooms was nearly always the hearth, 'designed to extend and bring to rest a main axis of the house' and exploit to the full the warm reds, oranges and browns of Mercer's tiles.

Although Arts and Crafts tile-makers contributed to public buildings on both sides of the Atlantic, it is in the USA that Arts and Crafts tiles make the biggest impact in the architectural philosophy of large civic buildings. By far the best example is the work of Henry Chapman Mercer for the Pennsylvania State Capitol at Harrisburg, his most prestigious and profitable installation. A Philadelphia architect, Joseph M Huston, was commissioned to design the building in 1902 and the following year he

Grueby & Co, founded in Boston, Massachusetts, in 1894, specialized in matt glazed tiles with relief decoration. *Above.* 'St George and the Dragon'. *Left.* Part of a floor at the Perkins Institution and Massachusetts School for the Blind. The raised pattern of the central tile helped youthful blind occupants to orientate themselves at corridor junctions.

commissioned Mercer to make some 4,877 square metres (16,000 square feet) of tiles for the floor of the great rotunda. These included nearly 400 of Mercer's new tile mosaics, allowing pictorial images derived from the history of the area to be constructed in shaped pieces. Mercer's rough-textured red floor tiles appear in strong contrast to the highly polished white marble walls. Mercer said that the tiles were 'hand made and hand smoothed' while the marble was 'planed and polished by machinery'. American tile historian, Cleota Reed, concludes that Mercer 'wanted his floor to be understood as distinctly American and not as dependent on European models and influences, as were the other decoration and the Renaissance revival architecture of the building itself'.

The desire to reflect American craft in new public places can be seen too in the choice of decoration for New York City's subway system (begun in 1900). The original specifications for its design included reference to a concern for 'beauty of material as well as efficiency', reflecting a climate of civic betterment. The consulting architects, George L Heins and Christopher Grant La Farge, made extensive use of tiles. In many cases large areas of tiling or mosaic, mass-produced and serving a purely functional purpose, were punctuated with ceramic plaques from a surprisingly large number of different makers, often with a strong Arts and Crafts character.

Stations on the lower Lexington Avenue line remain distinctive and memorable to this day through their continuing use. Thus Bleecker Street's white lettering on cobalt blue oval plaques came from the Grueby Faience Company in Boston who provided glazed ornament for 19 of the original stations. Fulton Street, by contrast, has a pictorial panel in relief made by the famous Rookwood Pottery of Cincinnati, Ohio, and depicting Robert Fulton's paddle wheel steamship. The station was part of the first expansion, in 1905, of the original subway system. Later extensions, opened in 1918, included scenic panels of mosaic-like appearance as used at Canal Street and Christopher Street stations and probably made by the Mueller Mosaic Tile Company. Attractive though the 'mosaic' pictures are, they lack the architectural presence of the earlier relief plaques whose craft qualities make them 'shine resplendent like a rich jewel roughly set'.

Bleecker Street subway sign, New York City, made by Grueby Faience Co, Boston (1904).

From the examples described it will be seen that the scale of development and use of craft-made tiles in the USA reached considerable heights at the end of the nineteenth century and indeed continued as a major theme in the twentieth, particularly with innovations in California. Impressive though this American achievement was, it should not obscure the continuing efforts of the craft tile-makers in Europe. Contrary to popular perception, the Dutch hand-painted, tin-glazed tile was never supplanted by machine production. Many firms in Holland continued with the traditional processes of manufacture and decoration. When the German tile historian, Paul Knochenhauer, visited the tile factories in Holland during the early 1880s he remarked that most things were done by hand and he was surprised that the Industrial Revolution had had so little impact on Dutch tile-making. Indeed from the 1880s onwards the Dutch were able to regain some of their former export market to Britain as the Arts and Crafts Movement fostered an appreciation of the qualities of handmade, hand-painted delftware in the form of both tiles and pottery. English delftware tiles, made in centres such as Lambeth and Liverpool, had disappeared by the end of the eighteenth century and the new market was wide open. Dutch tile-makers modified the size of some tiles exported to Britain so that their traditional size of 5⅛ inches square was enlarged to the by now standard 6 inches square. This enabled them to be fitted into mass-produced cast-iron fireplaces.

The revived British interest in delftware tiles stems at least partly from William Morris who, in the early days of his quest for blank tiles to decorate, had to turn to Dutch tileries for any handmade alternative to machine-made dust pressed tiles. His designs lent themselves to the tin glaze technique and several were copied in Holland by Dutch makers and imported to Britain, some apparently even being stocked at the Morris and Co. shop in Oxford Street, London. A number of specialist importers established themselves as more people sought handmade tiles. Several had Dutch family connections, including the two best known: Martin van Straaten and Murray Marks (whose business was subsequently bought by Thomas Elsley).

Dutch tiles are found in the fireplaces of a number of late nineteenth-century Arts and Crafts houses including Wightwick Manor, Wolverhampton, where they are overshadowed by the more famous De Morgan tiles. Others feature in houses designed by Norman Shaw, including his 'Queen Anne' style buildings in the model garden suburb of Bedford Park in West London. A particularly good range also still survives at Fanhams Hall near Ware, Hertfordshire. This lavish Jacobean mansion of 1900 incorporated antique Dutch tiles from the seventeenth and eighteenth centuries in major fireplaces but in the kitchens and service corridors new Dutch tiles, many with designs depicting traditional children's games, were used to line entirely the walls on a scale which would have far exceeded the supply of antique originals.

Traditional tin glaze decoration of tiles also continued in nineteenth-century northern France, with some particularly fine blue and white stencilled geometric designs being produced around Ponchon, near Beauvais. Lacking the Dutch tradition of export, these tiles were largely for local consumption.

Little known too outside France are the extraordinarily creative architectural ceramics of the Greber brothers. Their former workshops in Beauvais (built in 1911) still present passersby on the busy rue de Calais with a *tour de force* of their highly novel glazes and forms. The stoneware façade rises from a 'plinth' of blocks in blue/green whose glaze colours wash and run together like dappled sunlight on the sea. Above this pairs of lifelike chameleons ascend vertical strips flanking the windows whilst a cornice of slimy greeny-brown frogs runs across the top of the building. A large central panel depicts a potter and his wheel, reminding us of their stake in the French art pottery renaissance of around 1900. The building epitomizes the craft ceramics tradition but it is not inhibited by tradition. Everywhere are signs of innovation, of taking risks. Variations of glaze colours are almost wilful in their juxtapositions. Although the Grebers used plaster moulds to repeat elements for architectural use, their work is clearly that of the craft potter.

Architectural façades of a similarly striking character were emerging in Britain too at this time. The tiles and blocks of architectural faience from which they were constructed were made and decorated by hand in the craft tradition. The big difference, however, was that in many cases the work was done within the context of a large industrial factory. Doultons excelled at this duality and, whilst churning out tiles and sanitaryware for a mass market, they were able to allow a creative artist like W J Neatby the opportunity to realize ceramic façades of great originality.

Perhaps his most memorable work was the building for Edward Everard, printer, of Bristol. In a narrow street in the city centre he composed a façade of such strikingly colourful and decorative elements that people thronged the street for days after it was completed. An angel separates figures of Gutenburg, father of printing, and William Morris whilst above is the allegorical figure of Truth with a mirror and a lamp. It is unlikely that Neatby would have been directly involved with decorating all the tiles. Unlike the Grebers, he could delegate his designs to the craft skills of factory employees but the result is nevertheless extremely impressive.

Doultons ventured into the one-off crafts field on a number of other occasions, particularly with the memorial tiles in Postman's Park. This novel use of hand-lettered tiles was conceived by the Victorian painter G F Watts, to honour heroic men and women. It materialized as Postman's Park off King Edward Street in the City of London, a peaceful haven made up of three former churchyards. A wall was set aside for the tile panels, which were protected by a pitched roof. The tiles, all of them made by Doultons at Lambeth, were used to commemorate unknown heroes who ranged from a six-year-old boy to a 61-year-old railway foreman. Each tragic but often highly

improbable incident is described in stylish script on large tiles and the borders are decorated with either Art Nouveau flowers or a Renaissance urn pattern.

One final episode remains in the story of the continuing use of tiles in the craft tradition. That is the artist or architect who seeks expression through the medium of tiles applied to a building's surface. Here the work of Antoni Gaudì (1852-1926) in Barcelona stands out as unique in its scope and originality.

Gaudì's early work at Casa Vicens (1883-5) was, as luck would have it, commissioned by a ceramic tile manufacturer. The rubble stone and pink brick walls of the house are gridded by horizontal and vertical bands of tiling. In these more regular circumstances than his later buildings, unbroken square tiles in contrasting colours work well.

Gaudì's later projects, particularly at Güell Park (1900-14) in Barcelona, involve structures that are much more fluid and organic and it is here that his characteristic use of broken tiles comes uniquely alive. The terrace above the market hall, edged with snaking, serpentine-like benches and covered with broken tiles forming enigmatic patterns, is a unique but well-known testimony to Gaudì's genius.

Above. The former Greber brothers workshop in rue de Calais, Beauvais. Built in 1911, the façade of the building provides a memorable display of creative tiling and other architectural ceramics. The pairs of chameleons (left) ascend towards a cornice of frogs (top).

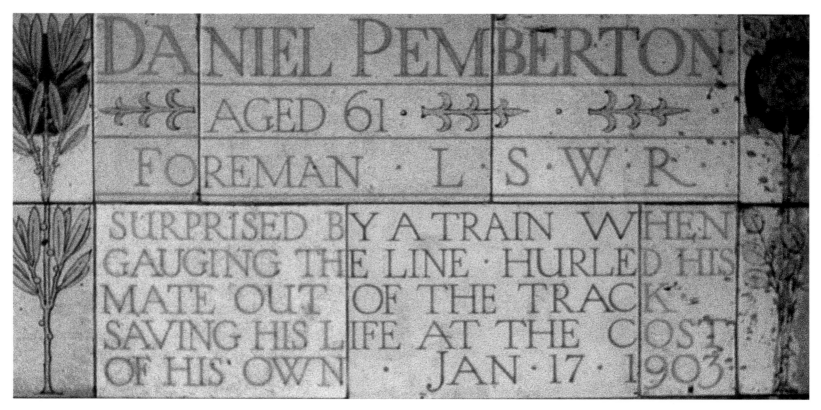

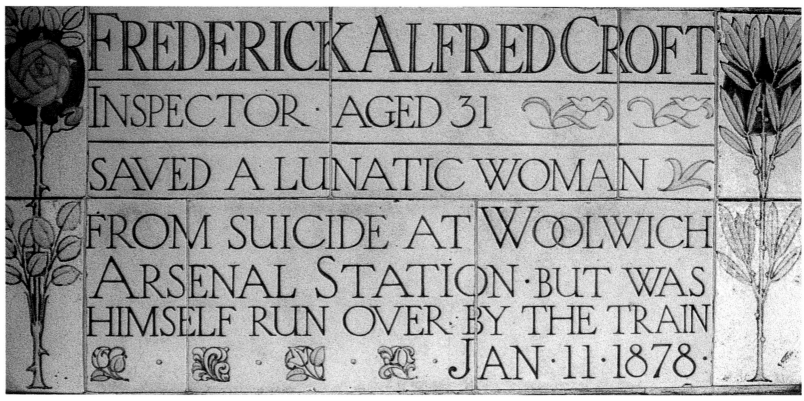

Tiles were for Gaudí an artistic tool and very few people even attempted to emulate him. The only mildly comparable example in Britain is the puzzling house 'Farrago' built in Hornsea in 1908-9 by a little-known Hull builder, David Reynard Robinson, for his retirement. The word farrago means 'a medley, a mixture, a hotchpotch' and the use of tiles, glazed sewer pipes, moulded bricks and other ceramic materials is at times so bizarre as to invite dismissal of the wilful assemblage of a lifetime's old stock by a local builder. But the wilfulness is subtle and frequently visually interesting. A history of the house by its owner, José Montgomery, reveals that 'in studying Robinson's creative use of tiles inside the house a number of visual displacements become apparent. He alters the colour of a tile or a number of tiles in a set sequence. He alters tiles in borders and corners or he changes the tiles themselves usually so subtly it is not immediately apparent. How a Hull builder came to produce the kind of tilework seen at Farrago in apparent isolation remains an unsolved mystery.'

Postman's Park, off King Edward Street, London. Hand-painted tiles by Doultons of Lambeth record the tragic and sometimes improbable deaths of unknown heroes.

Above. The organically undulating,
mosaic-clad ceiling of the hall of the
columns, Güell Park, Barcelona, by Gaudi
(1900-14). The medallions are by his
collaborator, Josep Maria Jujol.
Left and opposite. Casa Batllo, Barcelona.
The building started life as an apartment
block in 1877 but was transformed by
Gaudi in 1904-6. The deep central court
was reformed so that it opens out as it
reaches upwards and the colour balance of
the tiling gradually changes from all white
at the bottom to blue at the top.

Tiles in the Modern Era

The changes in the design and manufacture of tiles and their use in architecture since World War I have been very considerable. The story is a sophisticated one and really deserves a more detailed treatment than can be given here. The most commonly made assumption – that the use of decorative tiles has declined as the twentieth century has progressed – is open to question as modern buildings come in for a more objective analysis. The approach that will be adopted here will be to examine the fundamental themes of nineteenth-century tiling (which has formed the basis for the preceding chapters) in the light of the changes and new developments which have taken place between 1918 and the present day.

The notion of the successful union of art and industry, which was such a strong feature of mass-produced tiles in the nineteenth century, has changed radically. What was a happy marriage of two very different partners in the 1850s, 1860s and 1870s has, in the twentieth century, become an often strained and awkward relationship in which separation is all too obvious. In many cases large tile companies have been transformed from family business empires to multi-national corporations, with numerous amalgamations along the way. This should not imply that old methods are necessarily best, but it does mean that the input of educated, aesthetically experienced and well-travelled gentlemen such as Herbert Minton, George and Arthur Maw and Henry Doulton has not always been replaced in the new impersonal

The architectural context for tiles changed dramatically in the twentieth century, with the introduction of new styles and building materials.
Opposite. At the Hoover factory on the Great West Road, London, which was designed by Wallis Gilbert and Partners between 1931 and 1935, tiles provided bold bands of colour on a façade of gleaming white concrete and glass.

The Hoover factory, Great West Road, London, 1931-5. *Opposite.* Vividly coloured tiles provide dramatic emphasis for the cast concrete detail of the exterior.

Centre right and bottom. Bands of coloured tiles decorate the exterior and (centre left) are used in a similar way inside, along with newly fashionable terrazzo flooring. Both tiles and terrazzo were supplied by Carter & Co of Poole.

Above. In some of the washrooms, tiles have been displaced by a rival coloured sheet glass material called Vitrolite.

style of corporate management. Inevitably specializations in the tile industry were bound to occur as it developed and, even in the nineteenth century, aesthetic innovation was increasingly becoming the role of the professional designer. In the modern era the designer may have become all-important but the parallel specialization of financial control and management has helped to fragment the special union of art and industry.

There have been attempts to retain the virtues of this union in the modern era. In 1915 the Design and Industries Association was set up in Britain to help bring about a greater co-operation between professional designers and the manufacturing industry. Interestingly, it was two of the pioneers of that movement, Harold Stabler and Cyril Carter, whose company – Carters of Poole – made perhaps the strongest twentieth-century marriage of art and industry in the field of tiles (and other ceramics). In a succession of tiling projects, which were carried out from the 1920s up to 1960, eminent artists and designers such as Dora Batty, Edward Bawden and Peggy Angus made a distinguished contribution and Poole in Dorset became a major focus of innovation. Carters were a natural choice as a source of tiles and faience for those architects who were in the forefront of modern design. The buildings on which they appeared ranged from the aggressive Art Deco embellishments of Wallis, Gilbert and Partners' Hoover factory of 1931-5 to the restrained brown floor and cream wall tiles of the De La Warr Pavilion, Bexhill, Sussex (1935) – an important British landmark of the Modern Movement designed by Erich Mendelsohn and Serge Chermayeff.

Other manufacturers may have been less successful in integrating design and modern mass production, but all benefited from improved production technology in the twentieth century. For instance, the gradual elimination of lead from tile glazes removed the scourge of lead poisoning and its disastrous effects on the workforce. No longer were glaze dippers in tile factories required to drink daily pints of 'medicated beer', a special brew whose conventional ingredients were bolstered with sulphuric acid! This potion was thought to take harmful lead compounds out of the body. The concern which W J Furnival hoped would be generated by his almost evangelical *Leadless Decorative Tiles, Faience and Mosaic*, published in 1904 complete with appropriate recipes, has certainly been taken seriously. In addition, changes in fuel and kiln-firing have meant cleaner air with less pollution. Modern continuous gas-fired tunnel kilns not only produce less smoke pollution but are also more efficient users of energy. The latest Italian technology allows a wall tile to be fired in under an hour, as opposed to ten days in the nineteenth century.

Despite improvements in the speed and efficiency of making tiles today, one category which was ubiquitous in the nineteenth century, the encaustic tile, has almost totally failed to adapt to modern conditions. As the third chapter reveals, encaustic tiles were a major sector of tile production and use for half a century from

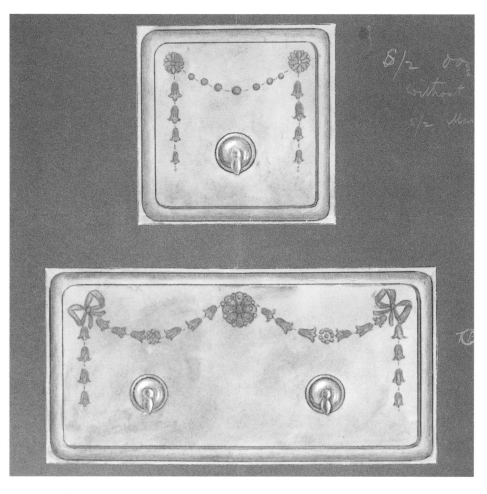

the 1840s. But they remained there, dinosaur-like and doomed to near extinction. Encaustic tiles made a fundamental contribution to the architecture of the Gothic Revival and it was this almost incestuous association with a particular style and use which was probably a significant factor in their decline, inhibiting stylistic changes as well as innovations in architectural application. After 1900, such small numbers of churches as were being built increasingly used marble or terrazzo for flooring and the tradition of patterned encaustic tiles was abandoned as the Gothic style itself adapted to the modern era. Despite this, several manufacturers continued making encaustic tiles as and when necessary up until World War II. But their designs remained essentially Gothic, and Art Nouveau- or Art Deco-inspired encaustic tiles are almost impossible to find in Britain or Europe.

Their labour-intensive method of production, using coloured clay inlays, has not advanced since the nineteenth century and this has also probably contributed to the slowness of any real kind of revival, which now seems likely to elude the twentieth century altogether. The technique and the desire to use it has not completely

In the 1920s and 1930s tile manufacturers attempted to respond to new trends in interior decoration and domestic services. These tiles, specially designed to house light switches and fit in with standard tiling, were offered by Maw & Co.

A characteristic bathroom tiling scheme of the 1930s by Carter & Co of Poole.

disappeared, however. In the 1960s Dick Swann of Leicester wrote his pamphlet *Tiles Old and New*, praising the medieval tiles in his local Roman Catholic church, St Mary De Castro, Leicester. He not only produced replicas of the old tiles (which are on display in the church) but also set out his proposals for a series of 24 new designs 'to be laid in the sacristy'.

Although apparently unexecuted, the designs are remarkable for their choice of contemporary visual symbols. These include a three-stage spaceship surrounded by planets and stars, an archetypal 1960s motor scooter (described as 'making the town a Hell for visitor and resident alike') and a television set complete with antennae! There is a wry mocking humour in some of the designs which include a trio of worshippers at the shrine of materialism (described by Swann in his booklet as 'the most popular religion of the twentieth century').

The Swann designs are characterized by a novelty and freshness of approach which is largely absent from other encaustic tiles made in the latter half of this century. Most of those produced have been intended for restoration projects of various kinds. Thus at Beauvais in France new tiles were made after World War II for use in the restoration of the ancient houses close to the cathedral. The original late fifteenth-century structures, which were destroyed by the German invasion of 1940, incorporated inlaid tiles as part of the infill material in the spaces between the timbers of the frame.

A similar philosophy of precisely matching nineteenth-century material lies behind the special unit run by H & R Johnson in Stoke-on-Trent since the 1970s. This has attempted to imitate the intricate designs and variety of inlaid colours of the tiles in buildings such as the Palace of Westminster in London and the Capitol in Washington DC, with a view to replacing worn floors.

The successful conservation of nineteenth-century tile pavements in cathedrals and public buildings remains a considerable challenge. Modern footwear may be softer and kinder to tiles but the cumulative grinding effect of grit particles continues to wear away the clay inlays, making replacement unavoidable in the long term. Meanwhile a small British firm, intriguingly named 'The Life Enhancing Tile Company', has begun production of a range of entirely new encaustic designs, unfettered by the constraints of having to match the past precisely.

If encaustic tiles and the Gothic Revival have proved to be something of a cul-de-sac in the twentieth century, the Modern Movement has opened up a new series of opportunities for using tiles in architecture. The part these tiles played has been very different to that of those tiles in the nineteenth century. Indeed many people find it difficult to reconcile exuberantly decorated nineteenth-century tiles with the rational simplicity of the Modern Movement and assume that tiles simply fell into disuse soon after the turn of the century.

In an unexpected way, tiles in modern buildings are a continuation of the cool, clean and hygienic theme which in the fourth chapter was seen to be such a feature of Victorian Britain. The main difference is that tiles in modern buildings offer not just a literal impression of cleanliness but, through the use of undecorated tile surfaces and sometimes of matt glazes and pastel colours, they contribute to the overall image of clean and functional architecture by producing a tight-fitting skin over simple rectangular shapes, smooth circular columns or gently curved forms.

In May 1939 *Architectural Review*, which was well known as a supporter of the Modern Movement, published an eight-page supplement on tiles. The first two pictures vividly demonstrate the clean and hygienic qualities of tiles in both the nineteenth-century literal and twentieth-century extended senses identified above. One picture shows the familiar elaborately moulded tiles on the walls and columns of the Refreshment Room at the Victoria and Albert Museum. Below is the far less familiar entrance vestibule to Highpoint ll, the block of flats at Highgate London, designed by Berthold Lubetkin and the Tecton group. Here the tiles are quiet and

Los Angeles Central Library, opened in
1926, was designed by Bertram Grosvenor
Goodhue without specific reference to any
defined historical style. Nevertheless,
brilliantly coloured ceramic tiles were used
to clad the building's crowning pyramid,
recently restored after earthquake damage
in 1987. Cracked tiles were replaced and a
new torch installed to symbolize the 'Light
of Learning'.

reticent, providing a simple but elegant wall-lining which is paired with rectangular glass blocks and smooth plaster. The caption to the pictures highlights 'the changed approach to the use of the medium over a space of seventy years'.

Tiles contributed to other Tecton buildings too, most notably at the Finsbury Health Centre (1935-8) whose splayed-out wings were seen as a pioneering 'megaphone for health' in this densely populated inner London borough. Plain tiles lined the internal walls and, along with translucent glass blocks, put into practice Lubetkin's socially motivated design process which ran 'Clean surfaces and bright colours produce cheerful effect – Air of efficiency gives confidence to the patients – clean and purposeful architectural character'.

Lubetkin's philosophy was a good deal more vigorous about materials than that which might have been demonstrated in the average British home at that time. Tiles, it is true, played a part in the decoration of bathroom and kitchen walls, since they provided an unfussy and easy-to-clean surface; but in general terms they no longer contributed to life in the home in the colourful and multifarious ways in which they had in the nineteenth century.

The fireplace still dominated the living-room in many homes in the 1920s and, although tiled, its form had by now altered considerably. Cast-iron as a framing material had given way to 'slabbed' fireplaces made up from reinforced concrete and tiles. Their form became lumpish and overtly architectural with integral tiled shelves and ledges, often adopting the stepped symmetrical shape of an Aztec temple and the fashionable image of Art Deco. Many of the tiles were by now plain mottles in drab brown and oatmeal colours. The tradition of an art gallery of picture tiles around the fire was usually reduced to one or a pair of 'highlight' tiles, featuring subjects such as galleons in full sail.

The demise of the tiled fireplace was undoubtedly hastened by new methods of domestic heating. At first the fireplace absorbed the gas fire and the wall-mounted electric fire readily enough and the slabbed, tiled surround offered a robust and easily cleaned surface close to the source of heat. Electric fires, with their chromed reflectors, went well with angular surrounds covered in tiles decorated with zig-zag Art Deco details. For many people this was the ideal evocation of the tradition of hearth and home, updated in the latest jazz moderne style and freed from the slavery of coal and ashes. During the 1930s, however, the radio began to challenge the fireplace as the focal point of the room. In a few bizarre instances tiled fireplaces were actually supplied with built-in radio speakers! After World War II, the spread of central heating and the establishment of the universal television set as domestic icon dealt a final blow to tiled fireplaces from which they are only just recovering.

Contraction of the domestic tile market was influenced too by the advent of alternative materials. The nineteenth-century rhetorical question 'To what use cannot tiles be put?' was turned on its head and in the inter-war years might have reappeared as 'What uses are left for ceramic tiles that have not been replaced by other, often synthetic, materials?'. Thus tiled front paths became concrete or concrete slabs; hallways were floored with wood blocks, terrazzo or cork tiles and an ever-increasing variety of sheet materials ranging from linoleum to vinyl. Even tiled bathrooms were under threat from the new coloured sheet glass material – vitrolite.

In Britain there were few architects at this time experimenting with tiles as a medium of decoration for private houses. The work of Edgar Wood at Royd House, Hale, Cheshire was wholly atypical. Wood built this reinforced concrete house between 1914 and 1916 for his own use and decorated the centre part of the curved front with tiles in bold geometric, arabesque patterns, pre-dating by a decade a similar use for tiles on cinemas.

The situation in the USA, however, was much more progressive. Here the development of decorative tiles gained great headway in the first quarter of the twentieth century. A combination of bold colours and relief decoration was used for tiles which found many uses in the home, not least as risers to steps and stairways.

One of the factors which inhibited the domestic use of tiles in Britain before World War II was the almost total reliance which tile manufacturers had on ironmongers' and builders' merchants for their marketing and distribution. In a prophetic article in *Design* magazine in August 1953 Mark Hartland Thomas foresaw the advent of retail tile shops and the benefits this would bring in allowing 'customers of both kinds, house-holders and architects, to rediscover the possibilities of tiling for decoration in many different situations and in large areas as well as small'. The subsequent increase in home ownership, together with a do-it-yourself revolution, has made tiles a very accessible form of home furnishing.

Late twentieth-century developments worthy of special comment include the tiled Aga cooker back. Derived from the Victorian tradition of tiled cooking ranges, these new versions are usually a much more personal expression of the owner's individual taste and aspirations. They may be custom-decorated to portray the family, the family cat or dog, or at least some evocation of country living, for which the Aga is the supreme symbol.

Although the pace of domestic tiling has slowed down in the twentieth century, the same cannot be said for tiling used for commercial premises and some types of public buildings. The ability of tiles to create styles, convey commercial messages and establish identity and to uplift and entertain on a grand scale has continued to be exploited right up to the present-day. Precedents established in the nineteenth century have been developed and expanded.

The tiled butcher's shop went from strength to strength in the first half of the twentieth century. Styles certainly changed (restrained neo-classical became popular)

Above. Watercolour design for the window of an auditorium and exhibition hall at Pasadena, California, 1931, by Gladding McBean of Los Angeles.
Below. The Mexican influence can be seen in this tile panel from the Biltmore Hotel, Santa Barbara, California, by Gladding McBean.
Opposite. Swan sundial panel designed and decorated by Maggie Angus Berkowitz of Milnethorpe, Cumbria, c. 1980, for installation on an exterior wall.

and mouldings got simpler, but the use of tiles remained paramount. As chains of shops in different towns, all owned by one company, were developed so tiles acted as a kind of ceramic livery, reinforcing the company name and image. Other types of shops also utilized the tile idiom and each adopted a distinguishing motif. For instance, all the Maypole Dairy shops had a hand-painted panel of 24 tiles made by Pilkingtons, which depicted a medieval maypole scene on a village green. David Grieg, the grocers of Scottish origin, used repetitive relief-moulded thistles in blue, gold and green.

Many distinctive shop tiles of the inter-war period were made by Carters of Poole. A farmyard series, designed by E E Stickland in about 1922 and made in both painted and stencilled versions, continued to be used by Dewhursts the butchers until the 1960s. Around 1925 Mac Fisheries commissioned some marine scenes from Carters, including Dora Batty's herring girl with a basket of fish on her head and Minnie McLeish's sunset scene with boats. Showing considerable marketing acumen, Mac Fisheries decided to use these (together with additional designs) for a series of ceramic fish paste lids and packaging labels.

Shop tiles for identity went beyond those selling food. W H Smiths, booksellers, newsagents and stationers evolved an elegant oak shopfront for its branches which incorporated charming pictorial panels telling the potential customer what was available inside, such as children's books, postcards and guides. The most complete surviving W H Smith's shop from this period at Newtown in Powys was restored in 1975 as the company's contribution to European Architectural Heritage Year.

A much more blatant piece of twentieth-century tiled advertising (also found in the stationery trade) was achieved when Samuel Jones and Co, once well known for their Butterfly Brand goods, erected a new factory building in Camberwell in the

The Katherine Hamnett shop in Glasgow's Princes Square development. Designed by Branson Coates Architecture and opened in 1988, the interior was inspired by Hamnett herself who enthused with the architects about Barcelona, Morocco and the exquisite possibilities of tiles. Although understated from the exterior, once inside the shop there is a richly tiled seat that starts near to the door but falls as it spirals around the room, eventually merging with the floor.

1920s. The firm used the Camberwell Beauty butterfly as its trademark and employed Doultons to produce a huge tiled version to sit atop their factory building. This ceramic lepidopteran measured 6 metres by 4.25 metres (20 feet by 14 feet) and consisted of 231 large tiles. The butterfly, in rich purple-brown, blue and yellow became such a celebrated local landmark that during World War II Lord Haw-Haw, the broadcaster of German propaganda, said on his radio programme 'Germany Calling' that the huge tiled panel was assisting navigation. Therefore, on the orders of Winston Churchill, it was painted over. The butterfly was uncovered again after the war and re-sited in 1983, following demolition of the factory.

Identity of a different kind had already been sought and achieved by the use of tiles on London's Underground at the turn of the century (see the sixth chapter) and the tradition has continued. When the older stations on the Central line were modernized in the 1930s, Frank Pick, vice chairman of the London Passenger Transport Board, chose Carters to design and produce a series of relief-decorated tiles showing familiar London buildings such as the Palace of Westminster, St Paul's

The tiled façade of a pharmacy in Las Ramblas, Barcelona.

Twentieth-century tiling has continued and developed its role of conveying messages to the consumer. Top. Paints, brushes and artists' materials from Lisbon, Portugal. Centre. Michelin men bouncing around a petrol pump in Spain. Bottom. A 1930s railway porter from Haarlem station, Holland.

Opposite. A striking and long-standing tile panel advertising Chile nitrate on the wall of a roadside barn in rural Spain.

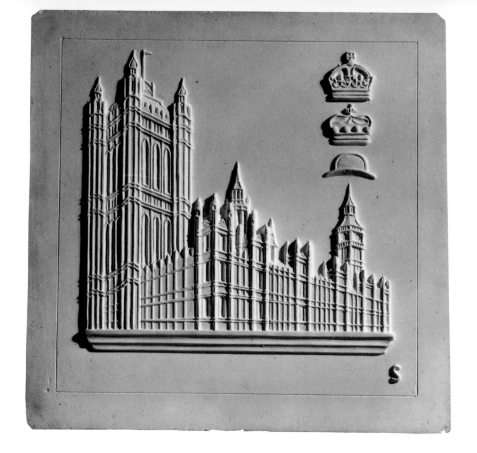

Two relief-decorated tiles from a series
designed c. 1938 by Harold Stabler and
made in spray-glazed creams and off
whites by Carter & Co for London
Underground stations.
Above. The plaster pattern for a
Westminster tile. Note the hierarchical
headgear for monarchs, lords and
commoners.
Right. 55 Broadway was designed by
Charles Holden as the modernist
headquarters of London Transport. Holden
and Cyril Carter (whose company made the
tile) were great friends and fellow members
of the Design and Industries Association.

Cathedral and the Crystal Palace. More recently, on the new Victoria line, a series of corny puns depicted on tiles has been used. These include a maze for Warren Street (designed by Crosby/Fletcher/Forbes) and five crowns in the form of a cross for Kings Cross (designed by Tom Eckersley), showing that tiles in public places can entertain as well as inform. Even newer schemes incorporating tiles have continued to be used and especially popular are the large profiles of Sherlock Holmes on the Bakerloo line platforms at Baker Street Station. The unmistakeable outline of Holmes, with deerstalker hat and curly pipe, is in fact cleverly constructed from hundreds of smaller profiles of the famous detective, each the size of a small dot. In this way the tiled decoration can have meaning from several yards away as well as from close up.

Plain-coloured, rectangular modern tiles used on a huge scale and with confidence and creativity. This tiled road cutting with artificial 'geology' at Telford, Shropshire, was completed in 1983.

Opportunities for using tiles on a grand scale have actually multiplied since the nineteenth century as steel and reinforced concrete buildings have increased in size, making huge areas potentially available for decorative tilework. When used on this scale, tiles no longer need to be individually decorated. Machine-produced rectangular tiles can be used in schemes where each tile is of a single colour and contributes as a dot to the overall pattern. One of the most successful of these modern tiled murals is the roadside cutting in Telford, Shropshire, in which bands of coloured tiles have been used to give a rock strata effect, complete with geological faults. This remarkable hillside of tiles, which covers 2,260 square metres (7,415 square feet), was designed by Kenneth Budd. Driving alongside the tiles at speed is an exhilarating experience which varies according to light conditions. In direct sunlight the colours of the tiles are rich and earthy and the 'rock strata' look strong and geological. When the sun moves round to shine obliquely along the varied surfaces of the tiles, a much softer, silvery textured sheen becomes apparent.

Modern, expansive tile murals feature strongly in the USA and are frequently associated with transport structures. The largely underground Philadelphia Market East railway station has been transformed into a tranquil woodland glade by the use of tiling representing full-sized leafy trees. In other situations more abstract patterns have been developed by artists attempting to reflect the kinetic activity of transport. The new Harvard Square station in Cambridge, Massachusetts (designed by Skidmore, Owings and Merrill) has large-scale tilework by the New York artist, Joyce Kosloff. The work comprises interlocking geometric-shaped tiles, some derived from the traditional Islamic star and cross arrangement. They are glazed in many bright colours, some solid and some with motifs or images. The whole is designed to be experienced on the move – as the public walks up or down the adjacent ramps so the patterns will unfold and change, revealing themselves gradually, rather than all at once as a picture panel does.

The strongly individual character of the tiling at Harvard Square station is a reminder of the enduring strength of the craft tradition in tiles. Since the nineteenth

In New York City efforts by tile artists range from bold creative statements to what might be construed as tile graffiti.
Left and below. Traffic lights garnished with ceramic stars and stripes.
Opposite. At 33rd Street subway station badly damaged original tiling has been surreptitiously infilled by ceramic artists. This has not only drawn attention to the plight of original tiling but has now fostered the legitimate involvement of tile artists in station refurbishment.

century, almost every decade has produced artists worldwide who have sought to use ceramic tiles as a creative medium of expression. During the early years of the De Stijl movement, between 1917 and 1920, its leader Theo van Doesburg designed tiled floors and glazed brick exterior panels for 'De Vonk', a holiday home for factory girls on the Dutch coast. The new Dutch artistic movement manifested itself through severe abstraction into straight line, square and rectangular forms which were readily adapted to the use of tiles in architecture.

Much more homely were the tile-decorating efforts of two English ladies from the 1930s – Sylvia Packard and Rosalind Ord. Their small business, which became Marlborough Ceramic Tiles, produced delightfully fresh hand-painted designs, some of which were made up into wooden trays or used in kitchens and fireplaces. The contrast with De Stijl could hardly have been more pronounced – but this extreme diversity is one of the most striking features of twentieth-century tiling.

The 1980s saw something of a renaissance of craft tile-makers and decorators in Britain. With low overheads and a flexibility which could meet the specific needs of clients and architects, they were able to survive the otherwise difficult economic conditions. In several instances the Government's Manpower Services Commission schemes and funding have provided a valuable starting point and at least two tile-makers have benefited from the Prince of Wales's Youth Business Trust.

One final, important and very distinctive ingredient remains in the cocktail mix of modern tiles. This is a respect, even veneration for nineteenth-century tiles, which has come about comparatively recently. In 1939 Arthur Lane of the Victoria and Albert Museum's Department of Ceramics wrote 'The turgid revivalism of the nineteenth century, conflating the styles of all previous epochs, made great use of tiles... Today, sickened by our nineteenth century excesses, we have practically discarded ornament.' By the 1970s, the pendulum had swung in earnest and buildings from 100 years before were beginning to attract widespread admiration for their colour, decoration and complexity. Tiles played an important part in this reversal and, far from being reviled as 'lavatorial' and 'having a dank, period appeal', they were seen to be worthy of study, preservation and enjoyment.

Gradually these things became reality. The Tiles and Architectural Ceramics Society was set up in Britain in 1981 and since then it has taken on the role of the national society responsible for the study and protection of tiles and architectural ceramics. The Tile Heritage Foundation (established in 1988) plays a similar role in the USA and numerous groups with similar, if more local, aims exist in several European countries (see the back of the book for details). Techniques for restoring, removing and re-siting nineteenth-century tiles have been developed and there is a new sector of tile output, from both industrial and craft producers, designed to meet the widespread demand for reproduction nineteenth-century tiles.

Right. Echo of the past. This newly tiled baker's shop in Amsterdam has used English tiles to recreate the instantly recognizable elements of the famous Harrods' food hall and to fulfil a nostalgic need for 'heritage'.

Below. Interesting use of geometry in Rupert Spira's tiles from the Froyle Pottery for exterior panels of an office building in Ludgate Hill, London, a project undertaken for Rosehaugh Stanhope Development plc.

In Amsterdam the supreme irony has emerged of a baker's shop which has recently been elaborately tiled – not in Dutch tiles and tradition, but with English tiles used to recreate directly features from Harrods' food halls in London!

The nineteenth-century tile tradition is a rich one, now widely appreciated and emulated. If we can avoid the pitfall of 'turgid revivalism', it can play an inspirational role in the creative design and use of tiles for the future.

Glimpse of the future? The elevation to Blackfriars Court, London, by John Outram, 1991. The building is designed to be clad with specially developed coloured concrete tiles, using aluminium strips to highlight the joint lines. Outram's inspiration came partly from the work of an old tile-maker he met in Cyprus. His design offers a renaissance of colour and decoration which combines tile traditions with modern creativity.

Directory of Architects and Designers

This directory covers the period of the nineteenth century and up to 1914 and includes those major architects who incorporated decorative tiles and architectural ceramics in their buildings. Artists and designers who were involved with work on an architectural scale are also included. However, tile designers and designers working within tile companies who had no control over the architectural context of their work have been omitted. They are covered in other publications aimed primarily at collectors.

The first part of each entry gives general biographical information, together with an overview of the individual's contribution to the architecture of the period. This is followed by specific examples of schemes where decorative tiles were used, though these cannot be completely comprehensive.

Berlage, Hendrik Petrus (1856–1934)

Born in Amsterdam into a middle-class family, Berlage studied briefly at the Academy of Fine Arts in Amsterdam but, recognizing his talents to be more suited to architecture, he enrolled (1875) at the Bauschule of the Eidgenössische Technische Hochschule in Zurich. In 1881 he entered the office of Theodorus Sanders, engineer, in Holland. In 1884–5 they jointly prepared designs for Amsterdam Beurs (Stock Exchange) and won fourth prize in a competition. However, the programme was shelved until 1896 when Berlage alone received the commission and completely reworked the design. He abandoned the original complicated massing and florid ornament and instead, using his own proportional system based on geometry, achieved an ordered, sober and somewhat monastic building. Berlage included a ceramic clock on the tower and internal narrative panels made by De Porceleyne Fles, Delft, in the sectiel technique (shaped pieces of tile following the lines of design). Despite his modern ideas, his use of tiles illustrates sympathy with the Arts and Crafts Movement.
Tiling schemes:
Beurs, Amsterdam, Holland. 1897–1903.
Holland House, Bury Street, London EC3. 1914–16. Headquarters building for W H Muller's Dutch shipping company. Extensive use of ceramics as external cladding and internal decoration employing glazed brick, tiles and mosaic.

Bodley, George Frederick (1827–1907)

Son of a doctor in Hull, he later moved to Brighton. In 1845–50 he was apprenticed to and lived en famille with George Gilbert Scott. He later reacted against Scott's brand of Gothic, being more influenced by the writings of Ruskin and an association with G E Street and William White who were in Scott's office at the same time. Butterfield was also a close and influential friend. Bodley's work was mostly ecclesiastical. He liked to consider a building as a whole, designing everything from ceiling and floor down to the last chalice and vestment. He also did college buildings at Cambridge. Early churches often had good tiled pavements but for later ones he used black and white marble.
Tiling schemes:
All Saints Church, Jesus Lane, Cambridge. 1864. Minton encaustic tiles in chancel.
St Martin-on-the-Hill, Scarborough, Yorkshire. 1861. Encaustic tiled floor.

Burges, William (1827–1881)

Son of a prosperous engineer, Burges was educated at Kings College, London. Greatly interested in medievalism, he was able to indulge this fascination while articled to Edward Blore (1844) and later while working at Matthew Digby Wyatt's office (1849). He was also influenced by the doctrinal teachings of John Ruskin and Pugin's great Gothic Revival work at the new Houses of Parliament but he most particularly admired and emulated French Gothic of the thirteenth century.
Tiling schemes:
Cardiff Castle, Cardiff, South Wales. 1865–81. For the Marquess of Bute. Burges's chief work which shows some of his best and most idiosyncratic tiling schemes. He used decorated tiles lavishly on the walls and floors, despite having railed against them in his 1864 Cantor lecture. The castle's floor includes examples of the *champlevé* technique, which is rare in England, being found more frequently in France. *See also* Gazetteer.
Knightshayes, Tiverton, Devon. 1868–73. House for Sir John Heathcoat Amory, MP and lace-making magnate, includes tiled fireplaces in the medieval style.

Butterfield, William (1814–1900)

Born in London and apprenticed to a Pimlico builder in 1831 at the age of 16, in 1833 Butterfield became an architectural student articled to E L Blackburn, a young antiquarian architect, and enrolled as a student member of the Architectural Society. In 1840 he set up his own practice and in 1842 moved to 4 Adam Street in the Adelphi. He was related to Wills of Bristol whose patronage was crucial at the start of his career. One of the most prolific Victorian church, college and school architects, his interest and use of constructional polychromy is remarkable for its inventiveness. He used tiles freely, creatively but judiciously, through geometric arrangement.
Tiling schemes:
All Saints Church, Margaret Street, London W1. 1849–59. Extensive floor tiling scheme. Atypical pictorial panels added later. *See also* Gazetteer.
Baverstock Church, Wiltshire. 1880–2. Wall and floor tiling – an example of the many and varied smaller churches in which he used tiles to great effect.
Ottery St Mary Church, Devon. 1878. Wall tile decoration in south transept – supplied by Simpsons, London.

Collcutt, Thomas Edward (1840–1924)

Born in Oxford and articled to R W Armstrong in London, Collcutt worked in the office of Mills and Murgatroyd and, for a short time, with G E Street. A prolific architect working primarily in the London area, he had two distinct styles: one for public buildings, such as the Savoy Hotel; another more relaxed style for private houses. Both styles included decorative tiles. He was commissioned to design several ship interiors where he used tiles extensively, frequently choosing De Morgan as the supplier, though allowing him great flexibility with the designs.
Tiling schemes:
1882–1911 numerous ship interiors mainly commissioned by P & O, for example, *Oceana* 1888, De Morgan and imported Dutch tiles; *Palawam* 1895, De Morgan tiles; *India* 1896, De Morgan tiles.
Imperial Institute, Imperial College Road, London SW7. 1895. De Morgan tiles for fireplaces. Private houses at Totteridge, Hertfordshire, included tiled fireplaces (possibly Medmenham Pottery tiles).

Crane, Walter (1845–1915)

Born in Liverpool but he lived most of his adult working life in London. Apprenticed in 1859 to W J Linton as a draughtsman on wood. Primarily known for his book illustrations, he also designed successful wallpapers (principally for Jeffrey & Co) and some textiles. Interior design schemes often included tiles in fireplaces – frequently De Morgan's. Crane was commissioned to design tiles for Maws and Pilkingtons. His designs for Maws' wall tiles relied on transfer-printed images with hand colouring. His series entitled 'Flora's Retinue' for Pilkingtons was in relief style with hand colouring. He produced no encaustic floor tile designs. His interest and expertise was in a decorative, not an architectural, effect. His small but significant contribution to art pottery involved producing designs, sometimes executing the decoration himself, for Wedgwood, Minton, Pilkington and Maw. He designed many items for national and international exhibition stands. From the mid-1880s he was a committed Socialist and founder member of the Northern Art Workers Guild. Opposed to art teaching outside the workshop, he worked energetically from within and established institutions to effect change. He published many papers and in 1898 became Principal of the Royal College of Art.

Day, Lewis F (1845–1910)

Lewis came from a middle-class background and, on leaving school, spent a period abroad before returning to England where he became entirely self-supporting and self-educating. He worked for two stained-glass firms initially but soon became involved with designing on a freelance basis for other materials as well.

His designs were mostly confined to two-dimensional or very low relief patterns, particularly for wallpaper, textiles and tiles. He was most influential through his writings on design which began in 1877. He produced a major series for the *British Architect* in 1878 and enjoyed a close association with the *Art Journal* and the *Magazine of Art*. He contributed regularly to the *Manchester Guardian*. A very practical designer himself, Day expected others in the field to have a thorough understanding of materials, design and their application to industry. Through his writing he was often able to bridge the gap between 'arty' Arts and Crafts designers, training establishments and industry. In 1897 he became Master of the Art Workers Guild. His important publications were: *The Application of Ornament* (1888); *The Anatomy of Pattern* (1889) and *Nature in Ornament* (1892).
Tiling work:
He designed tiles for Maws, Pilkingtons and J C Edwards, sometimes stipulating a slip-outlined decoration but most frequently demanding a lustre finish.

De Morgan, William Frend (1839-1917)
One of the most important potters of the late nineteenth century, De Morgan was an innovator both in design and technique. He started designing tiles for Morris, Marshall, Faulkner & Co in c. 1869 – many of these designs show a strong Morris influence. In 1872 he moved his studios from 40 Fitzroy Square to 30 Cheyne Row, Chelsea, the first of several relocations which were to mark the distinct geographical periods of his work. In 1882 he moved to Merton Abbey, in 1888 to Sands End Pottery, Fulham, where he entered into partnership with Halsey Ricardo. He studied Turkish and Persian patterns and colour and by 1879 his 'Persian' colours were good enough to supply Lord Leighton with additional tiles to make up deficiencies in his collection of Turkish and Syrian tiles being installed in the Arab Hall at Leighton House. De Morgan's tiles were used primarily in upper-class bathrooms, grand hallways and fireplaces, though they were also supplied to Barnard, Bishop and Barnard for insertion into the cast iron fireplace surrounds which were advertised in their catalogues.

Gaudi, Antoni i Cornet (1852-1926)
Born in Tarragona, Spain. His father was a copper-smith and boiler maker, his uncle a wood turner – skills which helped Gaudi develop his feel for materials and respect for tools and their users. His highly individualistic style of architecture drew freely on naturalistic forms, forging aspects of Gothic and Art Nouveau into a vocabulary all of his own. His buildings have humour; materials, colours, shapes and finishes are played with, frequently making bizarre juxtapositions. He used glazed architectural ceramics (in wild glaze colours) and tiles, sometimes whole but usually broken into pieces and re-assembled in a quasi-mosaic fashion peculiar to Gaudi. The strong Catalan craft tradition helped Gaudi to produce his work and for it to be accepted.
Tiling schemes:
Casa Vicens, Barcelona, Spain. 1883-5. Gaudi's first major private commission for Vicens – a ceramic and tile manufacturer. Extensive and exuberant tiling inside and out.
El Capricho, Comillas, Spain. 1883-5. Commissioned by wealthy tycoon Maximo Dioz de Quijano. Exterior main block has bands of relief yellow sunflowers alternating with green foliage tiles. Sunflowers and green lustre tiles on tower.
Güell Park, Barcelona, Spain. 1900-14. Finest example of Gaudi's collaboration with nature. Gaudi mosaic snaking wall and other examples throughout park including grand double staircase and grotesque creatures, dragons etc.

Godwin, Edward William (1833-86)
Godwin was born in Bristol and after education in London returned to be articled there to William Armstrong, City Surveyor, Architect and Engineer. He set up his own practice in 1854. Influenced by the writings of Ruskin and his friend William Burges. He was an early proponent of Japanese style.
Tiling schemes:
Town Hall, Northampton, Northamptonshire. 1861. Winning competition design included geometric tiled pavement for the corridor surrounding the Council Chamber. The floor did not survive but was replaced, using original drawings, in a 1992/3 restoration by Roderick Gradidge.

Dromore Castle, near Limerick, Eire. 1869-70. Fireplace surrounds.

Goldie, George (1828-87)
A pupil and later partner of M E Hadfield and J G Weightman, Goldie established a reputation for designing good churches and their attendant schools and houses, particularly among the Roman Catholic community. An extremely able designer of encaustic floor tiles, he produced many designs for both Maws and Craven Dunnills. His style was medieval Gothic extemporized. His work was exhibited at the Royal Academy in 1854-92.
Tiling schemes:
Chester Cathedral, Cheshire. Lady Chapel encaustic pavement.

Green, Leslie William (1875-1908)
Green attended Dover College and was then articled to his father Arthur Green (d. 1904), a Crown Surveyor. After studying at South Kensington, he spent a year in Paris. As an assistant he worked on numerous projects in central London. He set up his own practice in 1897. Although his working life was very short – he died aged 33 – he made a huge impact on the daily lives of millions of underground travellers; in 1903 he was appointed architect to Underground Electric Railways Co of London Ltd in collaboration with Harry Wharton Ford (1875-1947) who was staff architect (1899-1911). Green was responsible for the design of all the areas the public saw, from the station above ground to the train tunnels below, for the Baker Street and Waterloo Railway, Great Northern, Piccadilly and Brompton Railway and Charing Cross, Euston and Hampstead Railway. He designed 50 stations in five years and used tiles extensively to various ends – to present a clean overall uniformity, to accentuate certain areas, to inform passengers and to give a distinct and recognizable individuality to each station or line.

Jones, Owen (1806-89)
Born in London of a modestly well-to-do family, he was educated at Charterhouse before becoming a pupil of the architect Lewis Vulliamy and, briefly, of the surveyor William Wallen. In 1830 he embarked on a three-year expedition to the Continent and the Near East, carrying out his seminal studies of the

Alhambra, its decoration and colour with Jules Goury (1803-34) . In 1834 he set up in London as an architect and printer, finding no one capable of carrying out the scale of colour printing required for his drawings of the Alhambra. This published work and his later *Grammar of Ornament* (1856) – a monumental source book of ornamental style, form and colour – provided the inspiration for many designers and manufacturers. Fascinated by tile patterns in the Alhambra, during the 1840s and 1850s Jones involved himself in contemporary English mosaic and tiles. In c. 1840 he prepared ten elaborate and influential geometric designs for J M Blashfield (a developer of Kensington Palace Gardens and a terracotta manufacturer) who was experimenting in making mosaic and tessellated pavements. By the late 1850s he had also prepared designs for Wyatt and Parker (a building firm associated with Blashfield), Minton, Maws and Godwins. When the Crystal Palace Exhibition moved to Sydenham he used colourful Minton tiles in the Alhambra Court. His most important tile design, for the floors of the new Houses of Parliament, submitted in competition in 1843 and reported to have been favourably received by the public when exhibited in 1844, has been lost. Contemporary commentators described the design as 'Moorish'.

James and Lister Lea
A Birmingham architectural practice which dramatically changed the look of public houses from the mid-1800s onwards with a series of large and showy examples in the markets area, south of the Bull Ring, Birmingham. They created a theatrical form of architectural advertising, particularly in the smaller 'in street' pubs, and broke new ground by taking the structural and decorative terracotta detailing all the way to the top of the building's façade. The practice relied heavily on terracotta and tiles to create opulent effects at relatively modest costs. Terracotta usually came from Hathern Station Brick and Terracotta Co of Loughborough to whom the choice of decorative detail was left and the tiles were usually selected from Minton's catalogue, though specials were ordered as well.
Tiling schemes:
Many public houses in Birmingham

(some now destroyed) but The Woodman, Easy Row (1891), had a series of painted tile panels depicting scenes of 'Bygone Birmingham' (now demolished). The Bartons Arms, High Street (1899–1901) still has a good display of elaborate tiling in a variety of styles.

Lynam, Charles (1829–1921)
Born near Stafford, Lynam entered his father's architectural practice after leaving school and also qualified as a surveyor. In 1849 he established his own architectural practice. He made rapid progress though most of his work, with two notable exceptions, was in Staffordshire. He carried out designs for schools, hospitals, industrial and domestic buildings as well as a large number of church restorations. His three innovatory tile factories are the most remarkable of all his schemes.
Tiling schemes:
Minton Hollins Tile Factory, Old Shelton Road, Stoke-on-Trent. 1869. Decorative detailing in unglazed geometric and encaustic tiles over windows and a prominent name panel in mosaic. Extensive internal tiling, though this was probably conceived by Minton Hollins.
Craven Dunnill Tile Factory, Jackfield, Shropshire. 1874. Unglazed geometric and encaustic decorative detailing over windows.
Library, London Road, Stoke-on-Trent. 1878. Impressive regular array of tile panels (now very badly faded) above first-floor circular windows.
Maw and Co Tile Factory, Jackfield, Shropshire. 1883. Tile panel above main entrance bearing informative details of the firm.

Morris, William (1834–1896)
The son of a wealthy London stockbroker, Morris turned to architecture while at Oxford, under the influence of Burne-Jones' and Ruskin's writings. In 1856 he entered the office of G E Street. In 1861, encouraged by Ford Madox Brown, the company Morris, Marshall, Faulkner & Co was set up to produce well-designed decorative work. Tiles were some of the earliest products, though low firing enamels were unsatisfactory. They always used bought-in white glazed blanks, usually Dutch – their soft tin-glaze being more sympathetic to Morris's decoration than highly vitrified English lead glazes. Morris

always painted his tiles by hand – he objected to printed tiles, believing the character of decoration came from delicate brushwork. This attractive delicacy made his tiles quite unsuitable for the robust use to which they were meant to be subjected and very few survive. Realizing the unsuitability of his type of tile decorating, he turned instead to De Morgan or imported Dutch designs for decorating schemes and for customers to buy in the shop.
Tiling schemes:
Queens' College Hall, Cambridge. 1875. Fireplace tiles.
Peterhouse Hall and Combination Room, Cambridge. 1868–74. Fireplace with tiles also placed on hood of chimney.

Neatby, William J (1860–1910)
He spent his formative years in the north of England, gaining experience in several architectural practices. Later he joined Burmantofts as a designer and painter of tiles and architectural faience. In 1889 he moved to London to take charge of Doultons department of architectural decoration, where he stayed until c. 1900. It was here that he was able to carry out investigative work into new techniques for glazing and colouring ceramics and here that he produced his most memorable tiling schemes.
Tiling schemes:
The Winter Gardens, Blackpool, Lancashire. 1896. A series of 28 panels depicting females in extravagant costume (these panels are still extant but, currently, are covered and inaccessible).
Everard Building, Broad Street, Bristol, Avon. 1901. Remarkable polychrome tile façade.
Harrods Meat Hall, Brompton Road, London SW1. 1902. Hunting scenes frieze at clerestory level forming an idealized catalogue of the goods for sale below.
St Nicholas' Hospital, Gosforth, Newcastle-upon-Tyne. 1900. Proscenium arch in recreation hall bearing Art Nouveau scheme of foliage, birds and two female figures.

Pugin, Augustus Welby Northmore (1812–52)
Pugin was born into a family already involved in architecture. His father Augustus Charles (1762–1832) was employed by Nash as a designer of

Gothic decorations, and published books on French Gothic architecture. A W N absorbed all this and his immense antiquarian knowledge led to his own highly influential publications and designs. In architecture he was a firm believer in honesty of construction and materials. He carried the same tenets through to the applied arts where he was a brilliant designer – Barry engaged his skills for decorative detailing for the new Houses of Parliament. His conversion to Roman Catholicism gave new meaning to his life and work and brought the significant patronage of the Earl of Shrewsbury for whom he did Alton Towers and St Giles, Cheadle. Pugin's concern encompassed all aspects of his buildings and early on he became fascinated by tiles in their medieval context. Through his close friendship and technical collaboration with Herbert Minton, Pugin can be seen as a prime mover in the great revival of encaustic tiles.
Tiling schemes:
Houses of Parliament, Westminster, London SW1. Extensive pavements.
St Giles Roman Catholic Church, Cheadle, Staffordshire. 1841–6. Encaustic pavement.

Ricardo, Halsey Ralph (1854–1928)
Born of a professional family in Bath, Ricardo was articled to the Cheltenham architect, John Middleton; afterwards he was assistant to Basil Champneys. He spent a year in Italy, then set up a practice in London in 1878. He received many commissions through his father-in-law's civil engineering practice (Rendel & Robertson) including offices, an Indian railway station and many family homes. A great proponent of colour in architecture, he introduced faience and glazed tiles into many of his buildings and especially De Morgan tiles on interior surfaces – De Morgan was his business partner from 1888–98.
Tiling schemes:
55-57 Melbury Road, Kensington, London W14. 1894. Built for Sir Alexander Rendel – inside hall lined with peacock blue De Morgan tiles. Exterior – glazed brick chosen to 'repel adverse effects of age and climate'.
Howrah Railway Station, Calcutta, India. 1898. Designed in conjunction with Rendel & Robertson. Exterior of brick and coloured tiles.

8 Addison Road, Kensington, London W14. 1905. Extensive use of tiles and glazed brick inside and out – *see also* Gazetteer.

Scott, Sir George Gilbert (1811–78)
A prolific architect, Scott was concerned with the building and restoration of churches and cathedrals in Britain together with major public buildings such as St Pancras Railway Station, the Foreign Office, Whitehall and the Albert Memorial. He sketched medieval buildings and tiles during his childhood in north Buckinghamshire.
Tiling schemes:
Holy Trinity Church, Hartshill, Stoke-on-Trent. 1841. Designed floors and chancel dado for Herbert Minton with whom he developed an early connection. Also favoured tiles supplied by Godwins of Lugwardine, Hereford.
Lichfield Cathedral, Staffordshire. Geometric and encaustic choir pavement. Drawings exhibited at 1862 International Exhibition, London.

Seddon, John Pollard (1827–1906)
Seddon was born in London where his father, Thomas, had one of the largest furniture manufactories in the country. In 1847–51 he became the pupil of the classicist architect T L Donaldson. After a tour of the continent, he then set up a practice in London. He met his future partner, John Pritchard, a Gothicist architect in charge of the restoration at Llandaff Cathedral, Cardiff, who had been articled to Pugin and Thomas Walker. Pritchard's influence on Seddon's work was enormous, but the partnership ended abruptly in 1863. In many respects Seddon was an early 'conservation architect', expending great care in preserving ancient details. He was also well known for his skill in designing furnishings, such as font covers, pulpits, stained glass and tiles. He was probably a more prolific designer of tiles (primarily encaustic floor tiles and their arrangement) than any other Victorian architect, producing numerous sheets of designs for Maws (from as early as 1864 and including one of their sets of alphabet tiles), Godwins, Minton Taylor and other unspecified firms.
Tiling schemes:
Church of St Padarn, Llanbadarn Fawr, Aberystwyth, Dyfed. 1868–78.

Encaustic pavements, including tile incorporating duplex lamp in its design.
Castle House Hotel (now the University College of Wales), Aberystwyth, Dyfed. 1864. Hall floor.

Shaw, Richard Norman (1831–1912)
Born in Edinburgh, Shaw was articled to William Burn. He then embarked on a Continental tour, returning in 1859 to join the office of G E Street as principal assistant. In 1863 he set up his own practice, sharing an office with W E Nesfield (1835–88). Shaw became a highly successful and prolific architect of public and private works, frequently giving his public works a characteristic 'streaky bacon' effect by interspersing courses of cream brick or stone with red brick, as in New Scotland Yard, London. He consistently used the unifying force of red quarry tiles for the floors of churches and houses because he felt the place for colour was on the sanctuary or hall walls where he often specified Minton's stencilled designs.
Tiling schemes:
Cragside, Rothbury, Northumberland. 1870–c. 85. Extensive tiling on hall walls throughout house. Dutch tiled sunken bath.
Adcote, Little Ness, near Shrewsbury, Shropshire. 1876–81. House for Rebecca Darby – fireplaces with De Morgan tiles.
Low Bentham Church, Yorkshire. Wall and floor tiles.

Smith, Samuel Poutney (1812–83)
A prominent Shropshire architect, Smith made extensive use of encaustic tiles in church restorations and also private houses. His pavements employ a very large number of individual patterned designs, creating a busy and colourful effect.
Tiling schemes:
Holy Trinity Church, Leaton, Shropshire. 1859–72. Tile pavement.
St Mary Magdalen Church, Battlefield, Shrewsbury, Shropshire. 1861–2. Restoration, good Maw & Co tile pavement.

Street, George Edmund (1824–81)
Assistant to Sir G G Scott (see above) in 1844–49 (at the same time as White and Bodley). Already designing churches on his own account, Street undertook various continental trips resulting in published works (Brick and Marble in the Middle Ages [1855],

Spanish Gothic Architecture [1865]). In 1852 he set up his own practice in Oxford, moving to London in 1855. Apart from a few notable exceptions such as the Law Courts, London (which was won in competition in 1866), Street's output was almost entirely devoted to the Church of England – though competitions for Lille Cathedral (1855, unexecuted) and the Crimean War Memorial Church, Constantinople (1856) were entered and highly praised for their understanding of the different religious requirements. By the mid-1850s constructional polychromy had begun to appear in his designs and he was designing encaustic floor tiles for Maws and Godwins for use in his churches and their catalogues. He was an important link figure in the Victorian architectural training chain; Street nurtured Philip Webb, William Morris and Norman Shaw. In 1881 he became President of RIBA.
Tiling schemes:
St James the Less Church, Westminster, London SW1. 1859. Encaustic pavement.
The Law Courts, Strand, London WC2. 1866. Pavement with medieval-style encaustics.

Temple, Charles Henry (1857–1940)
Born in Kingston-upon-Thames, Temple completed his education in France. He returned to London to be articled to a firm of heraldic stationers and later worked for an Oxford Street engravers and illuminators. He joined Shrigley and Hunt, stained-glass manufacturers, where he gained a reputation for church decoration. He experimented with ceramics and set up as Temple & Messenger in Wandsworth. This venture did not last long; in 1887 he moved to Shropshire as Maw's chief designer; he had qualified as an Associate of the Society of Designers while in London. He did much to promote the reputation of Maw's work through his skill and versatility. He also developed and patented in his own name particular glazes, mostly eggshell, and a photographic process for tile decorating. In 1906 he left Maws and once again set up his own decorating studio, continuing to use Maw's blanks.
Tiling schemes:
Eye, Ear and Throat Hospital, Murivance, Shrewsbury, Shropshire. 1892. Three tile panels on staircase

depicting Faith, Hope and Charity. Designs exhibited at Royal Academy. World's Fair, Chicago, USA. 1893. Exhibition stand for Maw & Co. Elaborate architectural display which won awards and great publicity for Temple and Maws.

Viollet-Le-Duc, Eugène Emmanuel (1814–79)
Born in Paris, to a cultivated bourgeois family. He declined the Ecole des Beaux-Arts and chose instead to study with architects Huve and Leclere. He was very influential through his work and writings, translations of which appeared in English. His interests were strongly historicist with particular reference to the Middle Ages. In 1854 he published the first of ten volumes of his Dictionnaire raisonné de L'Architecture française du xie au xvie siècle (1854-68) which set him on a par with Ruskin as a leading proponent of the Gothic Revival. Much of his work was involved with restoration and he is known to have designed tiles for use particularly in his church restorations – usually made by Boulenger.
Tiling schemes:
Victoria and Albert Museum, London has two tile panels which he designed for the Château d'Eu as part of his extensive modernization programme.

Voysey, Charles Francis Annesley (1857–1941)
Voysey grew up near Hull and then in London. In 1874 he was articled to J P Seddon, and in 1879 he became assistant to Henry Saxon Snell. In 1880 he joined the office of George Devey. In 1882 he set up his own practice in Broadway Chambers, Westminster. Seddon and Devey did much to shape the form of his work. Voysey's own genius lay in creating the epitome of the English idea of home. The calm, uncluttered style of his houses was a welcome antidote to the over-ornamented houses of the preceding period, the more so through his meticulous attention to the detail of external as well as internal furnishings and fittings.
He designed furniture, metalwares, textiles and wallpapers as well as tiles which were mainly for Pilkingtons. Curiously, in his houses tiles were almost always set vertically around fireplaces – favouring rectangular rather than square tiles. In 1924 he

became a Master of the Art Workers Guild.
Tiling schemes:
Designed and painted tiles shown at Arts and Crafts Exhibition 1888 and 1889 and Glasgow and Paris International Exhibitions 1900 and 1901.
Capel House, New Broad Street, London EC2. 1906-9. Two offices with vertically tiled fireplaces using Medmenham Pottery tiles.

Wagner, Otto (1841–1918)
Born near Vienna, in 1857-9 he studied architecture at the Vienna Polytechnic Institute. In 1860-1 he attended the Royal Academy of Building, Berlin. In 1861-3 he completed his studies at the Vienna Academy. His architectural style was rooted firmly in the Renaissance period but, aided by scientific and technological progress, he evolved a new streamlined 'Vienna School' of architecture. His buildings and his many published works were seminal; his followers and pupils such as J M Olbrich and Josef Hoffmann were brilliant architects, carrying Wagner's theories into the twentieth century. He was a keen user of tiles (and, unusually, aluminium) for the thoughtful, controlled exterior and interior decoration of his buildings.
Tiling schemes:
Apartment house, Linke Wienzeile 40, Vienna, Austria. 1898-9. (Also known as the majolica house.) Upper five storeys (above street-level shops) have elaborate floral decorated tiles covering the façade – like an Art Nouveau ceramic creeper.
Ost Postsparkassenamt, Vienna, Austria. 1904-6. (Post Office Savings Bank.) Detailing of black and white chequerboard-effect tiling inside and out. External walls of courtyard faced with white and black tiles.

Waterhouse, Alfred (1830–1905)
Born the son of a wealthy Quaker Mill owner, in Aigburth, Liverpool, he began his architectural career apprenticed to a prominent Manchester architect, Richard Lane. He saw and sketched much on a continental tour that was to influence his later work. In 1854 he set up a practice in Manchester. His stylistic variety was great and his skill as a planner of a building's spaces unequalled. He enjoyed a sure understanding of colour in buildings and was most

enthusiastic about new materials, quickly seizing upon terracotta and tiles as new tools to be used with great effect. He used tiles from, and corresponded frequently with, Mintons, Godwins, Burmantofts and Maws and produced designs for Craven Dunnills. Many examples (beautifully coloured) of his tile arrangement designs exist in the RIBA Library, London, although in many instances the executed works have long since gone.
Tiling schemes:
Prudential Assurance Building, Holborn Bars, London EC1. 1880. Elaborate internal decoration using Burmantofts tiles.
University main building, Brownlow Hill, Liverpool. 1884 onwards. Wall tiling scheme.

Wood, Edgar (1860–1935)
Articled to Mills and Murgatroyd, a Manchester firm of architects (who had designed a house for Wood Senior, a cotton mill owner and strong Unitarian). Later Wood set up his own practice in his father's disused Park Mill at Middleton near Manchester. His works were mostly domestic, though he did some banks, churches and schools. In common with contemporaries such as Voysey, his style was refreshingly simple and somewhat advanced for northern industrial England. He also designed furniture and jewellery and in 1897 became a Master of the Northern Art Workers Guild (inaugurated by Walter Crane in 1896, Wood was a founder member). In 1911 he read a paper to the RIBA entitled *Colour as applied to Architecture.*
Tiling schemes:
Franco-British Exhibition, White City, London W12. 1908. Designed Pilkingtons Tiles pavilion.
33-37 Manchester Road, Middleton, near Manchester. 1908. Shop façades – the style of tiling here is very advanced – anticipating Art Deco.
Royd House, 224 Hale Road, Hale, Cheshire. 1914. Wood's own house with striking, colourful tile arrangement on central external wall of house.

Wyatt, Sir Matthew Digby (1820–77)
Born near Devizes, Wiltshire, and the brother of T H Wyatt, architect, to whom he was articled. In 1844–6 he went on a continental tour. In 1849 he reported to the Society of Arts on

the Industrial Exhibition held in Paris. In 1851 he was appointed secretary of the Executive Committee for the Great Exhibition. He carried out a number of important public and private commissions himself as well as collaborating with other architects (such as Sir G G Scott on Government offices, Whitehall, *see above*) and engineers (such as I K Brunel, on Paddington Station, London). Wyatt was an influential architect, designer and author of many published works such as *Specimens of Geometrical Mosaics of the Middle Ages* (1848) and *Specimens of Geometrical Mosaics* (1862) in which many of his designs for Maws, for whom he designed from 1850 onwards, are illustrated. His strong interest in tiles probably sprang from an early job recording Italian mosaic and tessellated floors that he was given by Blashfield, the terracotta manufacturer.
Tiling schemes:
Majolica fireplace for Maw & Co exhibited at 1862 London International Exhibition.
12 Kensington Palace Gardens, London. 1864. Moorish billiard room. The 1862 fireplace was purchased by Alexander Collie, a London and Manchester cotton merchant who owned 12 Kensington Palace Gardens and employed Wyatt to turn the kitchen into a new billiard room complete with majolica fireplace, elaborate matching tile dado (supplied by Maws), gilding, moulding and mirrors. Also geometric tiled floor (Maws) to edge of billiard table. Osgoode Hall (Law Courts), Toronto, Ontario, Canada. 1857–60. Design for Maws for extensive geometric pavements on two floors.

Gazetteer

This gazetteer brings together information on the history and location of important tiled buildings and schemes which survive from the nineteenth century and up to 1914. It is arranged according to the theme of the chapters and is intended to help the reader to find examples of the main uses of tiles in architecture and interiors.

Most of the buildings are working buildings and not maintained primarily to display their architecture. In some places, such as pubs, this will not be a drawback! In others, public access may be limited and appropriate arrangements for access should be made.

The gazetteer includes only selected examples and is biased towards Britain. Information about the location of tiles in architecture is welcomed by the Tiles and Architectural Ceramics Society who are compiling a comprehensive index for the UK (*see* Museum Collections and Organizations).

The Marriage of Art and Industry.
Arts and Industries Building, Independence Avenue, Washington DC, USA (part of Smithsonian Institution). Maw and Co geometric tiled floor restored in 1977 to celebrate the centenary of the building which houses original exhibits from the 1876 Philadelphia Exhibition, including English tiles.

Benthall Hall, Broseley, Shropshire (National Trust). In the main hall George Maw's geometric and encaustic pavement of c. 1860 can be viewed through two trap doors in the later oak-boarded floor. Remains of Maws' ceramic plant labels and crocus collection survive in the gardens.

Boulenger Tile Factory and associated buildings, Auneuil, France. Complete nineteenth-century tile-making complex. Despatch warehouse of c. 1883 extensively decorated externally with encaustic tiles which include commemorative medals and honours won at exhibitions. Manager's house tiled internally and externally. Boulenger 'Museum' of 1885 covered with encaustic tiles.

Craven Dunnill Tile Works, Jackfield, Telford, Shropshire (now Jackfield Tile Museum). The most complete surviving nineteenth-century tile factory in Britain, designed by Charles Lynam and opened in 1874. Tiled entrance hall and staircase with mosaic floor and wall panels. Elaborately tiled directors' lavatory. Exterior has geometric and encaustic tile infills over windows.

Maws Tile Works, Jackfield, Telford, Shropshire (now a craft centre). Tile factory of 1883 designed by Charles Lynam of Stoke-on-Trent. Exterior tile panel over entrance gate. Tiled entrance hall and staircase with 1914–18 war memorial in tiles. Floor of original showroom remains.

Queen Alexandra's House, Kensington Gore, London SW7. Building of 1887 originally intended as a hostel for students of the arts. Sir Henry Doulton donated the extensive ceramic decorations used internally. Dining room has 12 panels depicting famous figures from the history of ceramics and music. The designers and painters of the panels were J Eyre, J H McLennan, W J Nunn and E Lewis.

Royal Scottish Museum, Chambers Street, Edinburgh. Sample pavements of tiles from leading manufacturers adjacent to the Great Hall of Francis Fowke's building (1861–75). Original geometric tiled floor of main hall has now been destroyed.

Victoria and Albert Museum, Cromwell Road, South Kensington, London SW7. West or Ceramic Staircase designed by F W Moody and executed by Minton 1865–71. Relief faience panels and friezes on walls. Ceramic mosaic pavement to landing and tiled risers to steps. Ceilings, domes and spandrels have painted decoration on hexagonal tiles. Ceramic memorial to Sir Henry Cole (also designed by F W Moody) added in 1878.
Centre Refreshment Room 1868. Four tile-clad columns designed and modelled by James Gamble and made by Minton Hollins. Frieze at cornice level of letter tiles designed by Godfrey Sykes. Floor tiles (red octagons and black squares) by Maws. Grill Room 1868–70. Tile panels in blue and white designed by Sir

Edward Poynter. Smaller panels depict mythical subjects. Above are 16 large panels representing the months and seasons, painted by a class of female students from the South Kensington School of Art . Lavatories 1868. Walls tiled with octagonal tiles bearing lions, unicorns, crowns and V&A monograms. Made by Minton Hollins.

The Gothic Revival

All Saints Church, 7 Margaret Street, London W1. Designed by William Butterfield in 1849-59. Tiled floor uses geometric shapes of tiles as well as stone and marble to create ever-increasing complexity as altar is approached. Walls of nave have mixture of tiles and marble. North aisle wall, West wall and nave side of tower wall (1873, 1889 and 1891 respectively) have large pictorial panels of tiles with biblical figures designed by Butterfield, painted by Alexander Gibbs and fired by Henry Poole & Sons.

Cathedral Church of St Mary and St Chad, Lichfield, Staffordshire. Sanctuary floor 1861. Donated by Colin Minton Campbell as memorial to his uncle, Herbert Minton. Incorporates seven large circular tiles with designs of Old Testament scenes, reminiscent of medieval Chertsey tiles. Presbytery and Choir floor 1861-2. Patterned and geometric tiles from Minton with large *champlevé* roundels to an overall layout by George Gilbert Scott. Off Lady Chapel, walls of Bishop Selwyn's monument lined with painted tiles (Minton Hollins 1878) depicting scenes from New Zealand (including Maoris) and coal miners in Staffordshire.

Chapter House, Westminster Abbey, London SW1. One of the best preserved medieval tiled floors in Britain with replica replacements by Minton laid during the restoration of 1866-72 by Sir George Gilbert Scott.

Church of the Holy Innocents, Highnam, Gloucestershire. Designed by Henry Woodyer in 1849-51. Elaborate internal wall painting by T Gambier Parry is complemented by rich tile pavements in chancel and sanctuary.

Church of St John the Evangelist, 137

President Kennedy Avenue, Montreal, Canada. Baptistry floor tiles 1877 by Colin Minton Campbell. Chancel and sanctuary tiles laid in 1890s by Maws.

Church of Saint-Jean de Montmartre, 19 rue des Abbesses, Paris, France. Shaped ceramics by Bigot used to decorate reinforced concrete construction by Anatole de Baudot 1897-1904.

Hazlewood Castle, near Tadcaster, West Yorkshire. Gravestone to William Joseph Vavasour, who died in 1860, decorated with heraldic tiles.

New Palace of Westminster, London SW1. Tiles laid between 1847 and early 1870s. Extensive and elaborate encaustic tile pavements by Minton in St Stephen's Hall, Central Lobby, Lord's Lobby and the Royal Gallery. Fireplaces in Prince's Chamber have tiled cheeks.

St Edith's Church, Bishop Wilton, East Yorkshire. Designed by J L Pearson 1858-9. Sanctuary pavement of Godwin tiles in circular arrangements inspired by Jervaulx Abbey.

St Giles Church, Cheadle, Staffordshire. Designed by A W N Pugin 1841-6 who was also responsible for some of the floor tile designs which are used throughout the church. Inscriptions using encaustic letter tiles in north and south porches. Reredos of chapel of the Blessed Sacrament has porcelain tiles enriched with gilding.

St John the Evangelist Church, Rhosymedre, Clwyd. Church of 1837 with porch, aisles, chancel and sanctuary floors laid with J C Edwards geometrics and encaustics in 1887. Elaborate tiled reredos and dado made at Trefynant Tile Works in 1906 and erected as a memorial to J C Edwards.

St Peter's Church, Queen Square, Wolverhampton, West Midlands. Encaustic memorial tiles set diagonally into plastered west wall of nave near gallery steps.

Temple Church, off Fleet Street, London EC4. Restored 1841-2. The pioneering Minton tile pavement laid then was badly damaged by bombing in 1941. Surviving floor tiles were

relaid in the triforium of the rotunda.

Trinity Church, Copley Square, Boston, Mass., USA. Designed by H H Richardson and John La Farge 1873 onwards. Dust-pressed encaustic tiles, probably French, in west vestibule.

Cool, Clean and Hygienic
Dairies
College Farm, 45 Fitzalan Road, Finchley, London N3. 1882 dairy building (originally with thatched roof). Interior walls lined with Minton tiles including 'rustic figures' series.
Easton Park, Easton, near Wickham Market, Woodbridge, Suffolk. Octagonal dairy building of 1870 with geometric tiled floor and central fountain. *Pâte-sur-pâte* tiles decorated with flowers (Maws) in groups of four on walls between windows.

Fountains
Drinking fountain, Alexandra Road, Clevedon, Avon. Doulton-ware drinking fountain of c. 1900 with lower basin for animals. Glazed stoneware in rich colours, mainly green, brown and blue.

Butchers' shops
9 High Street, Axbridge, Somerset. Stall riser of decorative tiles with bull's head in blue in the centre. Pilasters of white glazed brick flank the doorway, one with bull's head.
11 Newport, Lincoln. Green glazed 'brick' tiling outside. Interior walls lined with tiles including four hand-painted panels signed and dated R W Jones, 1908. Panels depict cows, sheep and pigs.
30 St James' Street, Kings Lynn, Norfolk. Late nineteenth-century butcher's shop with six pictorial tiles of farm animals flanking the doorways.
Harrods Meat Hall, Brompton Road, London SW1. Elaborate scheme designed by W J Neatby and made by Doultons, 1901. Includes continuous high-level medieval hunting frieze. Jesse Smith, Black Jack Street, Cirencester, Gloucestershire. Art Nouveau-style lettering on a stall riser reading 'Pork Butchers'. Four-tile panel of pig's head in doorway.

Dairy Shops
Blake's Lock Museum, Gas Works Road, Reading, Berkshire. Displays three tube-lined tile panels from for-

mer dairy shop in London Street, Reading.

Public Baths
Beverley Road Baths, Hull. Elaborate interior tiling scheme of 1905. Lister Drive Baths, Liverpool. Tiled entrance hall and staircase of 1904.

Public Lavatories
Gentlemen's lavatory, Marketplace, Hull. Underground. Elaborate tiling and architectural faience with columns and friezes.
Gentlemen's lavatory, Pierhead, Rothesay, Isle of Bute, Argyll, Scotland. Built 1899-1900, designed by Rothesay architect John Russell Thompson. Tiled walls, floor of ceramic mosaic and 20 Twyfords ceramic urinal stalls decorated and glazed to imitate marble.

Hospitals
Bedford General Hospital, Kempston Road, Bedford. Designed by H Percy Adams and built in 1898. Twenty pictorial panels depicting nursery rhymes. Tiles made by Maws and decorated by W B Simpson and Sons, London. Artist and designer Philip H Newman
Paddington Green Children's Hospital, Paddington Green, London W2. Outpatients' Department was rebuilt in 1911 and 15 pictorial panels installed. Their subjects range from Peter Pan (after Arthur Rackham) and Scouting to topographical scenes of Finchingfield village and White Stone Pond, Hampstead
Royal Victoria Infirmary, Newcastle-upon-Tyne. The hospital was designed on the pavilion system by local architect W L Newcombe and hospital specialist H Percy Adams. Built between 1901 and 1906. Children's wards have 55 pictorial tile panels by Doultons. Artists include William Rowe, J H McLennan and Margaret E Thompson. Subjects are predominantly nursery rhymes and traditional children's stories.

Railway Stations
Haarlem Station, Jansweg, Haarlem, Holland. Rebuilt 1904 to designs by D A N Margadant. Widespread use of white and coloured glazed brick, together with tile panels, to convey information pictorially.
Shrub Hill Station, Shrub Hill Road, Worcester. Built c. 1865. Cast-iron waiting room etc. with majolica tiles

used to fill panels. Trade tile in recessed central bay indicates manufacture by Maw & Co, Broseley.

North Eastern Railway route maps
Examples of these survive at York, Scarborough, Whitby and Beverley railway stations, all in Yorkshire.

Guastavino tile vaulting
Grand Central Terminal, 42nd Street and Park Avenue N Side, New York, USA. 1903–13. Tile vaulting left exposed in parts of the lower level and in Grand Central Oyster Bar.

Tiles and the Home
Exteriors
Good examples of the external use of tiles on domestic houses can be seen in the following locations:
10 Stonegate, York. Façade clad in geometric and encaustic tiles (Maws) at first- and second-floor levels.

Amsterdam, Holland. Houses of 1880–1910 in streets around the Vondel Park to the west of the Rijksmuseum are especially rich in tiles, often in a strong Art Nouveau style. Particularly good examples are found at 2 Jacob Obrechtstraat, 62-68 Van Eeghenstraat, 77-79 Vondelstraat and 15 and 17 Jan Luikenstraat.

Beauvais, France. Avenue Victor-Hugo has a number of houses with exterior tiles and architectural faience by local makers, especially Greber. Numbers 12 and 15 are particularly impressive.

Crewe, Cheshire. This railway town, close to tile factories in The Potteries, has many examples of tiled floors and dados to the entrance porches of terraced houses. Nantwich Road and streets off it, such as Alton Street and Smallman Road, are particularly good examples.

Ghent, Belgium. Good Art-Nouveau tiling in houses in Prinses Clementinalaan and Koningen Elisabethlaan, both close to the railway station.

Glasgow. Tiled entrances to tenement buildings ('Wally Closes') survive in Glasgow's West End such as Hyndland district and in outer districts such as Gourock (Kempock Street and Cardwell Road) and Greenock (Margaret Street).

Roath and Pontcanna districts of Cardiff, South Wales. Tiled entrance porches are abundant here in late Victorian and Edwardian houses. Particularly good examples are Ninian Road which is adjacent to Roath Park and nearby streets such as Alfred Street (1891-6), Diana Street (1891-5) and Angus Street (1891-5).

Interiors
Domestic interiors using tiles are frequently in private occupation and the examples given are therefore restricted to those where access is possible.

Cragside, Rothbury, Morpeth, Northumberland (National Trust). Country house designed by R Norman Shaw 1869–84 for Lord Armstrong. Tiled dado to hallway and staircase. Blue and white Dutch tiles lining plunge bath.

Croesawdy, New Road, Newtown, Powys. An 1880s house of woollen-mill owner. Maws' patent mosaic floor to hallway. Tiled fireplaces and large tiles used in wooden panelled archway in hall.

The Grange (Art Gallery of Ontario), 317 Dundas Street W, Toronto, Ontario, Canada. Library fireplace with 22 Shakespeare tiles designed by J Moyr Smith for Mintons' China Works.

Highbury, 4 Yew Tree Road, Moseley, Birmingham 13. Designed by John Henry Chamberlain and built 1878-80 for Joseph Chamberlain (politician and no relation). Hall and staircase walls lined with tiles used together with marquetry and plaster panels. Several tiled fireplaces.

Linley Sambourne House, 18 Stafford Terrace, London W8 (Victorian Society). Tiled bedroom fireplaces.

Longfellow House, 105 Brattle Street, Cambridge, Mass., USA (US National Park Service). Bedroom fireplaces with English eighteenth-century printed tiles featured in Longfellow's poetry.

Valley Hotel, Ironbridge, Telford, Shropshire. Formerly Severn House and home of Arthur Maw. Geometric and encaustic tiled floor. Dado to hall and staircase and archway of high-relief majolica tiles.

The Architecture of Grandeur and Illusion
Cardiff Castle, Castle Street, Cardiff, South Wales. Painted wall tiles (1875-81) designed by William Burges and used in Summer Smoking Room and Roof Garden. Tile frieze in Nursery painted by H W Lonsdale. Encaustic tile pavements in Summer Smoking Room and (in the form of a maze) in Chaucer Room.

Castle of Sanmezzano, Valdarno, near Florence, Italy. A Moorish-style palace in Tuscany (1853-73) with lavish use of mosaics and tiles and including Hall of Peacocks with geometric tiled dado.

Leighton House, 12 Holland Park Road, Kensington, London W14. Designed for Lord Leighton by George Aitchison, 1864–66. Arab Hall (1877-9) has Syrian and Iznik tiles with additional work by William De Morgan and mosaics by Walter Crane.

Nevill's New Turkish Baths (now Gallipoli Restaurant), 7 Bishopsgate Churchyard, off Old Broad Street, London EC2. Interior of 1894 (below ground) has shaped tiles designed by architect G Harold Elphick and made by Craven Dunnills.

Public Houses
The Bartons Arms, 152 High Street, Birmingham 6. Built 1899–1901 for Mitchells and Butlers by architect Mr Brassington of James and Lister Lea. Impressive interior tiling by Minton Hollins includes a hunting scene panel in staircase hall.

The Church Tavern, Lichfield Road (junction with Waterworks Street), Birmingham 6. Built for the Holt Brewery Company in 1900-1 to designs by C H Collett. Street front covered in brown faience on ground floor. Tiling in Public Bar, Smoke Room and entrance passage in largely relief-decorated tiles of very varied colours by Maw and Co.

The Crown Liquor Saloon, Great Victoria Street (junction with Amelia Street), Belfast. Designed by Mr Flanagan. Exterior with tiles, faience and mosaic. Interior has geometric floor and ceramic bar front. All supplied by Craven Dunnills. Restored 1979–85 and owned by the National Trust.

The Mountain Daisy, Hylton Road, Sunderland, Co. Durham. Rebuilt 1900-2 by local architects W & T R Milburn. Back bar has ceramic mosaic floor, all walls fully tiled and quarter circle ceramic bar front by Craven Dunnills. Tile panels depict local scenes such as Cragside, Newcastle bridges and Durham Cathedral.

Civic Buildings
Bibliothèque Nationale, 58 rue Richelieu, Paris, France. The reading room (completed in 1868 to designs by Henri Labrouste) has nine domes filled with shaped ceramic tiles by Copeland of Stoke-on-Trent.

The Old Library, The Hayes, Cardiff, South Wales. Built 1880-82 to designs by Seward and Thomas. Entrance corridor lined with majolica, printed and painted tiles by Maws including designs by Walter Crane.

Osgoode Hall, Queen Street, Toronto, Ontario, Canada. Building work of 1857–60 includes the laying of a magnificent geometric tiled floor by Maws on the ground floor.

Pennsylvania Academy of the Fine Arts, Broad and Cherry Streets, Philadelphia, USA. Designed by Frank Furness and George Hewitt in 1872–6. English encaustic tiled floor and dado on ground floor.

St George's Hall, Lime Street, Liverpool. Perhaps the grandest encaustic tile pavement of the nineteenth century, made by Minton in 1853. Figurative border attributed to Alfred Stevens.

Town Hall, Rochdale, Lancashire. Designed by W H Crossland in 1866–71. Entrance hall has encaustic tiled floor made by Minton and designed by Heaton, Butler & Bayne. Twenty-one heraldic panels feature the Royal Coat of Arms, together with those of the County of Lancaster and Borough of Rochdale.

Town Hall, Westgate, Leeds. Building designed by Cuthbert Brodrick and built 1853-8. Entrance hall paved with 'civic encaustics' by Minton.
Commercial Buildings
10 Norfolk Street, Manchester (formerly Palatine Bank). Built in 1910 by Briggs, Wolstenholme & Thornely. Domed banking hall has three large

panels depicting Trading, Shipping and The Arts by A E Pearce and J H McLennan.

Bank of Scotland, Threadneedle Street, London EC2. Designed by J Macvicar Anderson, 1902. Glazed ceramic ceiling to main banking hall by Burmantofts of Leeds.

Lloyds Bank, Fleet Street, London EC4. (Originally The Palsgrove Hotel) Built in 1883 to design by G Cuthbert. Impressive entrance in coloured Doulton ware and mosaic. Adjoining corridor set with tiling displaying putti and swag motifs and heraldic panel. Banking area has tile panels showing scenes from Ben Jonson's plays.

Michelin Building, Fulham Road, London SW3. Thirty-four tile pictures on exterior brick piers depicting scenes of motoring successes on Michelin tyres. Building designed by François Epinasse and opened in 1911.

Pearl Assurance Building, St John's Lane, Liverpool. Designed by Alfred Waterhouse and built in 1890s. Burmantofts glazed tiles in browns, greens and pale yellow used to create complete tiled interior (including good fireplace) to former public office on north-west corner of building (now a wine bar).

The Craft Tradition

63 rue de Calais, Beauvais, France. Former workshops of Greber brothers, 1911. Remarkable decoration of façade includes life-like chameleons flanking the windows and greeny-brown frogs along the cornice. Large sculpted panel depicts potter at wheel.

Bristol Royal Infirmary, Marlborough Street, Bristol, Avon. Built in 1906–11 by H Percy Adams and Charles Holden. De Morgan tiled fireplace and overmantel in entrance hall.

Casa Vicens, Carrer de les Carolines 24, Barcelona, Spain. A house built in 1883–5 containing early work by Gaudi, commissioned by a ceramic tile manufacturer. The walls of the house are gridded with bands of tiling.

Clock Tower, The Triangle, Clevedon, near Bristol, Avon. Tiles made by Sir

Edmund Elton and presented, along with the tower, to mark Queen Victoria's Diamond Jubilee in 1897.

Debenham House, 8 Addison Road, London W14. Designed by Halsey Ricardo and built in 1905 for Sir Ernest Debenham. The exterior expresses Ricardo's theory of structural polychromy using white Doulton Carrara ware and turquoise and green glazed bricks by Burmantofts. Long entrance corridor has panels of De Morgan tiles and these are also used throughout the house in great variety for fireplaces and bathroom dados.

Everard Building, Broad Street, Bristol, Avon. Façade clad in Doulton's polychrome stoneware, designed by W J Neatby and built in 1900–1 for Edward Everard, printer.

Fonthill, Doylestown, Pennsylvania, USA. Remarkable house built by Henry Chapman Mercer for himself using re-inforced concrete poured in situ. It is richly and originally decorated with his own forms of tile.

Güell Park, Carrer Bellesguard 16-20, Barcelona, Spain. Built 1900–14 by Gaudi. Various structural and decorative elements of the park such as serpentine-like benches are covered with broken tiles in Gaudi's characteristic style.

New York City – subway stations. Arts and Crafts tiles, plaques and mosaics can be found at: Astor Place (Lexington Avenue Line, 1905). Relief brown beaver is a reminder of John Jacob Astor who made his fortune in the fur trade. Plaques by Grueby Faience Co., Boston. Bleecker Street (Lexington Avenue Line, 1904). Blue glazed tiles forming oval plaques bearing white lettering by Grueby Faience Co., Boston. Fulton Street (Lexington Avenue Line, 1905). Relief-decorated ceramic plaques by Rookwood Pottery depict Robert Fulton's steamship, the Clermont.

Perkins School for the Blind, 175 North Beacon Street, Watertown, Massachusetts, USA. Built c. 1913. Architect R Clipson Sturgis used relief-decorated Grueby tile features in corridors and some rooms to assist orientation of blind occupants.

Postman's Park, Off King Edward Street, London EC1. Wall covered with hand-lettered tiles made by Doultons commemorating heroic deaths. The idea was conceived by the painter G F Watts.

St George's Church, Osborne Road, Jesmond, Newcastle-upon-Tyne. Built by T R Spence in 1888–9. Chancel has glazed tiles with roundels of the Evangelists by G W Rhead.

Sunlight Chambers, Essex Quay, Dublin. Designed by E A Ould of Liverpool and built in 1901 as the Irish head office of Lever Brothers soap manufacturers. Exterior bears 12 long ceramic panels at first- and second-floor level illustrating the process of soap manufacture and use. These were probably designed by Conrad Dressler and made at Medmenham Pottery, near Marlow in Buckinghamshire.

The Tabard Inn, Bath Road/Acton Green, Bedford Park, Chiswick, London W4. Built 1880. Public bar has De Morgan tiles on the upper walls and saloon bar has fireplace with tiles above.

Wightwick Manor, Wightwick Bank, Wolverhampton, West Midlands (The National Trust). Built in 1887–93 for industrialist Theodore Mander to designs by Edward Ould. Fireplaces throughout the house use a wide variety of De Morgan designs, together with Dutch tiles imported by Thomas Elsley. Those in the billiard room fireplace are Dutch tiles of a design derived from William Morris's Daisy pattern.

Museum Collections and Organizations

Museums
Belgium
Kortrijk (Courtrai) Municipal Museum of Fine Art, Broeikaai 6, Kortrijk 8500, Belgium (eighteenth- and nineteenth-century Flemish tiles).

Britain
Birmingham Museum and Art Gallery, Chamberlain Square, Birmingham B3 3DH (industrial gallery which includes good examples of William De Morgan tiles). British Museum, Great Russell Street, London WC1B 3DG (nineteenth-century gallery).
Gladstone Pottery Museum, Uttoxeter Road, Longton, Stoke-on-Trent ST3 1PQ.
Jackfield Tile Museum, Ironbridge Gorge Museum, Ironbridge, Telford, Shropshire TF8 7AW.
Minton Museum, Royal Doulton Ltd, London Road, Stoke-on-Trent ST3 1QD.
People's Palace Museum, Glasgow Green, Glasgow G40 1AT.
Rowley's House Museum, Barker Street, Shrewsbury, Shropshire SY1 1QT.
Stoke-on-Trent City Museum and Art Gallery, Bethesda Street, Hanley, Stoke-on-Trent ST1 3DE.
Victoria and Albert Museum, Cromwell Road, South Kensington, London SW7 2RL.
William Morris Gallery, Water House, Lloyd Park, Forest Road, Walthamstow, London E17 4PP.
Wrexham Maelor Heritage Centre, 47-49 King Street, Wrexham, Clwyd LL11 1HR.

France
Musée départemental de l'Oise, Ancien Palais Episcopal, 60006 Beauvais, France.
Musée de la Céramique Architecturale, Auneuil (not yet open to the public – please address all correspondence to the Ecomusée).
Ecomusée des pays de l'Oise, 2 Rue du Franc-Marché, 60000 Beauvais, France.

Germany
Keramic Museum Mettlach, Schloss Ziegelberg, D-6642 Mettlach, Germany (Museum of Villeroy & Boch).

Holland
Boymans van Beuningen Museum, Mathenesserlaan 18-20, 3000 CG, Rotterdam, Zuid Holland.
It Noflik Ste Tile Museum, Eikenzoom 10, 6731 BH, Otterlo, Gelderland, Holland.
Huis Lambert van Meerton, Oude Delft 199, 2611 HD, Delft, Zuid Holland.
Museum het Princessehof, Grote Kerkstraat 11, 8911 DZ, Leeuwarden, Friesland, Holland.
Rijksmuseum, Stadhouderskade 42, 1071 XZ, Amsterdam, Noord Holland.

Portugal
Museu Nasional do Azulejo, 4 Rua Madre de Deus/Xabregas, 1900 Lisbon, Portugal.

USA
Cooper-Hewitt Museum (The Smithsonian Institution's National Museum of Design), 2 East 91st Street, New York, NY 10128, USA.
Fonthill Museum/Mercer Museum/Moravian Tile Works, Doylestown, Pennsylvania, PA 18901, USA.
Museum of Fine Arts, 465 Huntington Avenue, Boston, Massachussetts, MA 02115, USA.
National Museum of American History, Smithsonian Institution, Washington DC 20560, USA.
New Jersey State Museum, 205 W State Street, Trenton, New Jersey 08625, USA.

Organizations
Britain
Tiles and Architectural Ceramics Society, Reabrook Lodge, 8 Sutton Road, Shrewsbury, Shropshire SY2 6DD.
The national society responsible for the study and protection of tiles and architectural ceramics. It is open to anyone with an interest in tiles and decorative ceramics related to buildings. The society produces three publications: *Glazed Expressions*, an illustrated magazine published twice yearly; *Newsletter*, containing news items of a more immediate nature published four times a year and a *Journal*, a scholarly publication carrying articles

of original research and published biannually.
The Victorian Society, 1 Priory Gardens, Bedford Park, London W4 1TT.
The national society which exists to prevent the needless destruction of Victorian and Edwardian buildings of architectural interest and to promote understanding and appreciation of the architecture and decorative arts of the period. The society publishes a series of booklets entitled *Care for Victorian Houses*; number two in the series is *Decorative Tiles*.

France
GRECB (Groupe de Recherches et d'Etudes de la Céramique du Beauvais), 8 Avenue Victor Hugo, 60000 Beauvais, France.
OMAGE (Office Marlychois d'Archeologie et Groupe d'Etudes), c/o Bruno Bentz, 44 Chemin du Bas des Ormes, 78160 Marly Le Roi, France.

Holland
The Society of Friends of the Tile Museum It Noflik Ste, Treubstraat 29, 9402 KH Assen, Holland.

Spain
José Luis Porcar, Instituto de Promoción Cerámica, Diputacion Provincial, Plaza De Las Aulas 7, 12001 Castellon, Spain.

USA
Friends of Terra Cotta, Susan Tunick, 771 West End Avenue, Apt 10E, New York, NY 10025, USA.
Tile Heritage Foundation, PO Box 1850, Healdsburg, CA 95448, USA. The foundation is a non-profit corporation dedicated to promoting an awareness and appreciation of ceramic surfaces in the United States. It publishes a quarterly bulletin entitled *Flashpoint*.

Glossary

Architectural faience
A term evolved in the nineteenth century and used to describe large moulded or cast slabs or blocks of glazed and fired clay; these can be structural but are more often a purely decorative form of cladding. (Known as glazed terra cotta in North America.)

Bianco-sopra-bianco
(From the Italian, meaning white-on-white) A technique developed in Bristol during the eighteenth century; it enabled details to be painted in pure white on the bluish-white tin-glazed ground of the tile to give a subtle and original effect.

Biscuit tile
A tile after an initial firing which has fixed its dimensions and shape prior to decorating or glazing.

Champlevé
The technique whereby a resinous mastic composition is used to fill depressions or channels carved to form a design in a stone tile.

Cuenca
(From the Spanish, meaning a bowl) A technique whereby moulds were used to form the pattern as hollows in the surface of the tile, leaving a raised outline to keep different glaze colours separate. The technique was known particularly to sixteenth-century potters in Seville but it was also a forerunner to nineteenth-century dust-pressed imitations.

Cuerda seca
(From the Spanish, meaning dry cord) A decorative technique using black outlines (the dry cord) to separate glaze colours. This technique was known to the Moors who used it for elaborate polychromatic tile decoration. The process was revived in the nineteenth century. The black outlines, composed probably of wax thinned with spirit and mixed with powdered manganese, lay on the surface of the tile and the spaces between were thickly painted with coloured glazes which shrank from the greasy outlines during firing, the manganese remaining as the black outline.

Delftware
Derived from the Dutch town of Delft but applied to Dutch and English wares decorated in the following manner. Fundamental to this type of decoration is the opaque white tin glaze onto which a design is painted – polychromy is perfectly possible but blue is the favoured colour. The design invariably includes corner motifs and a central subject which tends to be landscape, figurative, etc.

Die
Metal or plaster-of-Paris plates placed at the top and bottom of the tile-forming box. These dies gave the front and back of the tile its particular pattern. They were always used in conjunction with a tile press.

Dust clay
Prepared clay (see *Plastic clay*) dried and ground to a fine powder, then sieved and sprayed with water to achieve a small percentage of moisture. This form of clay, used with a tile press, revolutionized the production of tiles in the nineteenth century. The dust clay could be fed into the mould-box of the press and seconds later, under pressure of the screw press (exerting some 30 tons of pressure) a firm, hard and compact tile could be lifted off. The other big advantage of dust clay lay in the enormous reduction in drying time before the tiles were fired.

Encaustic tile
A ceramic tile made either of plastic clay with slip infills or wholly of dust clay. The design on the tile is reliant upon coloured clays let into the main body of the tile rather than surface decoration. The coloured clays are fused together during firing; it is critical that the combining clays share precisely the same shrinkage rates.

Geometric tile pavements
Combinations of plain tiles of various geometric shapes (triangles, hexagons etc) and colours, the forms being made to bear a definite geometrical relationship one to the other.

Glaze
The impervious vitrified final coating which gives a tile its glossy sheen. The glaze is applied by dipping into or spraying onto the tile surface a

solution of powdered glaze suspended in water, then firing at a high temperature.

Guastavino tiled vaulting
The bonding of layers of tiles in a herringbone fashion to create a lightweight and fireproof vault which needs the minimum of propping during construction. This system originated in the Mediterranean countries and was perfected in the Catalonia region of Spain. It was introduced into America in the 1880s by Rafael Guastavino and his son (of the same name) and there it flourished under the new conditions.

Impressed tiles
Linear decoration impressed into a tile through the use of metal moulds bearing the design in raised outline. This form of decoration is sometimes known as counter-relief. During firing coloured glaze pooled in the outlines makes the pattern more distinct. Craven Dunnills and Godwins made reproductions of medieval tiles using this technique.

Lustre
The rich iridescent sheen used as a decorative effect on some wall tiles. The lustre finish was achieved by depositing a thin film of metal derived from metallic salts mixed with the glaze on the surface of the tile and fixed in a reducing atmosphere (ie the kiln was starved of oxygen at a certain temperature). Ruby lustre (derived from copper sulphate) was the most common but other colours, such as gold, green and blue, could be achieved through the use of different metal salts. Many manufacturers used this technique but De Morgan, Maws, Pilkingtons, Craven Dunnills and JC Edwards used it extensively.

Maiolica
Initially the term by which brightly coloured and sometimes lustre-painted Spanish wares were known in Italy. However, these soon became an Italian speciality. The painted decoration is applied over an opaque white glaze containing tin oxide.

Majolica tiles
Usually associated with relief-decorated tiles, though not exclusively so. Joseph François Léon Arnoux, the art director at Minton's China Works

(1849–92), is credited with the development of the opaque, brightly coloured 'majolica' glazes which sought to emulate the quality of fifteenth- and sixteenth-century 'Maiolica' or tin-glazed earthenware, with its brightly painted decoration.

Marquise tiles
Inlaid stone tiles which originated in and around St Omer in northern France. They probably inspired the thirteenth-century production of inlaid ceramic tiles in areas where coloured stones and marble were unavailable.

Mosaic
Small pieces of fired clay (glass and marble were also used to produce mosaic) cut with a guillotine and then sorted into colours and sizes ready for pasting, face down, onto full-size cartoons at the manufactory. These sheets were transported to the site of installation, cemented into place and the paper cartoon then removed from the face.

Pâte-sur-pâte
(From the French, meaning paste-on-paste) A process introduced into England c. 1870 by Louis Marc Solon who came from France and was employed by Mintons. It involved a time-consuming building-up of thin layers of slip using a brush, until the intended decoration was achieved. Some manufacturers, eg Maws, developed a mechanically formed and therefore cheaper version – though its effect was less subtle.

Patent mosaic
Made up of dust-pressed tiles, sometimes with irregular edges, which had the markings of mosaic pressed into their surface (which was covered with different coloured dust clays) to create the desired pattern. When these tiles were keyed into one another on the floor and cement brushed over the mosaic impressions, the resulting effect was quite convincing but completed at a fraction of the time and expense of real mosaic.

Plastic clay
(Ordinarily any clay that is mouldable) For nineteenth-century tile-making the raw clay (which was dug from the ground and contained impurities) would have been weath-

ered (that is, left outside for the weather to break it down) and then placed in a huge mixing machine (a blunger) with water and agitated until the clay and the water combined to the consistency of cream (slip). This slip then passed through a series of increasingly fine sieves and across a series of magnets which intercepted any particles of iron in the clay. If not removed, these particles would develop as specks in the tile later on and spoil it. At this stage the clay slip was either spread on plaster beds to dry or dried in filter presses. The clay was then ready for use.

Relief tiles
Tiles bearing a raised design; the design is formed when clay is pressed into a mould.

Slip
Clay mixed with water to form a liquid of a smooth pouring consistency.

Stoneware tiles
Made from a very siliceous clay or a composition of clay and flint which can withstand extremely high firing temperatures, thus rendering the tiles impervious to moisture and therefore most suitable for external application.

Terracotta
(From the Italian, meaning baked earth) The term generally applied to unglazed architectural ceramics and sculpture. In North America it also includes glazed architectural wares.

Tesserae
The individual units in a tessellated pavement. Strictly speaking, the term refers to mosaic but it was also applied to geometric tiles.

Tile press
A piece of machinery raised on four legs consisting of a box for the clay and a centrally positioned screw thread attached to an overhead fly wheel which, when operated at speed, produced several tons of pressure onto the clay in the box, thus forming the tile.

Tin-glaze
A glaze made by adding tin oxide to a lead glaze which, when fired, becomes an opaque white colour.

Transfer-printing (onto a tile)

The transfer of a printed image from a metal plate, wood block or lithographic stone by the application of thin paper or gelatinous 'bats' to the surface of the tile prior to firing.

Tube-lining
The piping of thin trails of slip onto a tile from the nozzle of a hand-held rubber bulb (a technique similar to cake icing) in order to form raised lines. These lines separate the areas of the coloured glazes which are applied secondarily. This method was especially suitable for 'one-offs' and small runs such as pictorial panels. A similar but mass-produced effect was achieved by using metal dies on which the outlines were depressed, thus producing raised outlines on the tile; these lines are always regular and of the same colour as the body of the tile.

Underglaze decoration
Printed or painted decoration applied to biscuit-fired tiles prior to a transparent glaze. Because the decoration is completely covered by a clear glaze fired at high temperatures, it is extremely durable. However, not all glaze colours can withstand such high temperatures and consequently underglaze decoration is limited.

Wall tiles
As distinct from floor tiles; wall tiles are generally made of earthenware clays and have a decorated, glazed surface (hand-painted, printed, tube-lined, relief-moulded etc.) which would be unsuitable for foot traffic. They tend to be thinner and the body is of a more porous nature than floor tiles.

For a more detailed list of tile decorating techniques see *Glazed Expressions* No 17, Autumn 1988 published by the Tiles and Architectural Ceramics Society.

Bibliography and Sources

Note: place of publication is London unless otherwise stated.

General
Allwood, Rosamond. *Victorian Tiles*. Wolverhampton Art Gallery, 1978.
Austwick, Jill and Brian. *The Decorated Tile*. Pitman House, 1980.
Barnard, Julian. *Victorian Ceramic Tiles*. Studio Vista, 1972.
Barnard, Julian. *The Decorative Tradition*. Architectural Press, 1973.
Furnival, William J. *Leadless Decorative Tiles, Faience, and Mosaic*. Stone, Furnival, 1904.
van Lemmen, Hans. 'Nineteenth Century Dutch Tiles' in *Journal of Tiles and Architectural Ceramics Society* Vol 1, pp1-7, 1982.
van Lemmen, Hans and Malam, John (eds). *Fired Earth: 1000 Years of Tiles in Europe*. Shepton Beauchamp, Somerset: Richard Dennis Publications, 1991.
van Lemmen, Hans. *Tiles in Architecture*. Lawrence King, 1993.
Lochnan, Katherine A. 'Victorian Tiles in Toronto' in *Canadian Collector* Vol 16, No 5, pp54-59, 1981.
Lockett, Terence A. *Collecting Victorian Tiles*. Woodbridge, Suffolk: Antique Collectors' Club, 1979.
Riley, Noel. *Tile Art*. Quintet, 1987.
Skinner, Deborah S, and van Lemmen, Hans. *Minton Tiles 1835–1935*. Stoke-on-Trent City Museum and Art Gallery, 1984.
La Céramique Architecturale des Années 1900 dans le Beauvaisis. Beauvais: Musée départemental de l'Oise, 1980.

Tradition and Sources
General
Berendsen, Anne. *Tiles: A general history*. Faber & Faber, 1967.
Forrer, R. *Geschichte der europaischen Fliesen-Keramik*. Strasbourg, 1901.
Lane, Arthur. *A Guide to the Collection of Tiles*. Victoria and Albert Museum, 1960.
van Lemmen, Hans. *Decorative Tiles throughout the Ages*. Bracken Books, 1988.
Meco, José and Marggraf, Rainer. *Fliesenkultur in Portugal*. Bramsche: Rasch Druckerei und Verlag, 1989.
Wires, E Stanley. 'Decorative Tiles, their contribution to Architecture and Ceramic Art' in *New England Architect*

and *Builder* Nos 14-17, 1960.

Middle Eastern and Islamic
Öney, Gonul. *Ceramic Tiles in Islamic Architecture*. Istanbul: Ada Press, 1987.
Petsopoulos, Yanni. *Tulips, Arabesques and Turbans*. Alexandria Press, 1982.

Medieval
Eames, Elizabeth. *English Medieval Tiles*. British Museum Publications, 1985.
Eames, Elizabeth. *Catalogue of Medieval Lead-Glazed Earthenware Tiles*, 2 vols. British Museum Publications, 1980.
Norton, Christopher. 'Medieval Tin-glazed Painted Tiles in North-West Europe' in *Medieval Archaeology* Vol 28, 1984.
Stopford, Jenny. *Monastic Mosaics – medieval tile pavements from great northern abbeys*. York: Bar Convent Museum, 1991.
Tillie, Willie. 'Flemish Inlaid Tiles' in *Glazed Expressions* 11, pp6-8, winter 1985.
Wight, Jane. *Medieval Floor Tiles*. John Baker, 1975.

Delftware
Hamilton, Suzanne C. 'Decorative fireplace tiles used in America' in *Antiques* Vol 121, pp768-775, February 1982. Covers eighteenth-century Dutch and English tiles.
Horne, Jonathan. *English Tin-Glazed Tiles*. J Horne Antiques, 1989.
de Jonge, CH. *Dutch Tiles*. Pall Mall Press, 1971.
Kelly, Alison. *Decorative Wedgwood in Architecture and Furniture*. New York: Born-Hawes Publishing, 1965 (see Chapter 15 'Tiles and Dairies'.)
van Lemmen, Hans. *Delftware Tiles*. Princes Risborough: Shire Publications, 1986.
Lewis, JM. *Welsh Medieval Paving Tiles*. Cardiff: National Museum of Wales, 1976.
Ray, Anthony. *English Delftware Tiles*. Faber & Faber, 1973.

The Marriage of Art and Industry
Archer, TC. 'On the Progress of our Art-Industries' in *Art Journal* Vol 13, pp333-4, 1874.
Benthall, Sir Paul. 'George Maw: A Versatile Victorian' in *National Trust Studies 1980*. Sotheby Parke Bernet, 1979.
Calder, Jenni. *Royal Scottish Museum: The Early Years*. Edinburgh: Royal Scottish Museum, 1984.
Herbert, Tony. 'Jackfield Decorative Tiles in Use' in *Industrial Archaeology*

Review Vol 3 No 2, pp146-152, 1979.
Herbert, Tony. 'Jackfield Decorative Tiles – A Victorian Art Industry' in *Design and Industry – The Effects of Industrialisation and Technical Change on Design*. Design Council, 1980.
Kay, Geoffrey. 'Charles Lynam – An Architect of Tile Factories' in *Journal of Tiles and Architectural Ceramics Society* Vol 4, pp21-28, 1992.
Maw, George. 'Appendix A. Catalogue of Specimens illustrating the Clays and Plastic Strata of Great Britain' in Reeks,T and Rudler, FW. *Catalogue of Specimens in the Museum of Practical Geology*, 1871.
McCarthy, James F (ed). *Great Industries of Great Britain*, Vol 3. Cassell, Petter & Gilpin, 1877.
Messenger, Michael. *Pottery and Tiles of the Severn Valley*. Remploy, 1979.
Physick, John. *The Victoria and Albert Museum: The History of its Building*. Oxford: Phaidon/Christie's, 1982.
Strachan, Shirley. 'Henry Powell Dunnill: A Victorian Tilemaster' in *Journal of Tiles and Architectural Ceramics Society* Vol 3, pp3-10, 1990.
Townsend, Everett. 'Development of the Tile Industry in the United States' in *Bulletin of the American Ceramic Society* Vol 22, No 5, May 1943.
Wood, Anne Mary (née Maw). Manuscript journal compiled after 1887. Held by the Maw family.
'Famous Art Workers: Messrs Maw & Co., Ironbridge' in *Journal of Decorative Art*, pp 135-142, September 1887.
'Report on Arts and Crafts Exhibition, 1888' in *Journal of Decorative Art*, pp4-7, January 1889.

The Gothic Revival
Beaulah, Kenneth. *Church Tiles of the Nineteenth Century*. Princes Risborough: Shire Publications, 1987.
Beaulah, Kenneth. 'Encaustic Tiles – a Nineteenth Century Viewpoint' in *Tiles and Architectural Ceramics Society Journal* Vol 4, pp15-20, 1992. This includes a reprint of two articles on encaustic tiles which appeared in the *Saturday Magazine* in 1843.
Brown, Philip and Dorothy. 'Obliterating Butterfield' in *Glazed Expressions* No 19, pp9-10, winter 1989–90.
Cartier, Jean. *Céramiques du Beauvaisis*. Paris: abc collection, 1984.
Crook, JM. 'The restoration of the Temple Church: ecclesiology and recrimination' in *Architectural History* Vol 8, pp39-51, 1965. For a contemporary account of the

restoration of Temple Church see *The Ecclesiologist* January 1842, No iii pp41-3 and *The Penny Magazine*, pp125-131 and 141-143, April 1843.
Cutts, Rev Edward L. *An Essay on Church Furniture and Decoration*. John Crockford, 1854.
Ferrey, Benjamin. *Recollections of A.N.Welby Pugin and his Father*. London, 1861.
Nichols, John G. *Examples of Inlaid Gothic Tiles*. London, 1841. Also *Examples of Encaustic Tiles*, 1842 and *Examples of Decorative Tiles*, 1845.
Pear, L Myers. *The Pewabic Pottery*. Des Moines, Indiana: Wallace-Homestead Book Co., 1976.
Shaw, Henry. *Specimens of Tile Pavements*. BM Pickering, 1858.
Thompson, Paul. *William Butterfield*. Routledge & Kegan Paul, 1971.
Wainwright, Clive. 'Encaustic tiles in the new Palace of Westminster' in *Tiles and Terracotta in London*, Tiles and Architectural Ceramics Society Tour Notes, 1981.
Annals of the Diocese of Lichfield, past and present; being a supplement to the Lichfield Church Calender, 1859. JH & J Parker, 1859. This lists churches receiving gifts of tiles from Herbert Minton.
'Church Building in Manchester' in *The Builder* 10 January 1880, p51.

Cool, Clean and Hygienic
Allsop, R Owen. *The Turkish Bath: its Design and Construction*. Spon, 1890.
Binney, Marcus, et al. *Taking the Plunge – the Architecture of Bathing*. Save Britain's Heritage, 1984. This includes a checklist of public baths in England and Wales up to 1939.
Collins, GR. 'The Transfer of Thin Masonry Vaulting from Spain to America' in *Journal of The Society of Architectural Historians* Vol 27 No 3, pp176-201, October 1968.
Green, Brigid G. *Milk for the Millions*. Barnet Library Local History Publications, 1983.
Greene, John, *Brightening the Long Days*. Gloucester: Tiles and Architectural Ceramics Society /Alan Sutton Publishing, 1987.
van Lemmen, Hans, 'Notes on Haarlem Station' in *Tiles in Amsterdam*, Tiles and Architectural Ceramics Society Tour Notes, 1987.
Morse, Barbara White. 'John Gardner Low and his original art tile fountain' in *Spinning Wheel* Vol 27, No 6, July/August 1971.
Pictures in Pottery – a note on some hospital wall decorations recently executed by

Doulton & Co. Ltd., Lambeth, London. Royal Doulton Potteries, 1904.
'Prince Albert's Dairy' in Architectural Review, pp414-6, December 1969.
Radkai, Marton. 'Cream of Dresden: The Pfund Dairy in Dresden' in World of Interiors, pp96-101, November 1991. An illustrated article on an 1892 dairy with Villeroy and Boch tiles.
Wilkins, Rachel. Turrets, Towels and Taps. Birmingham: City Museum and Art Gallery, 1984.

Tiles and the Home
Crane, Lucy. Art and the Formation of Taste. Macmillan, 1882.
Eastlake, Charles L. Hints on Household Taste. Longmans Green, 1878.
Hawes, Lloyd E. 'Longfellow, the poet, and Sadler, the tile printer' in Eleventh Wedgwood International Seminar. Dearborn, Michigan: Henry Ford Museum, 1966.
Herbert, Tony. 'Pictures round the fire' in The Traditional Fireplace, supplement to Traditional Homes Vol 4, No 11, pp18-24, November 1987.
van Lemmen, Hans, 'Art Nouveau Tiling' in Ceramics No 4, July/August 1986. Covers porch and exterior tiling on houses in Amsterdam.
van Lemmen, Hans. Tiled Furniture. Princes Risborough: Shire Publications, 1989.
Reed, Cleota. The Ward House. Syracuse, New York: Ward Wellington Ward Association, 1990.
Russell, Florence M. 'Close Encounters' in The Scots Magazine, pp527-533, February 1992. Illustrated article on tiled tenement closes in Glasgow.
The Use of Decorative Ceramic Tiles in Cardiff, c.1880–1920. Cardiff City Council, 1991.

The Architecture of Grandeur and Illusion
Atterbury, Paul, and Irvine, Louise. The Doulton Story. Stoke-on-Trent: Royal Doulton Tableware, 1979. Includes comprehensive list of the many impressive buildings featuring Doulton tiles, faience and terracotta.
Barnard, Julian. 'Victorian on the tiles the work of W.J. Neatby in ceramics' in The Architect, pp46-51, September 1971.
Crawford, Alan, Dunn, Michael, and Thorne, Robert. Birmingham Pubs 1880–1939. Gloucester: Alan Sutton, 1986.
Cunningham, Colin. Victorian and Edwardian Town Halls. Routledge &

Kegan Paul, 1981.
Curl, James S. 'The Victorian Public Houses of Belfast' in National Trust Studies 1980, pp54-65. Sotheby Parke Bernet, 1979.
Darby, Michael. The Islamic Perspective. The World of Islam Festival Trust, 1983.
Elwall, Robert. Bricks and Beer, English Pub Architecture 1830–1939. British Architectural Library, 1983.
Hitchmough, Wendy. The Michelin Building. Conran Octopus/ Heinemann, 1987.
Horne, AC, Jasieniecki, G, Liffen, J, and Rose, DL. 'A preliminary study of tiling on certain London underground railway platforms' in Glazed Expressions, pp4-5, summer 1982.
Knowles, Loraine. St. George's Hall, Liverpool. Liverpool: National Museums and Galleries on Merseyside, 1988.
Lyons, LB. A Handbook to the Pension Building. Washington DC: National Building Museum, 1989.
McWilliam, Colin. 'Cream of the Cafés' in Scottish Interiors Victorian. Edinburgh: Mowbray House Press, 1986.
Michail, MCT. 'The Castle of Sanmezzano' in FMR No 9, pp96-102, March 1985.
Pearson, Jenny. 'The Michelin Building' in Connoisseur, October 1975.
Pearson, Lynn. The Northumbrian Pub. Morpeth: Sandhill Press, 1989.
Porter, Venetia. 'William De Morgan and the Islamic Tiles of Leighton House' in Decorative Arts Society Journal No 16, pp76-79, 1992.
Sargent, Pauline. 'Painted Tiles by William Burges' in Antique Collector, pp101-108, March 1987. An illustrated article on painted tiles at Cardiff Castle.
Vickers,SJ. 'Architectural Treatment of Stations on the Dual System of Rapid Transit in New York City' in Architectural Record Vol 45, January 1919.

The Craft Tradition
Catleugh, Jon. William De Morgan Tiles. Trefoil Books, 1983.
Chase, Jim W. 'The Medmenham Pottery 2' in Glazed Expressions No 6, p3, spring 1984.
Dagnall, H. Postman's Park and its Memorials. Edgware, Middlesex: H. Dagnall, 1987.
Greenwood, Martin. Designs of William De Morgan. Shepton Beauchamp,

Somerset: Richard Dennis Publications, 1989.
Haslam, Malcolm. Elton Ware. Shepton Beauchamp, Somerset: Richard Dennis Publications, 1989.
Montgomery, Jose. Farrago – a History of the House and its Tiles. Leeds Polytechnic, 1984.
Montgomery, Susan J. The Ceramics of William H Grueby, The Spirit of the New Idea in Artistic Handicraft. Arts and Crafts Quarterly Press, USA, 1993.
Myers, Richard and Hilary. 'Morris & Company Ceramic Tiles' in Journal of Tiles and Architectural Ceramics Society Vol 1, pp17-22, 1982.
Myers, Richard. 'The Medmenham Pottery 1' in Glazed Expressions No 6, pp1-2, spring 1984.
Reed, Cleota. Henry Chapman Mercer and the Moravian Pottery and Tile Works. Philadelphia: University of Pennsylvania Press, 1987.
Sturgis, R Clipston. 'The Perkins Institution and Massachusetts School for the Blind at Watertown, Massachusetts' in The Brickbuilder Vol 22 No7, July 1913.
Taft, Lisa F. Herman Carl Mueller Architectural Ceramics and the Arts and Crafts Movement. Trenton: New Jersey State Museum, 1979.
Tunick, Susan. Ceramic Ornament in the New York Subway System. New York: Friends of Terra Cotta, 1989.

Tiles in the Modern Era
Hawkins, Jennifer. The Poole Potteries. Barrie & Jenkins, 1980.
van Lemmen, Hans. 'New Tiles and Mosaics in London Underground Stations' in Glazed Expressions No 12, pp6-8, summer 1986.
Swann, Dick, Tiles Old and New. Leicester, 1967.
Thomas, M Hartland. 'Tiles' in Design No 56, pp19-29, August 1953.
'Tiles' in supplement to Architectural Review Vol lxxxv No 510, pp261-8, May 1939.

Index

Page numbers in *italic* refer to the
illustrations

Acknowledgements

Authors' Acknowledgements
We are indebted to the following
for their help and advice in a wide
variety of ways:
Josie Adams
Kenneth Beaulah
Richard Bishop
Chris Blanchett
Julia Brant
John Carter and Susan Hughes
Helene Curtis
Brenda Greysmith
Ed Grusheski
Malcolm Hay (Palace of
　Westminster)
Heritage Tile Conservation Ltd (Chris
　Dellow and Jeremy Southorn)
Alan and Helen Holmes
Ann Hutchinson and Scott Lowe
Hans van Lemmen
Dr Katherine Lochnan (Art Gallery of
　Ontario)
John and Hilary Malam
many members of the Maw family
Rev Dom Bede Millard (St
　Augustine's Abbey Ramsgate)
Susan Montgomery
Arthur Moss
Richard and Hilary Myers
Steven Parissien
Dr Lynn Pearson
Cleota Reed and David Tatham
Pierre and Lise Rodien
Dr Joan Skinner
Dr Michael Stratton
Joe Taylor (Tile Heritage Foundation
　USA)
Robert Thorne
Susan Tunick (Friends of Terra Cotta
　New York)
Dr Clive Wainwright (Victoria &
　Albert Museum)
Jane Wainwright
Kit Wedd
Robert Weis
and many individual friends and
members of the Tiles and
Architectural Ceramics Society who
have fed us information over several
years.

Libraries and Institutions:
Boston Public Library, Mass., USA
British Museum, Department of
　Medieval and Later Antiquities
　(John Cherry, Beverley Nenk and
　Tracy Kemp)
Ecomusée des pays de l'Oise,
　Beauvais, France (Anne Maillard)
GRECB, Beauvais, France (Jean
　Cartier)
Ironbridge Gorge Museum Library
　(John Powell and Marilyn Higson)
Jackfield Tile Museum (Michael
　Vanns)
Keele University Library
Marblehead Historical Society, Mass.,
　USA (Betty Hunt)
National Museums and Galleries on
　Merseyside, Liverpool Museum
　(Myra Brown and Alison Pollard)
Shropshire Libraries
Smithsonian Institution, Washington
　DC, USA (Susan Myers and Bonnie
　Lilienfeld)
Stoke-on-Trent City Museum and Art
　Gallery (Debbie Skinner)
University of Wolverhampton Library
Wedgwood Museum (Gaye Blake
　Roberts)

Picture Acknowledgements
l=left; r=right; t=top; b=bottom;
c=centre
Peter Aprahamian, photographer 103,
144, 147, 151, 154, 155, 168-9, 174, 177,
178, 198, 199; Arcaid/photo Richard
Bryant 126, 200, 202br; Arcaid/photo
Lucinda Lambton 128; Avery
Architectural and Fine Arts Library
Drawings and Archives 111; Richard
Berenholtz, photographer 113, 192;
Maggie Berkowitz 210; Branson
Coates Architects 212 (photo Alastair
Hunter); Bridgeman Art Library 18;
Bridgeman Art Library/Victoria and
Albert Museum 180, 181; Cecil
Denney Highton, Architects 162t, 163
(photos Adam Woolfit); Martin
Charles, photographer 2, 4; ©
Country Life 79, 131, 164; Jerome
D'Arblay, photographer 98, 99, 158,
160, 170; Easton Farm Park 97t;
Edifice 100bc, 135bl, 135br; English
Heritage 27tl, 27bl, 27c, 27cr, 68, 130,
138, 139; Foreign and Commonwealth
Office 162b; Michael Harding, pho-
tographer jacket, 1l, 92, 94, 95; Robert
Harding 16, 17, 22t (photo Adam
Woolfit), 22b, 25tc; Hardy Holzman
Pfeiffer Associates 208, 209; Tony
Herbert, photographer jacket, 1r, 12t,
24, 25, 27br, 28t, 32, 33, 38, 39, 45, 46,
47, 48, 49, 56l, 58tl, 58tc, 59, 60br,
64b, 73, 75, 76, 80, 81, 82, 83, 84, 85,
88, 100, 101, 108, 109, 117, 119r, 120,
124l, 132br, 134, 135, 136, 140, 141, 157t,
161, 165, 173l, 184, 186c, 187l, 191b, 195,
196, 197, 214c, 214b, 217, 218, 221r;
Heritage Tile Conservation Ltd 106,
107, 185; Angelo Hornak 142, 175, 183;
Ironbridge Gorge Museum Trust 12b,
27tr, 31, 44, 52, 53, 55, 56r, 58tr, 58bl,
58br, 60bl, 65, 66, 67, 70, 71, 118, 119l,
124tr, 124cr, 129r, 132, 145b, 150, 152,
205, 206; Ian Jones, photographer
129l; Leeds City Art Gallery 114;
London Transport Museum 172, 173r,
216; Peter Machertich, photographer
202cl, 202cr; Magnus Edizioni 148,
149; John Malam 74; National
Museums of Scotland 64t; National
Museum of Wales 28b; National
Portrait Gallery 121; New York Transit
Museum 112, 219; John Outram, architect 222; Palace of Westminster 86,
87, 89, 91; Photo AKG London 10;
Pittshanger Manor Museum 116;
Cleota Reed, photographer 41, 97b,
119tl, 186t, 186b, 187r, 188, 191t;
Rochdale Town Hall 167; Royal
Institute of British Architects 145t;
Sainsburys 102, 104; Stuart Smith,
photographer 202t, 203; Rupert Spira
221l; Mary Swisher, photographer
211t; Theurer/Jonglet, photographers
50; Tile Heritage Foundation 135tl,
211b; Francesco Venturi, photographer 14, 15, 19, 20, 21, 123, 124br, 213,
214t, 215; Victoria and Albert Museum
8, 30, 34, 35, 37, 42, 61, 62, 63, 125,
182.